Amos H. Funk

My Life

and

Love For the Land

Amos H. Funk
My Life and Love For the Land

Copyright © 1998
Amos H. Funk
306 South Duke Street
Millersville, PA 17501

International Standard Book Number: 1-883294-76-2

Library of Congress Number: 98-67321

Printed 1998 by
Masthof Press
220 Mill Road
Morgantown, PA 19543-9701

TABLE OF CONTENTS

My Ancestors 1
Experiences In Our Early Years 3
My Penn State Experience 7
The Funk Family and the 1929 Depression 9
The Early Days 10
How Young is Too Young? 12
Our Family—A More Recent Look 14
Growing Vegetables and Small Fruit—An Interesting Challenge 19
My Remarks to New York State Growers—The Need to Adapt 21
My Trip to Ohio State With Dean Beattie—The Value of Research ... 28
Amos H—A Red Raspberry Named For Me 33
My Love For the Land—Where Did It Come From? 36
My First Sunday Morning Sermon—"The Christian Use of the Land" ... 39
I Speak to Methodists at Kansas City, Kansas 46
My Forty-Four Years With the Lancaster Conservation District 51
My Twelve Years With the Conestoga Valley Association 57
My Twelve Years With the Agricultural Preserve Board 67
The Background on the Second Most Important Meeting I Ever Attended ... 76
My Ten Years With the Lancaster Farmland Trust 92
The Pennsylvania Association of Conservation District Directors 112
My Twenty-Four Years With the Pennsylvania Conservation Commission 114
The Penn State Agricultural Advisory Council 116
My Appointment to the Advisory Committee to the U.S. Soil Conservation
    Service 117
Failure to Adequately Tell the Important Story of Agriculture 119
Presentations I Have Made 121
    The Paradise Rotary   *April 10, 1966* 121
    Farms Threatened By Urban Growth   *September 1, 1966* 125
    Lancaster Exchange Club   *August 1968* 127
    Pennsylvania Power and Light Conference on the Environment
        March 22, 1972 130
    Testimony on House Bill 1056   *May 1972* 133

The Pennsylvania Forum, Hershey, Pennsylvania *April 30, 1975* 137
Millersville Lions Club *May 27, 1975* 141
The Greater Lancaster Board of Realtors *March 16, 1977* 144
Funding Farmland Preservation Using Township Funds *August 1977* 148
Lancaster Tomorrow *May 10, 1978* 151
Getting Greater Farmland Preservation Support From Lancaster County's
 State Legislators *May 5, 1978* 156
Speaking for Farmland Preservation *May 20, 1978* 159
My Presentation to the Lawrence County, Pennsylvania, Grange
 March 29, 1979 162
State Grange Meeting at Trappe, Pennsylvania *April 5, 1979* 165
Lancaster County Farmer's Union *April 16, 1979* 175
Hunterdon County, New Jersey *May 5, 1979* 177
A 1980 Progress Report on Our Deed Restriction Program in Lancaster
 County *January 3, 1980* 181
History of Our $250 Per Acre Development Right Offer
 January 15, 1980 184
Pennsylvania Council of Farm Organizations, Harrisburg
 January 21, 1980 186
Spring Meeting of Pennsylvania Section of the American Society of
 Agricultural Engineers *May 2, 1980* 192
Special Meeting on Farmland Preservation at the Penn Harris Motor Inn
 September 22, 1980 197
The Farmland Preservation Bill That Became Law in Our Farm Market
 Greenhouse *December 1980* 201
Millersville Lions Club *January 13, 1981* 203
Adams County Extension Association *January 22, 1981* 208
National Association of Conservation District Directors' Annual Meeting,
 San Francisco *February 2, 1981* 214
The Pennsylvania Young Farmers Association, Hershey, Pennsylvania
 February 10, 1981 220
Garden Spot Young Farmers *February 18, 1981* 223
The Pennsylvania State Association of Township Supervisors, Pittsburgh,
 Pennsylvania *April 15, 1981* 226

Why Amos Funk Has Worked Hard to Preserve Farmland   *June 1980* 229
Farmer Attitudes and Their Effect on Putting Together a Deed Restriction
    Program in Lancaster County   *September 15, 1981* 232
Speech to the National Farm City Council   *May 29, 1981* 236
Open Market Committee of the Federal Reserve Bank
    November 10, 1981 241
Effect of the New Federalism and Reduced Spending on the Capitol Region
    March 17, 1982 244
How Modern Man Has Created His Own Farming Problems
    December 9, 1982 248
Can Lancaster County's Small Farms and Farm Families Survive?
    May 23, 1986 253
My Meeting With the West Donegal Township Officials
    November 20, 1986 256
Testimony on House Bill 442 and Senate Bill 156   *May 29, 1987* 260
My Meeting With Elizabethtown Young Farmers   *February 16, 1988* 262
The State's Role and History in Creating the Pennsylvania Conservation
    Easement Program   *November 15, 1990* 267
Congressman Walker's Hearing on the Environment at F&M College
    March 2, 1990 273
Funk Dedicates Lifetime To Conservation, Preservation, Ag Promotion
    February 22, 1992 277

DEDICATION

This book is dedicated to my wife, Esta, whom I love dearly. Her reassuring smile has always been there when problems arose. Her helpful hand has always been there when I needed a lift.

Thanks, Esta, for loving, inspiring, and encouraging me through sixty-two years of our marriage.

THANK YOU

Thanks to our first daughter, Grace Funk Wardrop, for her assistance on the word processor and her creative ideas on the book cover design.

Thanks to Grant Heilman Photography, Inc., for supplying the beautiful contour strips photograph used on the book cover.

# My Ancestors

I totally agree with the individual who said, "I am more interested in the kind of an ancestor I will be as compared with the kind of ancestors I have had." However, I feel strongly that many of our character traits are passed on from generation to generation. In addition, the environment in which we grow up also contributes to our character and the values we hold.

I am grateful that my wife, Esta, and I each grew up in Christian homes. All the Funk children benefited greatly from our Christian heritage.

I have good reason to believe one of my Funk ancestors was among the ten Swiss immigrants to settle in Lancaster County, Pennsylvania, in 1710. These early settlers took over a 6,600-acre tract in the Pequea Valley. My grandfather, Amos G. Funk, grew up near Central Manor on a farm that was deeded to the Funk family by William Penn.

Amos G. had to come to Millersville to find his future bride, Elizabeth Herr. Elizabeth's father, Christian Herr, owned the farm directly across the Slackwater Pike from where I now live. Of course, there is a connection. A number of years after the marriage of Elizabeth Herr and Amos G. Funk, they bought the farm directly across from Elizabeth's home and went to housekeeping there. My father, A. Herr Funk, was born and died in our log house which was built in 1823. He lived to be eighty years old. I, too, was born in that special house, and I hope I, too, can die there. Perhaps the Lord will allow that to happen.

Amos G. and Elizabeth Funk had four children. Their firstborn was named Christian; the next child was named Martin; the third child was a daughter named Elizabeth; and then my father, the baby of the family, was named Amos Herr Funk. However, through most of his life he chose to be called A. Herr Funk.

I also remember my grandparents on my mother's side. My maternal grandfather was Benjamin Eshleman. His wife's name was Anna Senft before marriage. The Ben and Anna Eshleman family lived in Red Hill, a small town in southern Lancaster County.

Ben and Anna Eshleman were blessed with seven children—five boys and two girls. The sons were named Edward, Oscar, Ben, Fred, and Earl. The daughters were my mother, Nellie, and her sister, Mable.

The children spent their childhood at Red Hill. Mother attended church at Marticville Methodist Church, where she played the organ.

My mother, Nellie Eshleman's, first husband was Abram Herr. Their marriage was blessed by the birth of a son. They named him Abram E. Herr. About two years after mother's marriage, her husband came down with tuberculosis. As happened often in those early days before penicillin, he died.

Sometime later my mother met and married my father, A. Herr Funk. A. Herr bought the farm from his father, Amos G. In 1911, following the marriage of my mother, Nellie, and A. Herr Funk, Mother's son, Abram Herr, came to live with them. Nellie and A. Herr had three children: Grace, my older sister; I was in the middle; and my sister Anna Mae, who now lives in California was the youngest. I suppose you could say we had the normal childhood. We all had to work on the farm, carry our weight, which didn't hurt us at all. We all had our chores to do. I seemed to take an interest in growing vegetable crops. My father had a milk route in the town of Millersville, as did his father, Amos G. They used a horse and wagon to deliver the milk. The milk was put in cans and tapped with a spigot into containers the customers would bring to the wagon when they heard the bell ringing.

Experiences In Our Early Years

My sister Grace did the things that most young girls do on the farm, as did Anna Mae. We never had a whole lot of extra money. We always had clean clothes to wear and we always had plenty to eat. My mother was a good cook. I would like to share an interesting incident that happened as we were growing up. It does not put me in the best light; in fact, I am a bit ashamed of myself.

Each Saturday evening we three Funk children took turns walking up to the corner of what was then called Applebutter Street and Slackwater Road. (That corner now has a much better sounding name: the intersection of Walnut Hill Road and South Duke Street.) We went to the corner to meet the ice cream man. We took enough money—I think it was fifteen cents for three cones. One particular Saturday evening, I went up there with my fifteen cents and ordered three chocolate ice cream cones. On the way home, I dropped one and somehow figured that I dropped Grace's. I don't know, since they were all chocolate, how I was smart enough to know that I dropped my sister Grace's, but it surely didn't make her happy. She wondered how I knew it was hers, but we worked through that. We did have some interesting times.

Another memorable thing I did when I was about three years old can be described as follows: My father's older brother, Uncle Martin Funk, and his wife, Aunt Sue, were visiting in our home. Somehow his brand new straw hat got on the floor, and I got great delight out of jumping on it and mashing it to pieces. Aunt Sue, who was very outspoken, was reported to point out to my uncle in no uncertain terms that Amos Funk, Herr Funk's son, will never amount to anything—he's too bad!

I recall another thing that we did that was interesting and significant. My dad had the milk route and my mother seemed to take an interest in raising chickens and gathering eggs from those chickens, and dressing chickens and going to market at the Central Market. We had a small stand about six feet long and four feet wide at the Central Market; the stand was number

111. My sister Grace and I accompanied my mother to the market at various times, and we got our first taste of selling to the customers. I liked it.

My dad had a small dairy herd that produced just enough milk to take care of our customers on the milk route in Millersville. We also took along things that my grandfather had planted, some blackberries and apples. It may be that as a result of my grandfather Amos G.'s interest in plants and trees that my intense interest in plants and small fruit and some trees started.

All of us children went to the Millersville Model School and Elementary School beginning in first grade, and later we went to what was then called Manor Township High School. In those days we had a choice of staying at the ninth grade at the Model School (junior high school) then, or else going to the high school. I chose to go to the high school because of the athletic program available there.

My brother, Abe Herr, who is eleven years older than I, was hired as coach at Manor Township High School. He had finished four years of college at Millersville Normal School, as it was called then, and he was hired as basketball and track coach at Manor Township High School. As I said before, I wanted to get involved particularly in basketball, hopefully on the second team at the high school. I went out for basketball and my brother was coaching me. He was tough. One time after we lost a game, he had gone over and pointed out to everybody else how bad they were and how poorly they played. He turned to me and said, "Funk, you have a yellow streak down your back a yard wide." Well, I never thought I had a yellow streak, but he thought so. I was always rather aggressive when I went for the center ball. But Abe and I got along all right. He was just trying to get my attention, which he did.

In my sophomore year at Manor Township, I made the varsity team, and during my junior and senior years I was varsity captain and county high scorer. Going back to my freshman year, that year we played in a cement block building. We didn't have any showers, and our dressing rooms were rather plain. We just had a room made out of siding—one for the girls, and one for the boys; or one for the visiting team and one for the home team, whichever it happened to be. That summer of 1926, the school board said to Abe Herr that if he was able to take the stones and dirt from the area under the gymnasium floor, dig out to a height that would accommodate one standing up in there, remove the material at no cost to the school board, then the school board would cement the area and put in showers. In 1927 and all of the following years, the basketball team did have showers and we appreciated it very much.

I was about the same height as I am now—5'10 1/2"—not very tall for a forward basketball player. But players weren't as tall as in 1998, the year I am preparing this book. We had three centers on our team: Sherman Hill was 6'1", Paul Shaub was 6'2", and Harold Hess was 6'6", so we had some reasonably good height at center. In my senior year we won the county championship. That was the first championship that was ever won by Manor Township High School. We didn't have big playoffs in those days. We just had an area playoff and we did win the district playoff championship. We won that game by one point, and that one point advantage came as a result of my sinking a medium long shot near the end of the game.

Abe coached me for the first two years of my basketball career. In my junior year we had a coach from Lebanon Valley. He wasn't the greatest coach in the world; his name was Smith. In my senior year we had a very good coach named Sam Brown. We had practically the same material in my junior and senior years, but we had better coaching. So coaches do make a difference.

I was not a brilliant student, about a B average. My best grade came in chemistry. I guess I could have gotten higher grades if I had tried a little harder. I had a lot of interest in all sports. I went out for track in high school, and the thing that I did best was pole vaulting. I did the broad jump and also ran the 100-yard dash, but wasn't fast enough nor could I jump far enough, but I could pole vault pretty well. In my senior year in high school we had a meet in Reading and I jumped 11'7 3/4" with a bamboo pole. That beat the old state record of 11'6". So I held the state pole vaulting championship for a number of years.

My sister Grace was also a very good basketball player. She was captain of the girls' team. They also won their championship. She was president of the Parrot Club. We didn't have a yearbook. That year, 1929, was a Depression year and it was pretty tough here in Millersville as well as everywhere. The Millersville bank closed and money was very tight. For two years my dad's tobacco crop was of poor quality because the weather was dry. We couldn't sell, so we had two years' worth of tobacco crop standing in the tobacco shed, losing weight while it waited to be sold. This is one of the few times I remember my father being worried. He had some bills to pay, taxes and so forth, and the total amount of money he needed was $3,500. The bank was closed; he couldn't borrow it from them. He couldn't borrow it from anybody no matter how hard he tried, so my Uncle Fred, who was secretary/treasurer of the Manor Township School Board, convinced the other board members that it was a good risk to let my dad have the money to pay his debts. This helped us out of a hole, and it shows how difficult things were in those years, 1929-1930, when no one had very much money. I remember well here on the farm that we had plenty of help from people who were willing to work for relatively low wages.

1930 Penn State Freshman Basketball Team. Amos Funk with the ball in the front row.

My Penn State Experience

After high school I was pretty well assured that I would go to Penn State. I had made up my mind; we had enough money. We did not know how severe the Depression would be or how it would affect us financially, so it was decided I would go from a small high school here in Millersville to a large university where the total enrollment was, I think, 4,000 in the fall of 1929. I went out for the basketball team, and there were 200 other young fellows who signed up to go out for the freshman team. Every day there would be a list posted showing the names of people who were still allowed to come out to practice and demonstrate their skills and allow the coaches to observe them to see if they were going to make the final cut. I think the number of people on the freshman team was about twelve in those days. I survived all of the cuts and did make the team. I was very surprised and pleased that someone saw in me enough of leadership that they would elect me captain of the freshman basketball team.

Following basketball, I went out for track as a pole vaulter. I made the track team as a pole vaulter and participated in the meets. I don't recall how high I jumped. One might ask: How were your grades? Well, my grades weren't too great. Probably a B student; I think in calculus I got a C. I think my problem was that I didn't study enough—didn't apply myself. The first year away from home and other things, including athletics, took a great deal of time. I enjoyed playing cards, which was a waste of time.

I guess the subject I liked least was calculus, and that's the reason I did so poorly. The subject I liked most was a lecture class by then Dean Ralph Watts, who spoke mostly about relationships and life. One of the things that I remember him saying was that he could envision in the not too distant future, instead of people caring for each other, each person would look out for himself and wouldn't care too much what happened to his neighbor. Here in 1998, we're just about there.

The dean of the School of Agriculture had a son Gilbert, who graduated from Penn State and had a roadside market in Blair County, Pennsylvania.

My sister Grace, her husband, Harry Kauffman, Esta, and I went out to see this market. We were very impressed by the market and also were impressed by the fact that Gilbert Watts, the son of the dean, wrote a magazine column in the *Pennsylvania Farmer*. I'll never forget one of the things he had in this column, because it is so typical of us human beings. He said there was a large rock in the driveway of his farm that he turned out for regularly. One particular day he was driving and thinking of something else and did not turn out for the rock. The truck he was driving ran over the rock, which projected up and broke the crankcase of the truck and caused considerable damage, and also cost quite a bit to repair. The point was that it would take a lot less time to remove the rock, which could be rolled off the driveway by one person, than to wait until you have this kind of problem.

When I came home from Penn State in June 1930, my brother Abe Herr took me aside and said, "Amos, I don't think you had better plan to be back in college in the fall because we won't have enough of money due largely to the fact that we didn't sell the tobacco and that the Depression reduced the income of everybody; I doubt if you can ever go back. But we'll see."

As I recall, I wasn't too upset by this. I don't know why, because I loved basketball up there. I liked the college life, but I started working on the farm helping Dad and Mother, working with my sisters. We had cows for that milk route I spoke about. We grew some tobacco, some corn, and wheat, general farm crops. Gradually because of my interest in vegetables, I persuaded my dad and mother to plant more vegetable crops. As those crops became greater in number and the yield was higher, we had to find a larger area to sell them than that 4'x6' stand in Central Market I spoke of earlier, stand number 111. When the other part of that stand (one-half a stand at that time) came up for sale, the lady who stood there decided she wasn't going to come to market any more, we rented it. It wasn't too long after that that another stand came up for sale in the Central Market and we rented that. We continued to rent additional stands and to take care of our increased production.

THE FUNK FAMILY AND THE 1929 DEPRESSION

For those readers who are too young to remember the Great Depression of the 1930s, I will describe some of the difficulties troublesome times created.

More than a quarter of the U.S. work force was out of a job. Hundreds of thousands of farmers lost their land. Their farms were sold at "sheriff sales" or other forced sales. On the U.S. Stock Market, the Dow Jones Industrial Average dropped nearly 400% to an all-time low of eighty-nine points in 1932. When one compares this low with some of the record-breaking-high stock averages in 1997 and 1998, it is easy to conclude things were very difficult in the early 1930s.

Another example is tobacco, an important cash crop in the past years at least, sold for twenty-five cents a pound in September 1929. In September 1931 and 1932, the price was two to four cents a pound, depending on the quality of the crop.

Other prices farmers received for their products in 1932 were:

Milk	75 cents to 90 cents a 100 pounds
Butter	25 cents a pound
Large eggs	8 cents a dozen
Potatoes	24 cents a bushel

This information should serve as an explanation as to why my sister Grace and I were willing to stand in the market for ten or more hours to sell as little as $35 worth of products for the entire day in 1938. Our lowest volume of sales dollars was on January 22, 1938. Eggs brought 20 cents a dozen that day. Our highest volume of sales in 1938, $136, occurred at the Central Market, Friday, September 16. This information was taken from one of my journals that I kept from 1938 until 1998.

One of our grandchildren, when told about the sale of $35 worth of products over a ten-hour period, asked, "How much did you get paid to stand in market?" The answer is: We did not get paid. We were glad to work for our room and board plus a little spending money when we could afford it.

THE EARLY DAYS

In 1939, total market high and low sales were about the same as 1938. Some prices may be of interest. Black raspberries, 30 cents a quart; tomatoes, 16 cents a pound; shelled lima beans, 20 cents a pint; and sweet corn 37 to 60 cents a dozen.

By 1943, things were getting a little better. Our lowest market was $50 and our highest market in ten hours of work was $380. Eggs were 45 cents a dozen; corn, 70 cents a dozen; black raspberries, 40 cents a quart.

There are some who look back with fondness to the good old days. I assure you, I am not one who wants to look back to those difficult days of the 1930s and 1940s.

The explanation of why our youngest sister is not mentioned in our selling experience is very simple. Anna Mae did not like to sell at the markets. In fact, whenever she could get away with it, she turned her back on the customers. As she describes her feelings today, "It was not my cup of tea." Sister Anna Mae did like selling. As soon as she was old enough, she got a job selling at Woolworth's 5 & 10 Cents Store in Lancaster. After high school, she got a good job at the Hamilton Watch Factory in Lancaster. Whenever she was able to do so, she helped us with numerous jobs on the farm. I am sure my sister Grace would agree with me: Anna Mae was the best looking of the Funk children. In fact, in her senior year of high school, she was selected May Queen.

Esta and I Bought the Home Farm

In 1950, my wife, Esta, and I bought the family farm on the Slackwater Road. With this purchase, I became the third generation of Funks to own the home farm.

Gradually we increased our acreage of vegetable crops and reduced the acreage of general farm crops. In 1952 we discontinued growing tobacco. As the acreage of vegetable crops increased, we needed to increase our marketing outlets to sell those vegetables. By the year 1963 when our youngest son, Fred, finished high school, we had eight market stands in the city of Lancaster and as many as six stands in nearby towns, such as Root's Market near Manheim, Green Dragon at Ephrata, and the Leesport Market that was held on Wednesday.

Operating up to fourteen market stands per week was quite an undertaking. Going to market four days out of each week did not allow one much time to do other things. It certainly was a challenge.

As I look back on it now, this marketing effort was very time consuming and required a lot of travel and many late hours of hard work, particularly loading and unloading the produce we had to sell and the produce left unsold at the end of the markets.

We did the best we could with the knowledge we had at the time. However, this marketing effort pursued in the 1950s and the 1960s could not be followed today in 1998. Labor costs are too high. Today, selling at Funk's Farm Market in Millersville is much more efficient and more satisfying to our customers.

One of the positive things about growing and selling vegetables and small and larger fruit is that an opportunity was provided to teach our children good work habits. Each of our children knew they were expected to perform tasks they were able to do. The smaller children did the simpler tasks like picking peas and pulling radishes; the older children did more demanding jobs.

Our children helped on market. As soon as they were able to sell, they assisted their mother at her market stand. As soon as they were able, they took over a stand of their own. This not only pleased them; it increased their resourcefulness and their ability to sell. Two of our sons are full-time salesmen; our three girls sell part time.

Although our oldest son had little interest in selling, he contributed greatly to our crop production program here on the farm. Amos was an excellent tractor operator and took very good care of the equipment he used.

Immediately after Amos graduated from high school, he informed me that he planned to enlist in the Air Force. Although this camê as a surprise, I certainly wanted our children to do what they thought would be best for them.

Amos did enlist in the Air Force. He served in various capacities including a flight simulator technician, field engineer, and electronic technician.

After he retired from the Air Force, he earned his associate degree while working as a field engineer with a commercial firm. In 1985, he made a career change to contract administration and is currently working for the Department of the Navy.

How Young is Too Young?

How young is too young to begin teaching our children good work habits? For Esta and me, all our children started assisting us in simple ways in our markets at the age of seven years. Simple tasks such as placing sweet potatoes neatly in oblong quart boxes and arranging stems of celery (stewing celery) in a square quart box were things they could do well, and the tasks challenged them. As they grew older, they were able to place the various vegetables our customers would buy into brown kraft bags. We were careful not to ask our children to do tasks that were too difficult for them. As they grew older and taller, they were able to wait on customers and make change.

I repeat, we tried not to ask too much of our children. However, as I look back on it now, asking our oldest child, Grace, at the age of sixteen (the age she was permitted to drive), to take our 1945 Diamond T truck with a twelve-foot bed loaded with produce to the Fulton Market in the city of Lancaster was a bit much. I am certain no other driver was available. I am very thankful she was able to make the delivery and arrive home safely. Perhaps this is an example of developing resourcefulness in children by asking them to do difficult things that are indeed within their capabilities when challenged.

Another example of my asking several of our children to accept a difficult challenge and then meeting it successfully involved selling early-maturing, yet surplus tomatoes to unknown buyers in an unknown market in the state of New York. Most tomatoes grown in New York ripen three weeks later than tomatoes grown in Lancaster County, Pennsylvania.

My goal was to move our surplus early-maturing tomatoes from a market in which there was an oversupply from home gardeners, as well as market gardeners, to a market in New York that is under supplied, with high quality homegrown tomatoes from Lancaster County or elsewhere. We had learned that higher prices could be obtained from the smaller retailers in

New York than would be realized at the larger wholesale markets. Therefore, our target was these smaller retail markets.

Our first effort to test the New York market came in 1959. We had too many tomatoes. The local market was weak due to oversupply. I discussed the matter with our two sons. I also explained my solution to the problem. I made it plain to them that the successful solution of the problem depended entirely on these two young sons. Andy was nineteen years old and Fred was fifteen years old.

My goal was to fill our 1952 International truck with 2 1/2 tons of our high quality tomatoes. Selling 250 twenty-pound boxes of tomatoes is no small task. I made it plain to them that they were to sell the entire load at the best price they could get. Their response was most gratifying. They said they would do their best to sell them at a good price. I was very proud of these two young sons when they did not hesitate in meeting this challenge. I was even prouder of them when they came home after their first trip and reported they had sold all the tomatoes at a price higher than I had suggested. Today, in 1998, both boys are in full-time sales, and they should be.

Another example of our third son's sales and managerial ability was demonstrated one year when we had too many strawberries for our normal markets. We learned we could rent a market stand at the Eastern Market near York, Pennsylvania. The problem, since the market was held on a Friday, was that all our market help was occupied at our normal market outlets. However, we did have fourteen-year-old Fred, our third son. Fred had already demonstrated he could sell with "the best of them." He could also manage a market stand effectively.

We got Fred a licensed driver and a helper. The first day ever in the Eastern Market, they sold over 1,000 quarts of strawberries, four bushels of sugar peas, and a substantial amount of other produce. Today, in 1998, Fred is the successful owner and operator of Funk's Farms and Greenhouses with the Farm Market.

OUR FAMILY— A MORE RECENT LOOK

On December 22, 1994, we successfully surprised my wife, Esta, on her eightieth birthday. It wasn't easy, but we did it. The gathering was held in the Family Life Center of the Grace United Methodist Church in Millersville.

Because we all love Esta so very much, we made a special effort to have all members of our immediate family in attendance. Present were the six children and their spouses, then living in five different states. Our eleven grandchildren and spouses of those married were present, as were our six great-grandchildren.

A total of 100 family members and friends, including Esta's 105-year-old mother, were able to join in the birthday celebration of a very special person, my dear wife, Esta.

At my request, our first daughter, Grace Funk Wardrop, assembled some interesting information about our family in 1994. It follows.

Esta Funk

> I am Mother's oldest child, or first child, as Mother likes Dad to say. I get to introduce the others to you. I was named for Dad's sister Grace Kauffman, whom many of you know and who we are happy to have with us tonight. I moved to York County more than thirty years ago, and I've been there ever since. For the past twenty-six years I've worked for the largest dental company in the world, which is headquartered in York. I'm presently a customer service supervisor. My favorite pastime is gardening.
>
> I met my husband, Jim Wardrop, in Sunday School. We've been married ten

years. Jim is a truck driver and about half cowboy. One hundred years ago he would have been a muleskinner. His favorite pastime is reading, and his favorite book is the Bible. He often says of Mother, she's more like Jesus than anyone else he's ever met.

I have two children. I'm very fortunate because they both live less than twenty-five minutes away from me. The oldest, a daughter Elizabeth, Beth as we call her, operates her own cleaning business. Her favorite pastime is gardening, especially herb and rose growing. Her husband, Rick Gohn, is an account representative for a central Pennsylvania office equipment company. He loves participating in all kinds of sports. Beth's son Ryan is Mother's oldest great-grandchild. He was twelve this year.

My son Wade Heath, Jr., or Rusty, is employed by an aluminum extruding company. He started there upon graduation from high school and has advanced to the position of night plant manager. His favorite pastime is fishing. Rusty's wife Kathy is an office manager for a title company. They have two sons, Ben, who is nine, and Jared, who is eight.

Amos Herbert Funk, Mother's second child, was named for his dad and his mother's brother, Herbert. After graduation from high school, Amos enlisted in the Air Force. He chose flight simulation as his specialty and continued in that field until retirement a few years ago.

When stationed in Sioux City, Iowa, he met his wife, Carol. They lived many different places during Amos's military career. They chose to live on the Gulf Coast of Florida after retirement from the Air Force in Milton near Fort Walton Beach. Amos is now working with the Department of Navy in contract administration.

Amos and Carol have three children. First, Amos III, who met his wife, Tracey, when visiting the farm with his family just before the family moved to Florida. Once in Florida, Amos III found that he missed Tracey so much that he asked KMart, where he was working, for a transfer to Pennsylvania and got it. He and Tracey married and are the proud parents of Chad, age seven, and Ashley, age three.

Amos is an assistant department manager for KMart in Ephrata. Tracey manages the floral greenhouses at the Masonic Homes. By the way, Tracey is responsible for the lovely decorations here tonight.

Second, David, and third, Vicky, are living in Fort Walton Beach, Florida. We are so happy that they are able to be here with us. It took some doing, but they made it. David always said he wanted to be a D.J. and he is at the Disc-O-Tech in Fort Walton Beach. Vicky is a senior waitress in one of the top restaurant chains in Florida.

Andy Myer Funk, Mother's third child, is the most like Mother's side of the family. His quickness and competitiveness made him a soccer standout in high school. He played soccer at Penn State until a broken leg shortened his college career.

Andy is an independent insurance broker. He's lived a number of places in this country, all the way to California, but his very favorite place is where he is now living—Virginia Beach. In fact, to hear him talk you'd almost believe he's a native Virginian.

Mother always said Andy was her best eater. That may explain why he's a great cook. However, his favorite pastime is sitting in his hot tub.

Andy has one daughter, Alecia. They are pretty much look-alikes. Alecia graduated from Kutztown College and is employed as a staff assistant for State Farm Insurance in the Harrisburg area. She loves the beach and she loves to ski. In fact, she will be visiting her Aunt June in Colorado in January for a ski vacation.

Frederick Allen Funk, Mother's fourth child, has followed the family tradition that the youngest boy stays with the farm. Fred always loved the marketing part of the business. After graduation from high school, he convinced Dad to convert an old chicken house into a small open air market. The market has grown to its present size—a year-round market employing 135 people. It's taken hard work and dedication and lots of planning and scrutiny.

Mother has the affectionate title of midnight market manager. As an example of how valuable her assistance is, when one of the expansion building projects was underway, Mother looked at the foundation and said, "This is out of square." No one listened, but Mother persisted. And sure enough, to the builder's dismay, she was right and it had to be redone.

Fred's wife, Jacquie, operates a jewelry replacement business. Jacquie was responsible for the punch and hors d'oeuvres we enjoyed before dinner.

Fred has two daughters. The older one, Kathy, graduated from Cabrinne College in Philadelphia. Until this present school year Kathy taught youngsters with learning disabilities in the Philadelphia area. She married her high school sweetheart, Jeff Kirk. Jeff is involved in retirement planning, investments, and insurance through Primamerica. Earlier this year they moved back to Lancaster County just a stone's throw from the farm, and started their family. Alex is Mother's newest great-grandchild.

Fred's second daughter, Kelli, graduated from the University of Pennsylvania, where she's earned her Master's Degree in Education. Kelli is teaching sixth grade science in the Philadelphia area.

Anna Mae, Mother's fifth child, was named for Dad's sister, Anna Mae Kritscher. After three brothers, I prayed hard for a little sister and was so happy when she was born a little girl. She's been a blessing ever since.

Anna Mae graduated from Millersville University. That same May she married Arnold Bennett, whom she met at the Fulton Market in Lancaster. She was selling vegetables and he was working for a paper company while attending F&M. Arnie often refers to Anna Mae as Esta Mae because she is so like Mother.

They are now living in Atlanta where Arnie has a private law practice, and Anna Mae works part-time for a party shop. Her most important job is being wife and mother. They have two children: Matthew, who will turn fifteen very soon, and Susie, who is twelve.

June, born in June, was Mother's sixth child. Being the baby, she was naturally spoiled. When just a young person, she became well known

Four generations of Funks in the sweet corn field. Sitting on the right is Amos H. Funk; standing on the right is Frederick A. Funk, son; standing on the left is Kathy Funk Kirk, granddaughter; and sitting on the left is Alex Kirk, great-grandson.

for original jokes called "Juney jokes." They had unrelated and unexpected punch lines that were somehow hilarious. She did have a more serious side. While in high school on the hockey field, she was called "the bull" for her fierce competitive behavior. She graduated from Harcum College in Philadelphia and was given the Harcum award for all-around achievement.

June met her husband, George Bianchi, while working as assistant treasurer in a New Jersey bank. George operated a gourmet restaurant and bakery down the street from the bank. They met over a spinach salad. George is a business builder. He started a croissant business, built it, then sold it. They moved to Colorado where they still live, built a high-end imported furniture and accessory retail business, and recently sold it. By the way, June was actively involved in both businesses.

George has often said of Mother that she truly lives the Scripture that "it is more blessed to give than to receive"(Acts 20:35).

June has one son, Justin, who just turned twenty-one. He is a junior at Towson State University in Maryland. Looking at Justin, it's not surprising that his favorite pastime is weight lifting. Justin plans to be a Drug Enforcement Administration agent.

Growing Vegetables and Small Fruit—
An Interesting Challenge

In my opinion, the one vegetable that has been most improved as a result of breeding is sweet corn. It has always been interesting to me how sweet corn color preferences have developed over the years. Here in Lancaster County, the corn of choice has been white sweet corn. The earliest white sweet corn I can remember was Stowell's Evergreen, an open pollinated variety, not a hybrid. However, when the first hybrid variety, Golden Cross Bantam, was introduced, because of the better quality of Golden Cross Bantam, the acreage planted to Stowell's Evergreen was sharply reduced. Our customers surely liked the sweeter taste of the new Golden Bantam hybrid.

As always happens in a country where free enterprise is encouraged, the white sweet corn breeders quickly began the development of steps needed to hybridize the white corn. Stowell's Evergreen hybrid and narrow-grained Evergreen were soon introduced.

Naturally the yellow sweet corn breeders proceeded to improve their products also. Although from time to time when we heard, read about, and tried a yellow corn that sounded outstanding, we received the same clear message when we tried to grow and sell it. Most folks in Lancaster and the surrounding counties prefer white sweet corn. I suppose it was only natural for corn breeders to reason that if some folks like white corn and others prefer yellow sweet corn, perhaps we could get much wider acceptance if an ear with a mixture of white and yellow kernels could be developed. This was done and this new corn called "Bi Color" type received outstanding acceptance in the New England states. Today in 1998, Bi Color corns are the corn of choice in New York. In western Pennsylvania, yellow sweet corn is preferred.

Today's sweet corns of all colors are much superior to the early sweet corns in eating quality, appearance, yield, and disease resistance.

These technological advances make it possible to produce a better product, of better quality. And even over a long period of sharply increased growing costs, growers are able to offer delicious sweet corn at reasonable prices.

Strawberries

Strawberry breeding over the years has greatly improved the strawberry varieties available to growers and consumers. The two varieties I first remember were Premier, an early berry, and Robinson, a mid-season berry. These berries were rather soft; they had a skin that bruised easily and, therefore, were very subject to rotting in the field or after they were harvested. Yields were rather low and disease resistance was non-existent.

Over the years, researchers in the U.S. Agricultural Research Service, in cooperation with specialists located in many land grant colleges in the United States, cooperatively have made vast improvements in strawberry fruit quality, yield, disease resistance, and other qualities needed to meet the requirements of specific growing areas.

For example, strawberries grown in Florida, California, or other areas where long distance shipping is necessary, the strawberry fruit has to have a tougher skin and firmer flesh than strawberries grown for "Pick Your Own" or for local sales. Strawberry breeders have accomplished a remarkable feat.

This having been said, we growers who raise strawberries for our local markets are certain the varieties we grow and the way we grow them cause them to taste better, and we know they are sweeter. The proof is in the eating!

Today in 1998 there is a concerted effort to produce strawberry plants that are resistant to soil-borne and other diseases. Developing plants resistant to insect damage, although somewhat more difficult, is also an important goal of strawberry plant breeders. Success in attaining these goals will reduce the amount of fungicides and pesticides needed to produce a marketable crop that is profitable for the grower. In addition, the cost to the consumer will be reduced.

My Remarks to New York State Growers—
The Need to Adapt

Leon Weber, a Penn State graduate in horticulture, worked for us during one summer over vacation.

Following his graduation, he secured a position as a horticultural extension agent in Suffolk County, New York. Apparently Leon saw something he liked about our vegetable growing program, because he was instrumental in inviting me to speak to a group of New York growers in Suffolk County at their annual meeting. My remarks follow:

When Leon Weber invited me here to share with you some of our vegetable growing experiences and observations, I had mixed feelings about accepting the invitation. The first questions I asked myself were, "What if I am a flop? How tough are those guys going to be on me?" Then I remembered the story of the fellow speaking at a Rotary Club dinner meeting in Texas. This invited speaker was doing pretty well, speaking at about 120 words a minute, when he noticed a fellow at the end of the speakers' table take out his six-shooter and lay it on the table. The speaker, not knowing exactly what the problem was, increased his delivery speed to 140 words a minute. As he looked hopefully around the room, he noticed another club member at the other end of the speakers' table take out his six-shooter and place it on the table. In desperation, he increased his delivery speed to 150 words per minute.

The president of the club, sitting next to the speaker, noticed the speaker was getting a bit desperate; so, he pulled on his coattail and whispered assuredly, "Don't worry, friend, it is not you we are after, it is the fellow who invited you." So, Leon, beware!

I live on a farm that has been in our family for three generations. My father spent his entire life on our home farm. My grandfather spent half of his life there; and, of course, I have lived all of my life there. They were in the dairy business and had a retail milk route in Millersville, then a town of 500 people, now a borough of 6,400.

Through my years in high school and college, particularly after college, I pressed my dad to allow me to grow additional vegetable crops. These crops were sold at a local farmer's market five miles from our home farm. Each year we grew a greater acreage of vegetable crops; until 1950, seventy-five percent of our acreage was in vegetables. It was in 1950 my wife and I bought the home farm of eighty-two acres.

By 1959, our acreage was too large for our home farm and we bought an additional eighty-nine acres near one of the dependable surface streams. The farm is eight miles away (which isn't good), but we do have plenty of water to irrigate. Irrigation has not been a major factor in the past several years, but it will be, I am sure, in the near future. We will have some dry years again as we have had in the past. I well remember the droughts of 1931-1932 and 1954.

We bought the farm eight miles away, which we call the Marticville farm, for irrigation and also to provide a site for a six-acre black raspberry planting. This farm is isolated from other vegetable farms and offered a degree of isolation from raspberry virus infection spread by aphids. Funny thing is, we never made much money on those raspberries for the simple reason that our production costs were too high and our yield per acre too low.

All of us in this room know that these are the two factors we can control. The price of our product is pretty much determined by supply and demand. Sure, we can decide to retail instead of wholesale. But even if we do this, our retail price is pretty much determined by the general prevailing price in the area.

Our average yield of raspberries over the period we grew them on this farm was 1,100 quarts per acre. After four years, we plowed them down. This year on a three-acre block of black raspberries, our yield was the highest we ever realized, 2,700 quarts per acre. We don't plan to plow them down, not when we sold them for $1.25 per quart.

In 1965, we purchased a farm of seventy acres that we were renting for five years, and on which we once grew five acres of red raspberries. We now grow one acre of red raspberries on this farm. With the high yields of new varieties developed by the late Dr. I.C. Haut of the University of Maryland and the prices we are receiving, red raspberries are the most profitable (net profit) crop we grow. This was not true when we had five acres, however. We retail most of the present acreage through our market.

I am quite sure raspberries are not an important crop here in Long Island. I used the example of red and black raspberries to try to illustrate a point. We thought we should have farms with isolation for raspberries and irrigation for raspberries and other crops. This was the principle motivation for buying the farm.

I am certain that the procedures we entered into do not represent the ultimate in long-range planning. There was not a lot of time spent weighing the alternatives. My main concern was: Could we swing it financially? Could we find a trusting banker? Even my father felt I should not buy the farm. In fact, he said to me, "Amos, you can't take proper care of the acreage you have now, why buy additional acreage?"

And you know, he was right! However, now with better herbicides and improved management procedures we manage to stay on top of things pretty well—not as well as we would like, but reasonably well. As an investment, we did all right. We had the two farms appraised this year and found the land value has increased over 350% in sixteen years, or approximately 22% a year. The farms have little or no development value, and we have done little to improve the buildings. Therefore, the increase is simply in value of land for farm use.

The irony of the matter, however, is that the same appreciation of land values that have increased our net worth is making it quite difficult for our thirty-year-old son to take over the farming operation. He is interested in growing and selling vegetables and small fruit. In my opinion, he has the managerial ability to conduct the business successfully. However, we are having difficulty coming up with a plan that he can handle financially.

We have been working with our extension people at the county and university level, an insurance company, a bank, and we are on our second attorney. We are getting a lot of ideas, but have not come up with a plan we feel our thirty-year-old son can handle. Being fair to our other five children does not make the problem easier. However, I am sure we will work something out.

We grow nineteen vegetables plus ten acres of strawberries and the red and black raspberries. Our goal is to grow what we can sell at our roadside market. If we have too much corn, as we did in 1974, we cut back the next year (10% in 1975). The great number of home gardens plus the favorable growing season caused us fits for about three weeks that year. We tried everything, we advertised more featuring corn, we reduced the price, we displayed corn more prominently, and we gave quantity discounts. However, we were reminded again what we knew before: When a crop is in oversupply, the best place for it is to let it in the field, or wholesale the product out of your selling area. We sent a lot of our corn to Washington, D.C., that year.

In 1975, I do not know how it was here in Suffolk County, but we had no serious problem of oversupply in our area for any of our crops. We matched production with demand rather well.

During the past ten years we have discontinued growing the following fourteen vegetables: beets, cabbage, Chinese cabbage, lettuce, bunching onions, sweet Spanish onions, pod peas, radishes, spinach, sweet potatoes, turnips, yellow corn, yellow beans, and pole lima beans.

We discontinued growing them for a number of reasons. Most of them were dropped because the volume sold was not great enough to justify the cost that growing a small area entails. Radishes and turnips were dropped because we could buy better quality than we could grow. On radishes, we were bothered with a black scruffing at the ground level on many of the plantings. We searched for answers but found no satisfactory ones. Now we are buying shipped-in radishes, and at least 90% of the time we can offer our customers high quality radishes. Soil applications of chlordane and deildrin nor diazonium sprays gave us satisfactory control of soil insects affecting the turnips we attempted to grow. Now we buy very nice turnips from a neighbor about four miles away who has found the answer to growing good turnips. He had fifty acres in 1975.

Sometimes when we get very busy, we discuss the possibility of cutting out several more of the crops we grow. With the exception of the fourteen crops I referred to earlier, we have difficulty reducing the number still further.

We have plenty of ground; in fact, we plan to plant ten acres of peaches on our Marticville farm in 1976. We are working closely with extension staff and several successful growers in the selection of the site, varieties, and other important facets in peach production. We are told peaches can be a good net profit item if well grown. We know it is an item that our customers like, and that there are times when we could not purchase an adequate and suitable supply within a reasonable distance.

However, with the exception of the peaches, we have not changed significantly the acreage of crops grown significantly in the past two years.

In 1973, of the fifteen major crops grown on which we have records, we have variation in net profit from a loss of $736 per acre on celery to a profit of $3,197 per acre on red raspberries and a net of $2,487 on staked tomatoes. Our records show that the average net profit from the fifteen vegetable crops grown is $825 per acre.

Now when I tell you that we grow 125 acres of small fruit and vegetables, some of you will multiply 125 x $825 and come up with a net profit of over $100,000 for our vegetable growing operation. The conclusion would naturally be that this guy is doing all right. Next summer all of you would be coming down to see me to see if I was lying or else to find out how we do it.

As most of you know, on the major crops we do not do that well. On our sixty acres of corn, we netted only $131 per acre; $178 on green beans, and, of course, on the five acres of celery we lost $736 per acre. Even on the best net profit crop, red raspberries, we can raise only one acre. If we increased the acreage, the net profit would fall because of the lower selling price.

Why do we grow celery when its production results in losing money for the farm operation? We grow celery because it is a traffic builder, the same as our advertising. People come to the farm to get high quality celery that is partially blanched either by the use of paper in the summer and fall, or by burying it in trenches for use from Thanksgiving to February 15. We trim it daily and give our customers a fresh product they cannot buy at the supermarket. I do not know how it is at your farm market, but it is hard to get customers out after November 1.

In addition to the need for celery as a traffic builder, I believe we can eliminate some of the problems causing losses in our celery program. Improving the level of moisture in the field and the addition of $CaCl_2$ and calcium nitrate has reduced the incidence of black heart significantly. The use of Benlate and Bravo has reduced the amount of blight and storage diseases. We also have been selecting plants that do not break down with black heart or that store well. It is a slow process, and I am sure my son would not have the patience or the inclination to follow the selection process. However, in our paper blanch program, we have reduced losses from 50% in 1972 to 10% in 1975.

In the spring we start our selling season (home grown products) with pansies about April 1. Asparagus and rhubarb start April 20. Then bedding plants May 1 to June 10.

We grow 20,000 potted tomatoes in three-inch pots for sale, plus 7,000 in three-inch peat pots for our own use. Hanging baskets and bedding plants are an important part of our vegetable growing operation. Not only does greenhouse production provide work in the winter for our key help, but it also provides 8% of the total farm income for the year.

We keep two sets of books, one for the farm operation and one for the farm market. Twenty-seven percent of the selling price of an item grown on the farm is designated gross profit for the farm market; 73% of the selling price of farm-produced products is gross profit for the farm.

Our strawberries start about June 1, as do our edible podded peas. Black raspberries start about June 15 to July 10.

We try to have staked tomatoes ready by July 4, but it is usually July 10 before we are picking heavily. Prices break sharply July 20 to 25. So in our area we are looking for a variety which, when set out May 10 (potted plants), will have some ripe fruit by July 4 to 10 and be over by July 25. The best commercial variety we have found is Jet Star. It surely does not fit the bill entirely, but it is the best thing we have available. We need smooth fruit, because many of our customers buy hot house tomatoes and will choose hot house over outdoor grown tomatoes unless the outdoor fruit is nice. This is true even when the hot house tomatoes are more expensive.

We are still working with several tomato lines originally supplied to us by Dr. Bill Hepler, now head of the Department of Horticulture at Penn State. These are open pollinated lines, and the one that looked best under our conditions is PS 3531. We have attempted to select several outstanding plants each year from this line. In 1975 it looked like we hit the jackpot. From ten selected plants, on July 18 we picked 4 1/2 pounds of ripe tomatoes from each plant. All of these were number one fruit, most of the fruit weighing six to eight ounces with no cracking and excellent interior. At the time of harvest, we were getting 55 cents a pound retail. Using the formula described earlier, this returns the farm 40¢ lb. x 4 1/2 lbs. per stalk = $1.80 per stalk x 6,000 stalks per acre = $10,800 gross per acre. The gross per acre return from our staked tomatoes in 1975 was $4,861. That is based on a yield of 11.2 tons per acre at 21.7¢ lb. over a picking season from July 1, 1975, to August 10, 1975. Naturally, in 1976 we will plant our entire early tomato planting to this line with enough Jet Star and Red Pack to compare performance.

The problem with PS 3531 is it is not resistant to verticillium or fusarium wilts. Dr. Hepler has several lines with PS 3531 as a parent that do carry resistance. If the new lines perform well, I am sure he will release them for trial.

Sweet corn starts with us July 10 with Spring White. We plant fifteen acres early and then plant three to five acres every five or seven days, depending on temperature and moisture conditions. Most years we can harvest corn to October 10. However, in the past two years, demand from September 20 to October 10 has been showing weaker trends in our area. The increasingly difficult problem of ear worm control after Labor Day is causing us to think about still further cuts in the acreage planted late and possibly an earlier cut-off period.

Later on in the fall we have the cool season crops. Celery, broccoli, cauliflower, and brussels sprouts are our principle fall crops.

We find cauliflower is a good traffic builder for our market. It also can be profitable with a little cooperation from the weather.

My Trip to Ohio State With Dean Beattie—
The Value of Research

Dr. James Beattie, then dean of Penn State's School of Agriculture, requested four individuals representing four different segments of Pennsylvania's horticultural industry, to accompany him and several of his staff to Ohio State University to share our views and experiences with several Ohio State growers, Ohio State faculty members, and several students. As I recall, it was sort of a "where are we now and where do we think the horticultural industry is going in the future" type of presentation.

My remarks on our experiences encountered while growing and marketing small fruit and vegetables on our three small farms follow:

As a vegetable grower for more than forty-five years, I can look back to where we have been. During that time we have to be considered a small grower, a family farmer. I represent the third generation on our farm. My father and my grandfather had a small dairy herd and a retail milk route. They also grew general farm crops.

After college, because of my interest in growing vegetables, we gradually increased the emphasis on vegetable crops. I worked for my father until 1950, when my wife and I bought the home farm. We purchased two additional farms and increased our acreage to 244 acres.

Our youngest son, Fred, came into the business in 1963. In 1976 we sold the home farm and the business to Fred. He rents the other two farms. Now I work for him. I have come full circle: First I worked for my dad and now I am working for my son.

As most of you know, our type of operation is very labor intensive. In 1973, 21,000 hours of hired labor were required to produce and harvest the twenty-two crops we grew for our roadside market.

Before 1952, high school students did most of the harvesting. After 1952 we hired an increasing number of Puerto Rican migrants. In 1966 the number of migrant workers peaked at twenty-three and we hired fifteen high school students.

Because of housing and other regulations, we have reduced the number of migrants hired to seven in 1978. Most of these men earn over $200 per week. In 1978 we employed no high school students. We needed the students. They were available but recent legislation made their hiring unfeasible.

In 1966 we grew thirty-two crops. Much of our production was sold wholesale. Since that time we have reduced the number of crops grown to seventeen and sell 90% of those crops through the roadside market. As a result of this change of emphasis, our sales are up and our labor costs are down, even at the substantially higher hourly rates.

By being more selective in the crops we grow (we are now down to seventeen from thirty-two crops), we can reduce our costs and increase our net profit.

As a general rule of thumb, if we can buy a minor crop of consistently good quality, we will not grow it. If we cannot make a profit on a crop three out of five years, we will not grow it. We will never return to twenty-three migrants and fifteen students; we can't afford to. Even with these shifts in management, it may be difficult for a small grower like us to remain in business. Perhaps new harvesting equipment can be developed that will be cost effective for the small grower.

However, there are things that scientists like you have done and can continue to do that will help you, can give us more profitable varieties. Let me cite several examples.

The late I.C. Haut, in cooperation with the folks at Beltsville, introduced the Marlate strawberry. Under our conditions, primary berries are produced of sufficient size and in sufficient numbers that our pickers can pick twenty quarts per hour compared to fifteen quarts per hour for Midway. This represents a 25% saving in picking costs. The Guardian strawberry offers still more savings because of its larger average size and a new selection that may soon be released by Dr. Gene Galletta, it is still larger in size plus it has some resistance to botrytis (as we observed it). This quality of rot resistance is important to strawberry growers for PYO and fresh market. Days between pickings can be increased a bit for market sales and less loss will be incurred in case of bad weather for PYO.

When I look back to tomato varieties like Bonny Best, John Baer, Valiant, and Marglobe, and compare these varieties with today's excellent varieties, such as Better Boy, Supersonic Jet Star, Red Pack, and a host of other fine varieties, it can be said of our plant breeders, "You have come a long way, baby," regardless of what anyone says about "hard tomatoes and hard times."

Although today most of the tomato breeding emphasis is on processing varieties, for obvious reasons, I feel there is an important place for small growers who do a good job of producing fresh market tomatoes. With this crop, harvesting and packing costs are also high.

In our own operation, harvesting, washing, and packing cost on our trellised tomatoes represent 30% of our total cost of production. Here again, the plant breeder has played and can continue to play an important role. Increasing the average size of fruit from 4.5 oz. to 6.0 oz. will result in a harvesting saving of between 20 to 25%. Increasing the resistance to cracking will also improve the profitability.

I have been observing a tomato selection sent to me for trial in 1973 by Dr. Bill Hepler, former head of the Horticulture Department at Penn State. I have been making selections from this line, as best I can, and in 1978 we had the best performance ever. Eighty-eight percent of the fruit graded #1 and the average fruit size was 6.4 oz. This selection produced 25% more early fruit than did Jet Star which is our best commercial early variety, and I have tried most of them. Ours per acre gross return exceeded $8,000 and even if our growing costs reach $4,500, we will still have a nice net profit.

The problem is, this line carries no resistance to verticillium and fusarium wilt and would be of little value in many areas, even if it were adapted. Bill Hepler made a start to introduce some V & F resistance into the line. However, his activities as a plant breeder were seriously curtailed when he was named head of the horticulture department.

Now since Bill has left Penn State, Dean Beattie is faced with the problems of finding a new department head. In addition, what recommendation can Dean Beattie or Walt Thomas make to the individual assigned to carry on Bill Hepler's plant breeding work. Can time and money be spent on developing tomato varieties for trellis and other fresh market growers who are relatively few in number and when there are so many higher priority needs to be met?

If research funding at the state and federal level were increasing instead of decreasing, there would be no problem.

Since this is not the case, one has to wonder about all this talk about helping this small farmer when research and extension funds are being cut to the point where providing the help needed is nearly impossible.

The use of herbicides is a very important tool in reducing our production costs. In 1978 the application of sencor and enide in split applications gave us the best weed control ever. This is the first year we have used sencor, and this is the first year we didn't have to cultivate or hoe. Quite likely some of you in this room were responsible for the development or clearance of this material. We appreciate your efforts.

Asparagus is a crop that has declined in acreage in Pennsylvania and in the northeast. In most cases, lack of per acre production or low prices for the processing crop, or a combination of both, have been the principal causes of this decline. In our area, fresh market prices are up sharply to $1.25 per pound for bunched asparagus and 85¢ a pound for 20-lb. bulk lots. During the past four years our yield per acre has been a low 2,185 pounds. At this level of production, harvesting and bunching costs represent 50% of the total production costs. However, even at this high labor cost we can net $600 per acre using $3.60 per hour harvest labor.

Dr. Howard Ellison's asparagus breeding program at Rutgers looks as though it will make available several lines of asparagus that will be resistant to fusarium wilt and rust. In addition, all the male hybrids lines I have observed have excellent horticultural qualities. Under our conditions the named variety Rutgers Beacon is superior to the Washington varieties and several of the all-male hybrids will easily outperform Beacon.

On our farm we are looking at fifty-two hybrid lines developed by Dr. Ellison and some varieties for comparison. From what I have seen, there is enough vigor and disease resistance in this new material to get asparagus production back to the 3,000 to 4,000 lb. per acre level. These new lines should help to keep us in the asparagus business using hand harvest, even at significantly higher wage rates. If and when a small harvester comes along at reasonable costs, we will look at it also.

I have no desire to go back to where we were with too many weeds, no herbicides, too many dangerous insecticides like arsenic of lead. I wouldn't mind spending some time in the DDT era, using a material safe to apply, effective in its use, and low in cost. It's only fault: it lasted too long. I have no desire to go back to those harsh, although effective, fungicides. I am sure if plants could talk they would agree.

All of us have to be disturbed by the many regulatory and funding decisions that are made by apparently well meaning but poorly informed individuals. Most regulatory measures increase the cost of producing food and fiber. Adequately funded research in most instances reduce the cost of production and prevent prices from rising too rapidly. If, indeed, there is a real concern to keep prices from rising too rapidly, why then are regulatory agencies receiving additional funding and our agricultural research receiving decreased levels of funding?

I am enough of an optimist to believe that those things that are best for this nation will prevail. I am enough of a realist to know that very little will happen unless we make it happen. There is an urgent need to keep telling our story to the right people. Perhaps those people should be different people than those to whom we have been speaking.

What do I see in the future, and I hope it is not in the too distant future? I believe research funds will be increased to their former levels with needed correction for inflation. I believe this because it has been proved that research and development is the life blood of any industry or any nation.

AMOS H—
A RED RASPBERRY
NAMED FOR ME

The story of the Amos H raspberry and many other raspberries is contained in a presentation I made in February 1993 to the State Horticultural Association of Pennsylvania. It follows:

I am, by nature, an individual who likes to try new things, including new varieties. Sometimes I try experimental lines that are only numbered and not yet introduced or named. This interest includes red and black raspberries.

The first raspberry variety we grew was Latham, introduced in 1920 out of Minnesota. It was a good mid-season producer with large fruit. The next variety we added was Sunrise. Sunrise had smaller fruit but was a week earlier. About the same time we tried St. Regis as an everbearer. We then replaced St. Regis with September, which was a 1947 introduction out of Geneva. After fruit quality and production was reduced by disease, we planted again.

Our next planting included not only Latham, but Taylor, introduced in 1935 by the Geneva station, and a few Newburg, introduced in 1929 out of Geneva. Latham and Taylor produced well. The flavor of Taylor was excellent. However, Newburg froze back severely nearly every year.

Not knowing much about the cause of winter injury in raspberries, we thought any variety that did well in the cold temperatures of Canada would certainly do well in Lancaster County. At this point, we ordered three Canadian varieties from Ed Lowder, a nurseryman from Anchester, Ontario. These varieties did not perform well on our farm.

In addition to the reds, we were growing the following blacks: Bristol, a 1934 Geneva, New York, introduction; Dundee, a 1927 Geneva, New York, introduction; and Cumberland, an 1896 Pennsylvania introduction.

In an effort to increase our income, we asked the Pennsylvania Department of Agriculture to certify the red and black raspberries we were growing. We hoped to propagate and sell plants from the above varieties. We rogued several times a year and sprayed for aphid control. The late Dr.

I.C. Haut, then head of the Department of Horticulture, University of Maryland, and Director of the University Agricultural Experiment Station, looked over the Pennsylvania Raspberry Certification list and saw this Lancaster County grower Amos Funk with nine varieties of raspberries listed. The number of varieties aroused his interest to the point that he paid me a visit in 1955. He was impressed enough by my level of interest that he invited me down to College Park to observe his breeding program and plots.

In a letter dated June 28, 1955, Dr. Haut spoke of efforts at USDA to "heat-treat" roots of Latham raspberries to kill any virus present in the stock. In this letter, he also spoke of two of his early selections, Anthretams and No. 5-420-5. He described them both as falling short on size.

On February 19, 1958, I received a letter from Dr. Richard Converse, plant pathologist USDA at Beltsville, exploring my interest in purchasing from Dr. H.F. Winter, Wooster, Ohio, 100 virus-free Cumberland black raspberry plants at ten cents each. The plan was that I would plant them on our farm in order that Dr. Converse could visit the field periodically and note the development of virus in these virus-free plants.

In a letter dated February 29, 1956, Dr. Haut wrote, and I quote: "No progress on the heat treatment on Latham. Guess I will have to go after this myself, some people get too easily discouraged."

My wife and I made our first visit to College Park on June 8, 1956. We were very impressed—44,000 experimental raspberry seedlings in one field.

In 1958, we received our first experimental red raspberries from Dr. Haut, 350 Sentry, 150 Sentinel, 50 Septer-3, and 50 Citadel.

The only experimental blacks we received from Dr. Haut were Allegany, which never performed well for us, and 134 J, now named Haut. Haut yielded 4,000 quarts per acre in our 1970 trials—our highest yield ever.

In February 1971, I received a phone call from Ted Stegmaier from Cumberland, Maryland. He did most of the propagation for Dr. Haut's experimental material. He explained he had approximately 1,200 black and red raspberry plants, including three numbered selections and ten named varieties. He said he wanted to move them and would sell the 1,200 plants for $200. How could I say no to that? Thirteen lines of red and black raspberries to observe. I said send them in April 1971. We planted them.

It was from this planting and my observation of the performance of other selections on our farm over the years that we decided on two spring-bearing varieties, Sentry and 449AB.

Dr. Harry Swartz was kind enough to name 449AB, Amos. Perhaps he did this because of my continued interest in this selection and my efforts to have 449AB, one of Dr. Haut's lost selections, propagated.

Thanks to Wendy Oglevee and her Phytolab, Inc., at Oglevee's in Connellsville, Pennsylvania, using a tissue culture technique, virus-indexed plants of Sentry and Amos were obtained and enough plants were made available for our planting of the two varieties in 1983. In our continuing effort to look for something better, we included ten plants each of Royalty and Titan. Although Titan yields heavily under our conditions, we do not like the appearance nor the taste of Titan fruit for our retail customers.

In 1990, by mutual agreement, propagation was turned over to Nourse Farms, Inc., in Massachusetts. Virus-indexed plants of Amos and Sentry are now available from Nourse Farms. I believe Sentry are also available from other sources.

In 1991 we set out a new planting of everbearing raspberries, 80% Heritage and 20% Ruby. Heritage has always been good for us. Ruby looks promising.

We also set out a new planting of blacks. We planted: Haut, 4%; Bristol, 36%; Jewel, 60%.

In 1992 we plowed down our nine-year-old planting of Sentry and Amos and planted in Methyl Bromide fumigated soil a new planting. Because of the very satisfactory performance of the variety Amos, we ordered equal amounts of Amos and Sentry plants. We ordered tissue culture harden-off plants from Nourse Farms Greenhouse.

As we continued to look for something better, we included ten plants of Harry Swartz's C.D.H.1, twenty-five plants of Tulamen, a 1990 Canadian Introduction, that may or may not be sufficiently winter hardy to be profitable. We also planted a few Royalty because of its later ripening.

Based on my experience, I would recommend to any growers interested in growing red raspberries: try Sentry along with the newly released cultivar Amos. As compared to Sentry, Amos is five days earlier, very important in our market. Berries are larger and equal in taste to the excellent quality Sentry. Amos is a very good cultivar for retail markets.

Amos produces half as many suckers as Sentry, reducing our labor costs over $100 per acre. The fruiting canes are thicker than those of Sentry. The early yield is double Sentry and the total yield is nearly equal to Sentry. Both cultivars are superior to Latham under our conditions.

My Love For the Land—
Where Did It Come From?

What caused me to care so deeply for the land? We can examine things that were not done to influence my thinking and the development of my interest in the conservation and wise use of our natural resources.

This love of land was not taught to me by my parents. My father used the best farming methods he was aware of. This did not include effective erosion control. I was not encouraged or persuaded by any of my teachers while I was in school at any level. I did not learn it at 4-H or FFA meetings.

Why in the late 1970s and early 1980s would I be willing to spend at least 1,000 hours per year going, almost without exception, wherever I was invited to encourage the wise use of our God-given natural resources, including the preservation of our best farmland? Although I was sometimes reimbursed for my expenses, I never accepted payment for my presentations.

Perhaps the best answer I can arrive at is contained in a presentation I made in my church, Grace United Methodist Church in Millersville, on Laity Sunday, October 14, 1990. My presentation follows:

Connecting Faith With Action
Amos Funk
Laity Day Sunday
October 14, 1990

When Bill Skelly asked me to speak briefly on how I connect my faith with action, the question prompted some soul searching on my part. I had never thought much about it. A great deal of the credit has to be given to my Christian mother. Not only for the things she taught us children in our home, but also for the fact she brought us regularly to Sunday School and church each Sunday.

As some of you know, it was at a combined Sunday School and church service that I accepted Christ as my Savior at the age of twelve. I believe with this act of accepting Christ as one's Savior also comes a commitment to turn over to the Lord the best of our ability, our time, and our energy to do the Lord's work. I doubt if I gave this matter much thought at the age of twelve. However, "all things are possible with Christ." For this reason, I believe a seed was planted in my subconscious mind at the age of twelve.

As my friend Henry Huber is finding out with his gardening, one must do much more than plant a seed if you want to harvest a crop. I feel the seed with which I was blessed was nurtured by a very special and talented Sunday School teacher named Edna Habecker. Each Sunday we would have to memorize several Bible verses. If we did well, she would give us a small reward. One Sunday I was given two verses to memorize. One was in the first chapter of Genesis, verse one: "In the beginning God created heaven and earth," and in the second chapter, verse fifteen: "The Lord placed man in the Garden of Eden as its gardener to tend and take care of it." In Edna Habecker's explanation of verse fifteen, she emphasized the importance of being a good steward of God's creation. In answer to my question, "What does being a good steward mean?" she pointed out one should not destroy or waste God's creation. I never forgot that statement.

Later while in high school, again in a Sunday School class taught by another excellent teacher, Elvin Brenner, father of Roy and Bob Brenner, we were discussing the book of Deuteronomy. Elvin Brenner pointed out to us that in this book and elsewhere in the Bible, we are taught that it is our duty to God as well as to one another, to honor the land, not destroy it, and to respect the plant and animal life upon the land.

This truth also made a lasting impression on me. I started looking around our farm to see if we were properly caring for the land. I noticed there was some serious erosion taking place on some fields of our farm. Not knowing what to do about the situation, I suppose I just filed it away in my mind as a problem. Some time later I met Abner Houseknect, a neighbor who worked for the U.S. Soil Conservation Service. He told me about his work and how farmers could reduce erosion on cropland and better protect the land and the environment. In addition, he invited me to accompany him to a meeting held by a group of conservation pioneers, including Arthur Brown, a former Penn State wrestler who had turned farmer, a Presbyterian minister named George Shea, and others. Incidentally, we met at the Memorial Methodist Church in Quarryville.

At this meeting, it was pointed out that by changing the field shapes and farming across the slopes of the hill in alternate strips of cultivated and non-cultivated crops such as wheat and hay, erosion could be reduced and more rain that falls on the land could be retained. By this procedure, the soil that God created would not be destroyed by erosion. After several trips to observe the farms where this new method of farming was in use, I was convinced this was the way to go.

At this point I approached my dad and suggested that we get the Soil Conservation Service to prepare and implement a conservation plan for our farm. I will never forget his response. He said, "Amos, I will never get used to or like those crooked rows. However, you probably will be farming long after I am gone and if you think it is a good idea, let's try it." What a response! What a dad! We had a conservation plan developed, and it was implemented.

Because of my enthusiasm for conservation farming, I was asked to serve on the Lancaster County Conservation District Board formed in 1951. I asked the county commissioners not to reappoint me in 1995.

In the early 1960s I became concerned about the loss of parts of a farm or an entire farm sold for development. I chose to call this "Real Estate Erosion," since we are still talking about the land God created. Land can be used wisely for development that is well planned and for farming, using approved conservation methods. It is most important to have a balanced mix of both uses in the proper locations.

I have tried to point out how a seed planted in my subconscious mind at the age of twelve and nurtured by two outstanding Sunday School teachers, assisted by neighbors and friends in and outside of Grace Church, caused me to pursue with considerable vigor the conservation of our soil and water, the preservation of farmland, and the protection of our environment.

My First Sunday Morning Sermon—
"The Christian Use of the Land"

On Sunday morning, June 25, 1978, I was invited to speak at our morning worship service at my home church in Millersville. The subject I was asked to speak on was "The Christian Use of the Land." My remarks were as follows:

Good morning! I consider it a privilege to be asked to speak to you. I wish I could say it is a pleasure to be up here, but it is not. I would rather be sitting down there with you. However, when Clyde Hess asks you to do something, it is difficult to say no. In addition, I believe most members of our congregation would like to do more for our church, but many of us are fearful of not doing an adequate job. Therefore, rather than risk trying and failing, we refuse and avoid the risk. I know I have been guilty of this a number of times.

I suppose I was more willing to accept this request because the subject I was asked to discuss is so very important to me and I am able to share my concerns with so many of you at one time.

Some of you may wonder how I became interested in conservation. It started in the late 1930s. I became aware of the serious erosion taking place in some of our fields (on our home farm). I had learned that by changing the field shapes and farming across the slopes of the hill in alternate strips of cultivated and non-cultivated crops such as wheat and hay, erosion could be reduced significantly, and more of the rain that falls on the land could be retained.

At this point, I approached my dad and suggested we get the U.S. Soil Conservation Service to prepare and establish a conservation plan for our farm.

I will never forget his response. He said: "Amos, I will never get used to or like those crooked rows. However, you probably will be farming long after I am gone, and if you think it is a good idea, let's try it." This is all

I needed. I was asked to serve on the Lancaster County Conservation District in 1950 and I have been serving since that time.

In the first chapter of Genesis we read, "God created the heaven and the earth." In the second chapter, verse 15, we read that the Lord God placed the man in the Garden of Eden as its gardener to tend and take care of it.

The question I would raise today is: Are we really taking care of the "Garden," the land in the Garden, the water that flows through the Garden, and the air above the Garden?

As it appears to me, the Lord in His infinite wisdom has given us the freedom of choice in many areas of our lives. We can choose to accept our Savior at an early age; however, all of us can cite instances when those who waited until the eleventh hour have not been refused. We can be active in our chosen church fellowship and thus enjoy the rich blessings of this marvelous association, or one can be less active and remain somewhat aloof and thus be denied these blessings and rewards.

So, too, as we live in this very expanded "Garden of Eden" we have choices to make. What kind of caretaker or steward will we prove to be? There are numerous examples to prove that if we make poor choices we will get long-range poor results.

As an example of poor stewardship, I would like to have you look with me at the Promised Land through the eyes and account written by W.C. Loudermilk, an early conservationist who made a conservation evaluation in a number of countries, including the Holy Land, in 1938 and 1939.

You will recall that after forty years of wandering in the wilderness, Moses stood on Mount Nebo in the Land of Moab and looked across the Jordan Valley to the Promised Land. He described it to his followers in words like these:

"For the Lord thy God bringeth thee into a good land, a land of brooks and waters that spring out of the valleys and hills; a land of wheat and barley and vines and fig trees and pomegranates, a land of olive oil and honey; a land wherein thou shalt eat bread without scarceness; thou shalt not lack anything in it; a land whose stones are iron and out of whose hills thou mayest dig brass."

I doubt if Martha Eckman, Mary Barley, or any others of you who may have visited the Holy Lands were shown this part of the Jordan Valley because, according to Mr. Loudermilk, it is not a pretty sight. He puts it this way, and I quote: "We looked at the Promised Land as it is today, 3,000 years after Moses described it to the Israelites as a land flowing with milk and honey.

"We found the soils of red earth washed off the slopes to bedrock over more than half the upland area. These soils had lodged in the valley where they are still being cultivated and are still being eroded by great gullies that cut through the deposited soil with every heavy rain.

"As the soil was eroded from the sloping part of the valley to the valley floor, the productive capacity of the soil was lost; when the productive capacity of the soil was lost, the people moved out. In fact, in one part of the Jordan Valley, of the 161 sites once populated, 124 are now abandoned."

I would conclude from this happening that up to a point, God will let undesirable things happen if we do not do our part. However, I know very well that very little that is desirable or worthwhile can be accomplished without God's help.

I doubt if this kind of massive erosion will ever take place in this nation, for a number of reasons. However, right here in our county soil erosion has taken its toll over the years. This is particularly disturbing when it is pointed out that 100 years are required by nature to form one inch of topsoil. According to a 1940 survey conducted in Lancaster County, one-fourth of the area surveyed lost 75% of the topsoil originally found there; one-half of the area lost 50% of its topsoil, and the remaining one-fourth of the area lost less than 25% of its topsoil. Here in Lancaster County, there were eight to twelve inches of topsoil before the land was first farmed.

In a national study completed in 1975, it was found that in parts of the state of Iowa, one bushel of soil was lost by water erosion for every bushel of corn produced. Soil is being washed away on our nation's cropland at the average rate of nine tons per acre per year.

So the next time you take a cross-country flight and look down over all that farmland, think about the tremendous loss of soil that is taking place. The average annual erosion ranges from a height of twenty-three tons per acre in Mississippi to a low of one ton per acre in California, where most of the cropland is quite level.

Our conservation district has encouraged and assisted farmers in the county until now nearly one-third of the farms are adequately protected from serious erosion. We have also worked with builders and developers under the provisions of the Pennsylvania Clean Streams Law, assisting them to adopt such measures that will reduce erosion from the building sites.

Yet, after every heavy rain most of our streams are chocolate brown as a result of the sediment load they are carrying. It is obvious we are not doing enough. Howard Manning and his company are doing their part by encouraging farmers to disturb the soil loss during planting preparation, and after planting, by using a procedure called minimum tillage. This method leaves a mulch on top of the soil and this tends to prevent erosion. It looks very promising.

In the 1950s we were concerned with the loss of soil by rain-induced erosion. In the 1960s, we developed a new concern; we became concerned about the loss of entire farms or parts of farms when they were taken out of production for industrial or residential developments.

Because of my interest and concern in this area, in December 1967 I was appointed by former Governor Shafer to an eighteen-member committee and given the charge to develop a plan to preserve Pennsylvania's agricultural land.

After two years of work, we presented our report and recommendations to the governor. He and others complimented us on the report and described it as a good report. Unfortunately, to date, few of the recommendations have been implemented. Naturally, this has been very frustrating to me. However, we are still trying.

Each year, it seems more and more of our good farmland is lost to urbanization. As an extreme example, I would cite Suffolk County, Long Island, in New York state. Here is a county with excellent farmland similar to Lancaster County. It is a bit larger in area than our county. However, in the past forty-two years, 87% of the agricultural land has been taken out of production to accommodate the one million new people who moved into the county.

To those who say it couldn't happen here, I would point out that today Lancaster County leads all counties in the state in the rate of development. Thirty-three percent of the county is now urbanized. In fact, eight of the twelve farms nearest our farm in Millersville are owned by developers. While crops are now grown on these farms, quite likely development will be their future use, not farming.

For some reason, people and industry are attracted to the best farmland. To date, approximately one-half of Pennsylvania's best soils, the levelest, easiest to farm, and least erodable, are already converted to non-agricultural use. The reason: It is easier to build on these soils and it is cheaper to build on these soils.

A look at a soils map of Pennsylvania will show that most of the best agricultural land in the state is located in southeastern Pennsylvania. There, too, is where most of the industry is located and where most of the people live. The same situation exists in Lancaster County. Most of the development has taken place on the relatively level, rich limestone soils in the county.

Think of the Borough of Millersville. It is built on some of the levelest land in Manor Township, of which it was once a part. Don't get me wrong. I am not criticizing anything done by the Borough of Millersville—I wouldn't dare!

With an early Borough Council member Elvin Brenner, three former mayors, a current council president, Bill Kreider, plus several former council members and other borough officials, either present this morning or members of this congregation, again I repeat—I wouldn't dare level any criticism at the Borough of Millersville. All I will say to you officials, past and present, is congratulations for doing a good job and thanks for getting involved.

While most of our building in the past has been on prime farmland, I trust most of our future development will be guided away from our best agricultural land.

In addition, I would hope we would use less land for each home or apartment that is built. I would like to emphasize several points at this time. I am not against growth. I favor reasonable growth and guided growth.

I believe we can accommodate the projected 3,000 new housing units per year in Lancaster County if the housing density is increased toward the goal set by the Lancaster County Planning Commission. If this could be done, the projected 200,000 increased population in our county by the year 2,000 could be housed on less than 25,000 acres of land. There have been periods in our recent history when, for every 100 increase in population, seventy-five acres of agricultural land have been taken out of production.

If we do as poorly in the future as we have done during one ten-year period in the past, six times the 25,000 acres would be needed.

This would be a mistake and would surely represent poor stewardship on our part. I think it is time we treat land as a valuable non-renewable resource, rather than just an economic unit to be traded at will without any thought of the future impact of such action.

Many of us are asking the same question as asked recently by U.S. Assistant Secretary of Agriculture Rupert Cutler when he asked, and I quote: "How long can our nation permit the kidnapping of prime farmland for housing and industrial use before we gravely endanger our ability to meet the food needs of our people and our food commitments to the disadvantaged people of the world?"

According to the most recent census figures, Lancaster County is losing 8,000 acres of agricultural land per year to non-agricultural use. We still have nearly 400,000 acres of farmland left. If something isn't done about this loss, in fifty years there could be less than 100 farms left in what was once the Garden Spot of America, the leading non-irrigated agricultural county in the nation.

As I pointed out earlier, Lancaster is now the fastest developing county in Pennsylvania. Can our county continue to be the fastest developing county and still retain its position as the leading non-irrigated agricultural county in the nation? I doubt it.

Lancaster County is a county that the Lord has really blessed. Percentage-wise, our county has twice as much good fertile soil found as the remainder of the state.

None of us can take credit for the soil we find in our county. God in His infinite wisdom saw fit to allow this special soil to be formed in the county. Then, one can almost see the Lord directing an energetic, frugal people to His fertile land.

As a result of this unique combination of a special people, God fearing and hard working, and some of the most fertile soil on God's earth, Lancaster County has earned the reputation as the Garden Spot.

Although there are sixty-seven counties in the state, Lancaster County is responsible for nearly one-fifth of the state's agricultural product value.

As I pointed out earlier, land that is best for farming is best for everything else. It is best for industrial and commercial building; it is best for building houses, motels, and shopping centers.

Former Secretary of the Interior Steward Udall, speaking at Hershey some time ago, said that if he were to pick an ideal community east of the Mississippi River in which to live, he would choose Lancaster County. Apparently a lot of people agree with him. In the ten-year period of 1960-1970, Lancaster County's urban population grew 26%—six times the state's average.

You see, this is our problem: Our county is just too attractive. I am sure a lot of counties in the state wish they had this problem. I am fearful that unless we guide development a lot more carefully, and hopefully slow down the rate of growth, Lancaster County will not continue to be an attractive place to work and live.

Well, what can be done about the problem? In the interest of time, I do not think it would be appropriate for me to discuss the various proposals being advanced.

It is gratifying to report that at least we in Pennsylvania are past the study stage and are in the implementing process. On June 15, a number of us met with the House Agricultural Committee in an effort to develop land use legislation that will help. We also have had four meetings with the county commissioners in an effort to move ahead at the county level.

I would trust this morning some of you, hopefully many of you, have been persuaded that it is important to use the God-given resource of land more wisely. Discuss the problem with your friends. Study the proposed legislation. Support it if you can. Get involved, and by so doing you will have made a start in discharging your Christian responsibility concerning land use.

Ever since the book of Deuteronomy was written so many centuries ago, we have been taught that it is our duty to God as well as to one another to honor the land and to respect the plant and animal life upon it. On the whole, humankind has not lived up to that teaching very well. Today we are beginning to face up to the fact that we must not further delay, and further disregard will only add to the cost and compound the difficulty.

This venture is compelling, not as animals are compelled by brute force or irresistible instinct, but as free men and women are compelled by their reason, their knowledge, and their conscience. Human beings who recognize that they are placed on this planet by a loving and merciful God cannot disregard the calling to be responsible stewards of the incredibly beautiful, interesting, and bountiful world in which He has made us citizens. The time to start is now.

I Speak to Methodists at Kansas City, Kansas

A nationwide conference called by leaders of the Methodist Church was held in Kansas City, Kansas. I believe the year was 1980.

Selected Methodist farmers representing various segments of the nation's important agricultural industry were asked to prepare papers and speak to the assembled Methodist Church leaders regarding the farm crisis, low farm prices, increased production costs, and loss of too many farms due to foreclosures. These problems were being faced by too many farmers. My remarks to those attending were as follows:

My name is Amos Funk. I am a member of Millersville, Pennsylvania, Grace United Methodist Church, with a membership of 422. I am currently serving as president of the trustee board. My son and I are the only active farmers in our church.

We raise vegetables and berries on 244 acres in Lancaster County. We sell 95% of our products on our roadside market located on the farm. In addition to our key year-round help, this summer we are providing summer jobs for nearly forty college and high school students. They help us and we like to think we are helping them.

Perhaps one the biggest problems facing farmers today is the lack of understanding. People do not comprehend the tremendous financial burden a young farmer has to bear in order to start farming even back in Lancaster County, Pennsylvania, where the farms are comparatively small. In most instances, an investment of nearly one-half million dollars is needed if a young farmer plans to make a living exclusively from farming with no outside income.

In most cases, a young farmer will not be able to pay off the farm during his lifetime, and quite likely, through much of his lifetime his indebtedness will be nearly one-third of his assets. In most cases, his financial progress will be measured by the increase in his net worth—hopefully excluding the appreciation of his land. It is not an easy road to travel. Farming today is challenging, interesting, and certainly not an occupation for the faint-hearted.

Another area of lack of understanding is the thought that a "cheap food policy" is good for consumers and, therefore, is good for our nation. This could be the most important issue we can discuss during this conference.

If we Methodist farmers can convince the non-farmer representatives of our church attending this conference that, in the long run, a cheap food policy is bad for our nation, in my view this consultation will have been very much worthwhile!

There are powerful forces at work in our country as well as other nations in the world, urging the pursuit of a cheap food policy, making it difficult for the man or woman on the land to reap the reward for the innovations he makes.

Consumers the world around welcome such a cheap food policy and politicians respond, whether capitalist or communist. As nations become less agricultural and more urban, the incentive base for the farmer becomes less certain. It becomes more susceptible to political pressures and special interest dealings.

Most farmers are troubled by organized efforts to promote the meatless dinner—the beef boycott—and eat one less hamburger per week.

If it were not so tragic, we would have to smile at the scare campaign whipped up several years ago by the American Bakers Association that bread prices would go up to a dollar a loaf unless we impose export quotas on wheat. As most of us know, wheat prices have declined to below the cost of production, and bread has not been reduced in price; the price has actually increased.

The longshoremen got into the act when they refused to load Gulf export grain that was destined for Russia, on the pretext of keeping living costs under control while they did some fancy maneuvering of their own to increase shipping subsidies.

Almost unnoticed by most of the non-farming Americans during May through August 1977 was the official pleasure in Washington as farm prices declined four straight months in a row. The four-month decline of 15.2 % in farm prices was heralded each month as an indicator of only modest future rises in retail food prices. This seems most unrealistic in face of escalating farm production costs for the farmer.

The drop in farm prices masked the rise in nearly every other price category and permitted the Washington price watchers to interpret the overall showing of the price gain as evidence that inflation was coming under control.

It seems unrealistic to single out the farmers of this nation as the group on whom politicians and others depend to reduce the rate of inflation through a manipulated cheap food policy.

In order to remain in business, farmers must make a profit. Too often in recent years, this profit margin has been too small or non-existent.

This is a major problem that contributes to the farm crisis in this nation today. The latest instance of manipulation to maintain a cheap food policy in spite of its effect on the farmer, was President Carter's decision to raise beef imports by 200 million pounds. This was done against the advice of Secretary of Agriculture Bergland.

Pennsylvania's Secretary of Agriculture Kent Shelhamer, himself a Democrat, decries this decision and issued a strong statement against this action. I will quote some of his remarks.

"In the short run, consumers may save a penny or two when they buy hamburgers, but in the long run, beef producers who managed to stay afloat financially will be forced to keep their herd size down. That means consumers will have to pay higher prices for a longer period of time."

Some of us wonder why steel imports are being reduced and beef imports are being increased. Shouldn't we have the same set of rules for both groups?

We hear a lot about the high-priced beef at $1.68 per pound, when our closest competitors, the residents of Great Britain, are paying $3.86 for the same cut.

Norman Borlang, a plant pathologist who won the Nobel Prize in 1970, said that food costs less in the United States than anywhere in the world compared to the money available to pay for it.

On the farm, the cost of food has not risen nearly as fast as has the cost of processing, transporting, and marketing that food has increased.

In 1977, farmers in this nation were paid approximately 56 billion dollars for the food they produced on their farms. It cost 58 billion dollars to process, package, and distribute this food. This is the first time in the history of the country that it cost more to market the food we consume than it cost to produce it.

Wray Finney, then president of the American Cattleman's Association, called attention to those facts at a 1976 news conference held in Denver, Colorado, in 1976. I will quote from his remarks: "For twenty years, average food prices rose relatively slowly. This was made possible because farm productivity increased 5% a year and thus absorbed most increased production costs. Result: On the farm, food prices rose very little.

"Up to 1971, about 95% of all food price increases ere caused by higher costs and margins for transporting, processing, and marketing farm foods.

"Farm prices continued to fluctuate with changes in weather and supply and demand, *but farm to retail price spreads increased nearly every year.*

"In the early 1970s, farm prices rose significantly in response to shorter supplies and increased world demand, but the relentless increase in off-the-farm margins still accounted for *half the increase in average food prices*. During the past two years, more than *three-fourths of the food price* increases were caused by higher marketing charges.

"Labor costs represent half to two-thirds of the margins between what the farmer is paid and consumer costs at the market in certain segments of the off-farm food industry and wage increases without comparable improvements in productivity, have been the biggest single factor in price spread increases in recent years.

"Average cattle prices have risen significantly when compared to prices received several years ago, but cattlemen helped keep these increases under control with a 65% improvement in their output per man hour in just the past ten years.

"During the same ten-year period, the price spread between what the farmer received and what the consumer paid increased 74%. A major factor in this was labor cost increases. Wage rates in the meat processing industry climbed 77% compared with a productivity increase of only 30%.

"In the supermarket business, wage rates rose 82% but there was a 5% decline in productivity."

Although I know very little about the cattle or meat industry, I believe the numbers Mr. Finney brings to our attention apply to most segments of the food industry.

A look at the history of the American farmer and American agriculture should be ample proof that we farmers are not very good at matching anticipated demand with planned supply. If the price or prospective price of a crop or livestock product increases to the level where a profit can be realized, in most cases we farmers rush in with far too much vigor and soon we have an oversupply and prices are reduced.

Therefore, family farmers by their very nature in generations past, and hopefully in generations to come, will be the best possible insurance of an abundant supply of nutritious food at reasonable prices.

The problem is, and will continue to be: Is farming profitable enough to attract the best possible young people who, by their ability, commitment, and fortitude, can overcome the many problems ever present in the operation of a modern farm or ranch?

Again, I repeat a statement I made earlier: Farming is not an occupation for the faint-hearted.

MY FORTY-FOUR YEARS
WITH THE LANCASTER COUNTY CONSERVATION DISTRICT

Most of the decisions farmers have made in the past on the use of their land have been voluntary. The size and shape of the fields and the crop rotation used was up to the farmer. A look at any old atlas will reveal the square or rectangular fields, and in many cases the rows running up and down the hill.

In the middle 1930s I became aware of the serious erosion taking place on some of our fields on our home farm. I had learned that by changing the field shapes and farming across the slope of the hill in alternate strips of cultivated and non-cultivated crops, such as wheat and hay, erosion could be reduced significantly, and more of the rainfall that falls on the land could be retained.

At this point I approached my dad, for whom I was working, and suggested we get the U.S. Soil Conservation Service to prepare a conservation plan for our farm to control soil and water loss.

I will never forget his response to my proposal. He said, "Amos, I am certain I will never like or get used to those crooked rows; however, you probably will be farming here long after I am gone, and if you think it is a good idea, let's try it!" That was all I needed.

In 1939 we made a voluntary decision in our farm management by requesting the U.S. Soil Conservation Service to prepare a conservation plan for our farm. Since then we have completed conservation plans on our other two farms.

I would point out to you we practice what we preach! In 1950, a conservation district was formed in Lancaster County. I was asked to serve on the original board and I continued serving until 1995.

In the early days our chief mission was to encourage farmers to request the U.S. Soil Conservation Service to prepare a conservation plan for their farms. Although we have worked hard, our conservation district has not been as successful as I would like. Less than 2,000 of our 5,000 farmers have voluntarily requested USDA help to reduce soil and water loss from their farms, even though USDA provides their technical help free of charge.

In fact, the sediment load in most of our Lancaster County streams is higher now than in 1950, when our conservation district was formed. One does not need an instrument to measure the sediment load of the Little or Big Conestoga; we only have to look at the color of the water after a moderate to heavy rain. However, sufficient evidence has been developed to indicate commercial development and the accompanying earth-moving activities in Lancaster County add as much sediment to the streams as does farming activity.

In the opinion of the majority of Pennsylvania's legislators, not enough was being done to maintain the water quality in the streams in the commonwealth. Therefore, on July 31, 1970, the legislature amended existing legislation and Act 275 was passed. This act was called the Clean Streams Law. This act contains numerous provisions, including one on earth-moving activities for which an erosion control plan must be prepared. This covers developers of all sizes and farmers. The Clean Streams Law states that by July 1, 1977, all farmers must have a conservation plan for their farm if they plow any ground.

The history of the Lancaster County Conservation District from the very beginning in 1938 was one of problem solving, idea sharing and volunteerism.

Soil erosion, the problem that prompted the creation of the first district in the area of the county south of Route 30, remains a serious problem today.

The district supervisors, as they were then called, were: Chairman, Hartwell Roper; Earl Groff, father of Wade Groff; Arthur Brown; Earl Hoffecker; and H.H. Snavely. These district officials solved the problem of an inadequate supply of earth moving equipment by buying the equipment needed, hiring an equipment operator, and doing the needed earth moving work for a fee.

The district encompassing the entire county was created by a county commissioner resolution on February 24, 1950.

Elected to chair the new board of directors was Arthur Brown from the early board. Other directors were county commissioner member H.R. Metzler and J. Homer Graybill, William Fredd, and Amos Funk.

Since finances and budgets are on the minds of many of us these days, it may be of interest to note that on September 19, 1952, the original district turned over $2,167,000 to the new district. These funds were generated by earth moving user fees earned by the district.

Our district bought two $1,000 government bonds, leaving a balance of $167 for district use. We operated the district for five years on the $167 plus interest on the government bonds. I assure you that we had to make a little go a long way in those days. Nearly 100% of our efforts were volunteer.

With very little money and no staff except our Secretary-Treasurer Wayne Rentchler, a full-time Vo-Ag teacher at West Lampeter High School, most of the telling of the conservation story had to be done by the district directors. We would accompany SCS technicians Whitey Reese, Abner Houseknect, or County Conservationist Martin Muth. We, as farmer directors, would tell other farmers why we have a conservation plan on our farms and why we think the farmer we were visiting should give it a try. In those early days our success rate was about 25%. This was not high but encouraging.

We were encouraging contour rows, alternate strips of cultivated crops and uncultivated crops, such as hay or wheat. We encouraged a four-year rotation of crops, where possible. We also encouraged crop land terraces and diversion terraces where needed. Our objective was to keep the raindrop where it falls.

My good friend Arthur Brown did not choose to continue as a board member, and I was elected chairman of the Lancaster County District Board in 1952. I served as chairman for eighteen years. I resigned as chairman in 1970 to make room for Aaron Stauffer, who then became chairman. I retired from the district board in 1995, having served on that board for forty-four years.

The emphasis of our district program has changed over the years. Our early goal was to keep the soil in place—prevent erosion. Next, our goal was to retain as much of the rainfall in the soil through reduced runoff. As more manure and fertilizer was applied to the soil to obtain higher yields, reduced soil erosion into our streams became even more important to avoid serious pollution of our underground and surface water supplies.

Now in 1998 our district has been given the additional responsibilities of nutrient management and many related activities. The district staff has grown from zero to sixteen and our district budget has grown from zero to $735,000 annually.

In May 1957, we got our first appropriation of $500 from the county commissioners. Believe me, it was appreciated.

As the conservation district was asked to take on more program responsibilities, to solve more problems for the county and the commonwealth, we found our unpaid volunteer directors could not get the job done.

Nancy Burkhart was hired as secretary in 1965. She was our first paid employee. As of 1998, she is still a valued employee.

In 1971, we persuaded Henry Hackman, a former district director, to accept the position of our part-time district manager. We paid him for his services. This was a first for our district.

Today our district is being asked to be involved in more and more problem solving efforts, including erosion and sediment pollution control, nutrient management, and air and water quality.

To meet these demands our district staff in 1990 had grown to twelve. However, the entire district program is directed by the seven unpaid volunteer district directors.

From the very beginning to the present, we have received very valued support and assistance from the U.S. Soil Conservation Service and other cooperating agencies. We are greatly indebted to all of them for their help.

In 1951 when I was first named a director of the Lancaster County Conservation District, 26% of the county's cropland was planted to corn and 8% was in tobacco and potatoes. The remaining 66% was planted in close-growing crops such as alfalfa and hay, oats, rye, and wheat. In those days, Lancaster County soil was eroding at the rate of less than three tons per acre per year.

Contour plowing and planting, with considerable emphasis on the construction of terraces and diversions, were the practices we stressed over the years.

It is a bit discouraging after thirty years of effort to learn the soil erosion is worse than it was back in 1951 when we started. The question might be asked: "Where did we go wrong?" Perhaps it is not so much that we have failed, as it is that a complete change in our farming practices has taken place.

For a number of reasons farmers have changed their cropping practices. Corn acreages have increased from 113,000 acres in 1960 to 200,000 acres in 1980, a 177% corn acreage increase in twenty years. If the acreage in other row crops is added to the corn acreage, we find we now have in Lancaster County 71% of our cropland planted to row crops and only 29% of the cropland planted to close growing crops—erosion preventing crops like alfalfa, other hay, wheat, and barley.

We are creating problems at a much faster rate than we can solve them. Erosion loss now averages over nine tons per acre annually on the county's cropland and represents a 200% increase over the rate of erosion in 1951.

I was talking about this county soil loss at a meeting and Earl Newcomer was in attendance. After the meeting, Earl told me he just could not accept those soil loss figures. He said, "I have been doing custom corn picking for years and there are fewer gutters I cannot cross than in years gone by."

This is true, we are doing a better job of controlling gully erosion. What is hurting us and our soils is sheet and rill erosion. It is hard to observe nine tons of soil loss per acre, since it is a loss of a layer of soil approximately as thick as nine sheets of notebook paper.

The problem is that when one spreads that nine tons per acre (the average soil loss per acre over the 318,000 acres), the total annual soil loss in the county exceeds twenty-five million tons. That's a lot of soil.

The amount becomes more meaningful, however, when the total county soil loss (twenty-five million tons) is divided by the weight of an acre of topsoil six inches deep, which is 1,000 tons. By this procedure, we find we quite likely are losing the production capacity of soil equal to 2,500 acres each year when we lose nine tons per acre.

The disturbing thing about this soil loss is that in addition to the value of the soil itself, carried along with the eroded soil is any fertilizer or manure that has been applied for the crop.

A recent study in the county pointed out that a nine-ton per acre soil loss would carry with it at least $10.00 in nutrient loss per acre; the accumulated loss could total two million dollars annually. The question might well be asked how can that be when in 1980, all Lancaster County farmers spent less than $1 2/3 million for fertilizer, according to the 1980 Pennsylvania Crop Reporting Service, 8,020 tons of 12-10-10 equivalent.

The answer is as follows: According to the yet unpublished data gathered for the Lancaster County Land and Water Resource Study, farmers in the county in 1979 produced more than five million tons of manure enough to apply more than sixteen tons to every acre of cropland in the county in that year. It is then safe to assume that at least an average of ten tons per acre is applied to most of the corn crop and at least $5 per ton for the manure, there is a $50 per acre nutrient application for manure alone. There are some who believe the nutrient loss exceeds $20 per acre, thus doubling the value of nutrients lost to four million annually.

What I have attempted to do is try to demonstrate that we do have a long-range and a short-range problem and that it will pay us to do something about the problem.

The next thing to consider is what to do about it. Can we throw more money at the problem? That would help, but quite likely we will not have more money, at least not more ACP funds for cost-sharing help.

In fact, the President's budget proposed a nearly 400% reduction in ACP funding for 1983. Congress may or may not reduce that cut. It certainly will be difficult to live with.

Where does that leave us? I think that leaves us with conservation tillage—no-till or minimum-till.

We know that three tons or more of uniformly distributed residue per acre left on top of the soil can reduce erosion 85% on moderate slope lengths. We also know the more passes that are made over the field with either the disk or the chisel, the less residue will be left on top.

Conservation tillage is moving forward in Iowa, Illinois, Ohio, New York, Maryland, and in parts of Pennsylvania. Although chisel plowing is used rather widely in Lancaster County, no-till or conservation tillage, allowing considerable crop residue on top of the soil has not moved ahead very rapidly.

My Twelve Years
With the
Conestoga Valley Association

The Lancaster County Conservation District, encompassing the entire county, was established by the county commissioners in 1950.

A board of directors was appointed in 1951. A number of years later, after Henry Hackman had been appointed to the board, we were sitting in the old county courthouse. We were early for the scheduled meeting of the Conservation District Board. As we waited, Henry shared the thought that protecting the county's soil, water, and other natural resources was a difficult task. Henry posed the question, "Wouldn't it be great if we could persuade interested urban people to assist us in our conservation efforts?" He reminded me as to the strength additional numbers provide. Remember, in those early days the Conservation District had very little money and no paid staff.

Henry Hackman's idea made sense to me. However, I had no idea how to make it happen.

Some progress had been made in Chester County as a result of the formation of the Brandywine Valley Association. We did not do much about Henry's idea except think about it and talk to several people. One of those people was Earl F. Rebman.

For many years, Earl had been a "voice in the wilderness," trying to drum up support to protect, use more wisely, and beautify the Conestoga Creek and the area that surrounds it.

Earl Rebman expressed interest, but not much happened until we went to several meetings at the Brandywine Valley Association in Chester County, headed up by our good friend Robert Struble, who later in his life became county commissioner in Chester County. Robert Struble would extol the benefits and the actions that were taken by the Brandywine Valley Association there in Chester County. He surely made it sound good, as though it was a worthwhile thing to pursue. But still nothing happened in Lancaster County until March 17, 1956, when I happened to be president of the Millersville Men's Club. We met on Saturday nights once a month. On this particular night, because of this interest of Earl Rebman, Henry Hackman, and others, we invited Robert Struble to be our principal speaker. He was a very promotional speaker, able to get one's attention and motivate individuals to action, and he just stirred up enough interest to cause the Millersville Men's Club to support the formation of a Conestoga Valley Association in Lancaster County to preserve the Conestoga River. Everything went fine except, as happened with other organizations with which I was involved, we had a lot of enthusiasm, but no money. At that time during the meeting, March 17, 1956, Earl Rebman got up and said, "I am very anxious to have this Conestoga Valley Association formed, and so I'm going to underwrite the cost of the organization for one year." He had no idea what it would cost, but he felt so strongly that he would do it.

That was the first step. Seventy-five club members were in attendance, along with some guests who were invited: Earl Rebman, Max Smith, Henry Hackman, John Haverstick, Robert Biolo. They represented the Game Commission and Izaac Walton League, etc. So that was a start on March 17, 1956.

The next action that was taken was at a meeting held in Earl Rebman's store at the corner of Water Street and West King Street in Lancaster. I acted as temporary chairman of that meeting, and Earl Rebman was the main spokesman. The Society's aims as Earl outlined them were:

1. The promotion of the soil conservation projects of Lancaster County farms through a system of education which would include more contour plowing, strip farming, and proper planting to conserve a dropping water table and prevent erosion and to see that the water is retained in the land where it falls for the best use of the moisture.
2. The development of the clean stream program for the Conestoga Creek.
3. The development of a program of planting and planning of recreational areas on the banks of the Conestoga for picnicking, boating, swimming, and fishing activities.

The eventual inclusion of the entire county as a conservation and development program, particularly the small streams in the western part of the county which empty into the Susquehanna. In addition, Earl pointed out that the financing for the program will take several years to complete and will come through the cooperation of all persons interested in such a program. He added that the interest in some sort of conservation organization has been evident since 1904, when the Lancaster Chamber of Commerce drew attention of its members to the need for a clean-up program along the Conestoga, particularly as a source of Lancaster's water supply.

Earl Rebman stressed that the charter should permit the association to buy and sell real estate and proposed that the efforts be made to have the property along the streams deeded to the organization. "Some day," he said, "at least one side of the stream will be public property."

Considerable discussion arose over the choice of the name of the association. Before the Conestoga Valley Association was approved, much of the discussion involved the aim and scope of the group with several of those present pointing out that there was considerable interest in improving the tributaries as well as the main body of water.

Professor Frederick S. Klein of Franklin and Marshall College told the group that the college is extremely interested in the proposed program and the Geology Department plans to make a survey of the stream, and equipment could be made available to the organization. Mayor Kendig C. Bare cited the proposed program as one that will benefit all parts of our county and proposed the cooperation of the city. A similar project along the Conestoga on a much smaller scale was begun in 1930 by a group of cottage owners in the Ephrata area. William S. Bixler, secretary of the Lancaster Livestock Exchange, told the group how a two-mile stretch along the old trolley line from Brownstown to Diamond Station had been reclaimed.

The next meeting of the organization was May 31, 1956. This meeting was held in the meeting room of the Lancaster County Bank on 138 North Queen Street in Lancaster. The major purpose of this meeting was to sign the organizational charter drawn up by Attorney Rengler; it had to be signed by the officers, which we did at that meeting. I guess one could say that now we had an organization and also the officers were elected at that meeting. I was elected president; Henry Hackman was vice-president; secretary, Ben Landis; and Earl Rebman, treasurer. We had a troop of thirty-three directors who said they would be willing to serve. Included in that group was Henry Stacks, editor of the *Intelligencer Journal*, and many others.

At my first formal meeting as president of the Conestoga Valley Association, I outlined several concerns. One was, we need more than the present 138 members of the Conestoga Valley Association; my goal was cited as 1,000 members from a county such as Lancaster. I appointed John Kirk, who works with the Pennsylvania Forestry Association, as chairman of the Membership Committee. Also, I mentioned that in order to make a determination of the purity of the water of the Conestoga at this time, it might be well to request a water quality study. I was then authorized to send a letter to the Pennsylvania Department of Health requesting a water quality study.

As an example of some excellent work by my friend Carl Lefever, Carl sent a number of letters and made some visits to Mr. E.S. Matters, Superintendent of Billings at PP&L. After the signing of some legal documents, an agreement was reached whereby the Conestoga Valley Association was given permission to clean up and make ready for improved recreational use, two sites along the Conestoga Creek, near Safe Harbor. On Thursday, November 28, 1957, thirty-one volunteers met following a treat of delicious donuts and other goodies supplied by neighbors and supporters living along the Conestoga above Safe Harbor. A start was made to clear and prepare for recreational use the first of three recreation areas along the Conestoga. Trees were burned, submerged trunks were pulled out, the surface of the land was leveled, and debris was collected and hauled away. This was an excellent example of how volunteers will respond to leadership. I thanked everyone who was helping. We had tractors, we had dump trucks, we had everything we needed, including help from the president of Millersville University, Dr. Bill Duncan. We had Millersville Explorer Boy Scout Post #345 also helping to do what they could. Boy Scout leaders David Bishop, Larry Eckman, and Ronald Snavely helped clean up. Milt Dietrick and my friend Ben Eckman also helped to clean up.

On January 1, 1958, we had an even more successful gathering of a group of volunteers. One hundred five volunteers came to help CVA prepare a second picnic area.

Using the information I acquired from our effort on Thanksgiving Day when we cleared the first recreation area, we decided to clear a larger, five-acre area located at the confluence of the Little and Big Conestoga Creeks on New Year's Day 1958. I used some experience I got from that earlier effort, and we got twice as many men involved—sixty men—and we had forty-five Boy Scouts from all over different parts of the county. The Explorer Scouts from Millersville spent half of a holiday in the Conestoga Creek.

A group gathered on a second such holiday work party to prepare recreational areas. The Boy Scouts were under the direction of the Rev. Richard Bishop, the pastor of Millersville Evangelical and Reformed Church. Warren Hershey and William Maurer, all of Millersville, directed that Explorer Troop #45. Explorer Scouts from Post #345 were under the supervision of Milton G. Dietrick and Ben Eckman, both of Millersville. Things went well. Esta's brother Aldus brought his tractor and someone else brought a tractor. I had asked a welder to come and bring his welding equipment in case we broke anything. Bill Flannagan was kind enough to supply that equipment. We had lots of chain saws and axes and lots of hands and strong backs on that day. I was certainly pleased. Lancaster Bakery supplied donuts for everybody—120 donuts—and we had free milk from one of the dairies close by. So we had a lot of contribution from many people who wanted to help us. In addition, a passing motorist saw the work and stopped and offered help for this worthwhile project. It was very gratifying to be able to complete this project.

I would like to cite another area of support for our efforts in the CVA. At a meeting attended by thirty-five members of the Lancaster County Implement Dealers Association, they unanimously voted to become sustaining members with a membership fee of $25. This was the third sustaining membership group supporting CVA—the other sustaining memberships are held by the Kiwanis Club of Lancaster and the Millersville Men's Club. What happens when we have these sustaining groups? We find that members tell friends in other groups, and they also help. For example, the Men's Club of Mountville donated some tables. We also got tables from Conestoga Lion's Club, quite likely the result of some effort from Carl Lefever. So all these efforts together helped to make what we attempted to do more worthwhile and make the total contribution to the community more meaningful.

Meeting on the County's Supply of Water

Since one of our goals of the Conestoga Valley Association was not only to preserve the quality of the water, but also conserve the quantity of the water that we have to provide for water in the future, we thought it was appropriate to hold a meeting on water. On January 3, 1958, starting at 8:00 p.m., we held a meeting in the Lancaster County Poultry Center on the Roseville Road. We were lucky enough to have Robert Stuble, Executive Director of Brandywine Valley Association, as a moderator. Our principal speaker was the Honorable Maurice Goddard, Secretary of Forests and Waters of the Commonwealth of Pennsylvania. We had the remarks by the Honorable Tom J. Monahan, Mayor of the City of Lancaster, and also invocation by Rev. Leroy Fegley, Pastor of Otterbein U.B. Church in Lancaster. Members of the panel were Charles P. Abraham, Superintendent, Department of Water, Lancaster City; R.A. Hamilton III, President of Hamilton Equipment Company, who sell and service irrigation; William C. Hine, Industrial Assistant to President of New Holland Machine Company, and Paul Hess, Electric Power, President of Safe Harbor Water Power Corporation, and G.A. Reinhard, Jr., Industrial Director of Engineering at Armstrong Cork Company. The meeting was well attended.

One of the participants in the meeting was Arthur J. Sinkler, President of Hamilton Watch Company, and he made a very important, short statement:

"Conservation is everybody's business." This picture was painted by all. Water is presently being consumed, polluted, and wasted at an alarming rate in Lancaster County, and it's not too late to remedy the situation. Dr. Goddard told the audience that unless we learn to conserve our natural resources, we will fall into the lot of North Africa, China, and other nations that were once great. He called water our second most important resource, outranked only by land. We mishandled the land, he said, we pollute the water, we consume the water. In order to maintain world supremacy, we are going to have to conserve water. He congratulated the audience and CVA for its approach to the problem, using statistics on rivers in Pennsylvania and bordering states, and demonstrated that the four rivers can be regulated through the construction of reservoirs. This, along with intensive conservation of land, he said, will provide the answer. You can increase or reduce runoff depending on how you handle the whole watershed, he said. The change in river flow, he emphasized, will be determined entirely on whether or not people care about the land. He told those gathered together that you have shown by being her tonight that you cared. Please preserve the land. Mayor Thomas Monahan told the meeting that the fruit of the CVA is coming into the point of reality.

Charles P. Abraham, Superintendent of the Department of Water in Lancaster City, said that the use of water in Lancaster City did not reach a billion gallons a year until the year 1890. By 1900, the use had doubled to two billion gallons, and by 1930, the amount of water needed was three billion gallons a year. By 1957 it may be as much as sixteen million gallons of water a day on hot days of summer. The use of water by industrial users is also an important factor in the total use of water. Superintendent of Water Abraham pointed out the amount of water needed by industry in the year 1957 in Lancaster County was as follows: Armstrong used on the average 1,100,000 gallons of water per day; RCA used 1,250,000 gallons per day; New Holland Machine, 1,000,000 gallons per day. Another ten major industries averaged about 160,000 gallons per day.

On April 12, 1958, at 8:00 p.m., a meeting held in the Lancaster County Poultry Center featured as a topic Sewage Disposal and related water problems. At this meeting the invocation was given by Levi Brubaker; the opening remarks by Charles Pierce, Lancaster County Commissioner; speaker was Francis E. Pitkin, Bureau of Improvement and Development, Department of Commerce, Harrisburg, Pennsylvania. The panel was moderated by County Agent Smith and the panel included: Sam Bard, President of Lancaster County Boroughs Association; John H. Gehr, Regional Sanitary Engineer; Edward Edgerly, former District Engineer; Pennsylvania Department of Health; Robert Epley, Sanitary Consulting Engineer; and Dr. John Hess, Department of Geology, F&M College, Lancaster, Pennsylvania; and Henry Wooding, Agricultural Extension Agent, Penn State University.

An Early Attempt to Clean Up and Protect Rock Ford (Hand Home)
On Saturday, July 26, 1958, fifteen volunteers started cleaning up around the Hand Home area (Rock Ford), took away some of the trees that had fallen down, boarded up with plywood the windows so vandals would not destroy any more windows. We worked until about 3:00 p.m. Saturday afternoon and got the place looking much better.

Rock Ford Reclamation
The Junior League had the money available to begin the necessary work on Rock Ford, according to Mrs. Elaine Holder. Various plans for restoration of Rock Ford had been thoroughly examined by the committee of the Junior League, in consultation with Dr. S.K. Stevens, Executive Secretary of the Pennsylvania Historical and Museum Committee; Earl K. Newton, Chief of the Bureau of Museums and Historical Sites; Architect Bumbaugh, one of the League's restoration architects in the United States and the man responsible for the painstaking restoration of the Ephrata Cloisters, was called in for estimates. Bumbaugh figured out a first class, all the way thorough job would require a maximum of $75,000, including $25,000 for furnishings. An alternate plan of restoration suggested by Newton on the Historical Commission would involve occasionally consulting an architect to work in close conjunction with local contractors to get the job done. Maximum estimated cost for such a job would be $20,000 to $30,000 and would include the paved parking lot, the complete heating facilities, plus landscaping. The Junior League envisions the makeup of a possible foundation which would include these organizations. All of them have indicated willingness to cooperate. The Colonial Dames of Lancaster County, Historical Association, the Pennsylvania Historical and Museum Commission, will provide the research only. No money is available here at present.

As I review some of the minutes and early plans of the CVA in 1957, I have outlined in general why at the September 25, 1957, meeting we had all this discussion about the General Hand Home and what might be done. It seems that wasn't enough to have on our plate; we also approved by board action going ahead with the historic tour with the cooperation of the committee that was formed. The committee members who agreed to serve were: Dr. Herbert Beck from F&M; George Hargus; Carl Lefever, who was very knowledgeable and very interested in the history of Lancaster County; William Kreitz; and Levi Brubaker, who was a Master Farmer. It was the interest of all of these people who thought it made sense to go ahead with this tour for people who weren't familiar with the historical significance of many sites that are present in and around the Conestoga Creek, as it was then called.

The itinerary for the tour was very interesting. We would gather at the County Historical Society, a new building on Wheatland Avenue, and we'd follow the water's edge to the ancient dam and lock still impounding the Conestoga above it. Then to the Conestoga at the waterworks. Stop at the Conestoga Lancaster Sewage Plant. Visit the site of both Monument and Chesapeake Street entrance to a cemetery carrying the name of some of the prominent people—James Buchannan, who was the only president from Pennsylvania who lived there; Governor Schultz; Henry Muhlenbe; and others whose graves overlook the Conestoga from the heights of Greenwood. Travel on a finish path to the Conestoga Boulevard; visit Reinhard's Landing, an important part of the life of Lancaster. Visit Rock Ford, home of Washington's Ad. General Edward Hand. Edward Hand was born in 1714 and died in 1802. He built the mansion that we talked about in 1785; it took until 1786 to finish it. He was a medical practitioner and occupied this house until his death. Washington was entertained here at tea in 1791.

Following the Old Factory Road to William Henry's gun factory, which was leased by Henry during the Revolutionary War; he was one of the majors in the Continental Army. Henry was Superintendent of Arms for the Army and he had between fifty and sixty gunsmiths working for him consistently, making muskets and rifles. Visitors to Meylin Gun Shop generally recognize the birthplace of the Pennsylvania, or so called Kentucky, rifle. Martin Meylin was born in 1670 and died in 1749 and built the Pennsylvania gun shop in 1714. It was the earliest known rifle. The Pennsylvania type was made here prior to 1745.

The Christian Herr House in Lancaster County was the oldest residence in the county built in 1719. Christian and Hans Herr were two of the ten Swiss immigrants, including Mylin, Miller, Kendig, Funk, Franciscus, Bowman, and others who took over the tract of 6,600 acres here in Pequea Valley in 1710. The Funk mentioned very likely was one of my ancestors, though I don't know the first name. However, I do know that my grandfather, Amos G. Funk, referred to earlier in the book, took over ownership after his father, grandfather, or earlier ancestor had some problems with finances, and that farm in Central Manor was deeded to one of the Funks from William

Penn. So it is an old property, and probably this Funk mentioned, one of these ten Swiss immigrants, was one of the Funks that I would have as a forefather.

It was suggested that they then would follow the Conestoga trail to the Postlethwaite's Tavern, where the first courts of Lancaster County were held. Lancaster County was erected from Chester County in 1729. On August 5 of that year, the courts were opened here at the Postlethwaite's. Foundations of the first jail are nearby. A town plan was presumably for the county seat when court was first held in Lancaster on November 2, 1730, in which year the town was named Lancaster, so named by John Rief of Lancaster, England, who was one of the justices of the court of the Postlethwaite's.

Then we went to the confluence of the Conestoga and the Little Conestoga, one of the beauty spots of Lancaster County and the site of the first known traders' post. At 5:30 we stopped at the Safe Harbor Picnic grounds, owned and operated by Safe Harbor Water Power Corporation. It was also the site of the ironworks at one time in Lancaster County. There the party lunched and were guests of the Safe Harbor Water Power Corporation.

The Second Annual Meeting

The second annual meeting of the CVA was held at the Lancaster County Farm Bureau Meeting Auditorium. Among other things, I presented the annual report.

Between 1956 and 1957, there were ten monthly meetings, one quarterly meeting, an annual meeting, and six special meetings. Divine guidance from ministers of the Gospel representing various churches in the community opened the meetings and participated in the discussions. A brochure outlining the objectives of the CVA was assembled and distributed to all members. If I remember correctly, the Lancaster Newspapers contributed significantly to the brochure. I don't remember if they paid it all or if they reduced the price of the printing.

During the annual meeting the illustrated lecture on the heritage and challenges of Lancaster County was presented by Vice President Henry Hackman, largely at his expense. This lecture had been shown to many groups and organizations who were interested. Total membership to date was 321. A goal suggested for the next year was that every member get five new members. The following progress was made toward meeting our long-term objectives:

Stream pollution—meetings with three separate state agencies were held to determine the state of pollution of the Conestoga.

A request was made to the Pennsylvania Game Commission to make a biological survey of the Conestoga.

Pete Bosser reported 100,000 fish were killed by pollution in the last six months in the Conestoga.

A clean streams bulletin will be mailed quarterly to all members. Less than 26% of the 7,951 farms in Lancaster County, or 2,000 farms, are now following recommended soil conservation practices. As president of the Conservation District, I assured everyone that we will do all we can to increase this amount of protection given to our precious farmland in Lancaster County, but it is a slow process and farmers don't move very rapidly. I also suggested that a joint committee be appointed representing farmers and sportsmen to improve the relations between the two groups.

As is often the case, the early years of an organization are the most difficult and, therefore, are the most challenging. For this reason, I have included only the first several years of the history of the Conestoga Valley Association.

I served nine years as president of CVA and three years as a director.

As of June 23, 1998, CVA is still going strong. The organization is carrying out their mission, as the present leaders see that mission. The task of natural resource conservation and wise use continues to be challenging. We appreciate any and all who assist in reaching that goal.

MY TWELVE YEARS
WITH THE
AGRICULTURAL PRESERVE BOARD

There are a number of ways to preserve farmland. It was decided here in Lancaster County the preferred method of accomplishing this goal was through a legal document called a deed restriction. In all cases in Lancaster County, the legal agreement is entered into voluntarily. We would have it no other way!

In the early days of Lancaster County's Agricultural Preserve Board, the term deed restriction was chosen to limit the use of farmland. The reason: The very strong sentiment of our plain sect farmers against any government involvement in their farm operations. We thought the Purchase of Development Rights might be misconstrued to mean government intervention.

Later, following many meetings, visits with small groups of farmers and excellent assistance from our local newspapers, we were able to use Purchase of Development Easements with no difficulty.

The following explanation of terms might be helpful:

What are the financial benefits to donating a conservation easement to the Trust or to the Preserve Board? To encourage nationwide efforts to protect land, the U.S. Congress enacted IRS regulations that allow a landowner to claim a federal income tax deduction when he places a conservation easement on his land (subject to specific conservation tests). The federal income tax deduction may benefit the landowner financially in exchange for the restrictions he is placing on his land with the conservation easement. The IRS requires the landowner to have an appraisal of the value of development rights. The Preserve Board or Farmland Trust staff can assist landowners in finding an appraiser for this specialized purpose.

Selling the conservation easement at a bargain sale price. Lancaster Farmland Trust has made cash payments to more than a dozen farmers for a portion of the appraised development rights. As a privately-funded organization, we don't have enough funding to pay the full appraised amount. Instead, we may offer the landowner a portion of the appraised value in cash, and the farmer can use the remainder of the appraised value as a federal income tax deduction. This option is called the bargain sale of an easement. Although the County Agricultural Preserve Board pays full value, there is a long waiting list for that program. Lancaster Farmland Trust does not have a waiting list and can act quickly to preserve a farm when the farmer wishes to do so, but we don't have enough funding to pay the full appraised amount. Therefore, a farm owner needs to evaluate which program best meets his needs.

If farm owners are interested in receiving a relatively small amount of cash for an easement ($0-$500 per acre), they should talk with Trust staff, and the Trust's board will consider making an offer based upon the farm's location, development pressure, soil quality, and the size of the Trust's fund balance.

The first ever meeting of the Lancaster County Agricultural Preserve Board was held on April 9, 1980. In attendance were James E. Huber, County Commissioner; Amos H. Funk; Aaron C. Stauffer; Charles Conrad; Phyllis Whitesell; Paul Whipple; and William Forrey. Others in attendance were Commissioner Robert Boyer; Commissioner Jean Mowery; John Ahlfeld, Director of the Planning Commission; and Sandy Coyman of the Lancaster County Planning Commission. Gerald Heistand of the Lancaster County Conservation District and Bob Williams of the *Pennsylvania Farmer*, with headquarters at Camp Hill, were there, as was Curt Harler, writing for *Lancaster Farming*. At the organizational meeting I was elected chairman, Aaron Stauffer was elected vice chairman, and Charles Conrad was elected secretary.

As I look back now we gathered together as members of the Lancaster County Preserve Board. We met because we wanted to meet and we were able to meet because the County Commissioners had declared a Preserve Board and named members of the board. But we surely did not know where we were going, or how to get there to save farmland. We were certainly plowing new ground. A lot of questions were asked and not too many answers were forthcoming.

Even before the Lancaster County Commissioners had named the Agricultural Preserve Board, they named the individual who was very helpful in moving us toward the position where we would be able to ask the County Commissioners to create our Preserve Board. This individual was Attorney James Thomas. He helped a lot as we discussed the possibility of forming this board to preserve farmland. It made me feel very good that the Commissioners chose him to be our solicitor. He had a good background; his father was a Mennonite preacher and stood in the Lancaster Central Market beside us. He had a fine family. That was a good start.

Aaron Stauffer pointed out his position: As a representative of the farming community on deed restriction programs, he said that participating farmers will be making a financial sacrifice; therefore, farmers expect the county to provide adequate resources for a successful program. Also, he believes farmers would like assurances that this program will provide long term preservation of agricultural areas. Mr. Paul Whipple, another board member, indicated that he had contacted several farmers for their reaction to the proposed program. He said they are generally taking a "wait and see" attitude. He will stay in close contact with these farmers for future reference.

From the very beginning, Aaron Stauffer and I felt that we shouldn't attempt to preserve all the farmland in the county, knowing full well this would be impossible. We did feel it was important to save the best land in the county, and that best land should be located away from major highways and sewer installations, and some distance from towns that had already been developed because both Aaron Stauffer and I felt that there would be a future problem between farmers and non-farmers when disputes about odor, noises, dust, and dirt came up. Non-farmers would not appreciate the farmer's position, and the farmers wouldn't understand why these complaints were hurled at them because they were there before the non-farmers moved into an area in most cases.

Bill Forrey, a good friend and high school classmate of our son Fred Funk, represented the builders on our Preserve Board, and he said the builders would go along with this and also take a "wait and see" attitude. It was very important to keep the preserved areas that we designated on the map and attempt to preserve away from sewered areas. Aaron Stauffer and I thought it made sense to do it. Our hope was that we could satisfy the builders' concern in this matter and, in fact, later on we did refuse to preserve some areas that the individuals wanted to preserve; we felt that they were in an area that should be developed because of the nearness to water and sewer. We have always taken what, in my opinion, was a realistic attitude toward preservation, not trying to do the impossible.

One of the things needed in any new organization at the start was appropriate stationery. Phyllis Whitesell suggested we get 500 letterheads and 500 envelopes at a cost of approximately $28 each. Larry Skromme moved and his motion was properly supported that 1,000 letterhead and envelopes be ordered; not a big expenditure of money, but it was a start.

As has been the case in most organizations that I've been involved in, one of the things that restricted our progress was the lack of money. At our May 9, 1980, meeting, it was pointed out that we had the balance in the treasury for the Preserve Board of $3,000 John Ahlfeld pointed out that the Community Development Program had designated $33,000 to cover the administrative costs of the Agricultural Preserve Board. That's better than $3,000, so we got started.

Since Pennsylvania has a township form of government, I knew from the beginning that we had to get the Township Supervisors supporting our efforts or we wouldn't move very far, and certainly not very fast. At our June meeting I invited Elam Herr and Bill Counts of the Pennsylvania Association of Township Supervisors to attend our next meeting to get a feel for what they think about what we are doing and hopefully to gain some support. It was also pointed out by Gerald Heistand that there are nine townships that now had effective agricultural zoning ordinances out of the sixty-six in the county. A meeting held on June 20, 1980, was the first meeting that we were able to accomplish one of our goals, and that was to have an Amish farmer on our Preserve Board. We were able to persuade David S. Fisher in the New Holland area to participate on our board. We provided transportation for him whenever he needed it because it was a rather long drive with horses. So on this date at the first meeting he attended, his presence and his participation was greatly appreciated.

As I have already pointed out, although community development funds allocated $33,000 for administrative costs, we had no money in the budget for buying deed restrictions. We weren't sure how the County Commissioners would react to any action the board took, but we thought we would take an action. We made a budget request for $500,000 to the Commissioners for acquisition of deed restrictions. Since we had already decided that, here in Lancaster County with very little money available, the amount of money per acre we should offer would have to be modest and quite likely would interest only the most dedicated landowners who, because of their dedication, would choose to restrict the use of their farmland for agricultural use only, by signing a legal document called a conservation easement. The use of the land, as described above, would be assured.

We were told by our county solicitor there was no enabling legislation to permit us to go ahead with our plan to preserve farmland as we envisioned it. With the help of Jim Thomas and resources from the Department of Agriculture, we drew up a bill called 1793 to see if any agreement existed among the various interested groups to get this passed in the State Legislature. At this particular meeting of our Preserve Board on June 20, 1980, Senator Gib

Armstrong came and discussed with us some amendments that had been suggested. We decided to okay the amendments that were presented and see what happened next. It was not easy. Even if we don't have enabling legislation, we thought we had to go ahead, so at the July meeting we decided that we would ask the attorney assigned to us, Jim Thomas, to prepare a legal document to restrict the use of land dedicated for use for agriculture forever.

Bill Forrey, representing the builders, said he thought this procedure would be more likely supported by the building industry if the deed restrictions were only accepted in Agricultural Preserves. This made sense to me. I didn't know how the Board would feel, but I could support that concept. David Fisher, our Amish member on the Board, said that quite likely the Amish would be wary of the proposed restrictions. Their fear was that it may be a trap to get them dependent on the government. Of course, they are very reluctant to do anything that is part of government. So the problems continued to be with us. We just had to try to meet the problems and find solutions to these problems.

We had all these plans for preserving farmland, yet we had no money. We asked the County Commissioners for $500,000. Mr. Huber correctly said that we hadn't spent anything yet, so the County Commissioners were reluctant to allocate that kind of money. Except for talking about it, we didn't make any decisions. No decisions were made by the Commissioners. At the July meeting, we did formally accept the idea that since we had so little money, we would limit our offer to interested farmers who agree to preserve their farms and farmland for a period of twenty-five years at a figure of $250 an acre.

Another recommendation came from Attorney Thomas, our solicitor. He said that he was concerned because we were having so much trouble getting support for the original legislation, House Bill 1793. By the way, I think I said Gib Armstrong was a senator at this time. In August 1980 Gib Armstrong was a member of the House and later became a senator.

Since we were having trouble with House Bill 1793, Jim Thomas suggested that quite likely we may be able to get further by amending Act 442. So, since we didn't know what else to do, we thought we would authorize him to do that.

At our September 19, 1980, meeting we made a very important step forward. The Preserve Board decided to give higher priority to the formation of agricultural preserves in townships that have adopted strong agricultural zoning. This made good sense to me, and I am glad the Board supported it.

I wanted to move ahead more quickly, as I usually do. I was slowed down by action by two of our Board members who were less sure than I was about the direction we ought to go. Charles Conrad and Larry Skromme both moved that we should not set a dollar amount on the incentive payment to farmers. Charles Conrad was especially concerned that this was a good idea, but that it was premature. I didn't agree with the action that was taken; it was supported. Now we took a step backward. Also at our September meeting, Commissioner Huber said that he was presenting amendments to Act 442 at the annual meeting of state association of county officials at the sate level.

Noah Wenger attended our October 3, 1980, Preserve Board meeting and he reviewed for us the various acts, mostly House bills, that had been passed over the years, helping to help farmers stay in business and making it easier for them to stay in business. There wasn't too much in there that I could see that lent itself to preserving farmland. Representative Wenger pointed out that the designation of contiguous areas for preservation would eliminate any farmers who wish to participate in preserve areas that would not be developed in any case amended. Mr. Ahlfeld noted that much of the language that appears in the table under Act 442 is not contained in the language of the amendment. Mr. Thomas stated that in his opinion more detail is needed in the amendment language, especially in the section on the area of deed restriction. Representative Wenger added that he supports the concept of the amendment, but he must be cautious as he has healthy respect for individual property rights. Mr. Ahlfeld pointed out that programs as proposed would not affect the individual unless he voluntarily joined the program.

At our October 17, 1980, meeting, we discussed more amendments to Act 442, and we had some opposition to amendments. We had some major core amendments. It truly wasn't easy as I look back on it now in 1998. We had a tough road to travel.

Finally some good news. January 16, 1981, I reported to the Board that the Township Supervisors Association, the Grange, the Farmers Union, and the County Farmers Association were all supporting Agricultural Preserve Board proposed amendments to Act 442. The State Farmers Association would not commit itself to support the amendments. Commissioner Huber reported that the State Association of County Commissioners had expressed its support for the amendments. Phyllis Whitesell asked of the Lancaster Board of Realtors had been contacted. They had not, but they were considered for future encouragement of accepting higher density involvement.

It was also announced by John Ahlfeld that the County Commissioners had officially passed a resolution appointing a Board. I guess we were appointed then, but not officially at that time.

At our March 20, 1981, meeting I informed the Board that the Farmers Association of Pennsylvania will not support the amendment until Ag District Bill 143 and Senate Bill 127 are acted upon. It was anticipated that this will take at least until June. Mr. Ahlfeld added the possibility that the proposed Ag District Bill would serve the purpose of the Board. Mr. Thomas stated his opinion that the District Bill would not solve the Preserve Board's potential legal problems.

At the July 31, 1981, meeting another action was taken. The County Planning Commission was asked to develop a job description for a full-time executive director with a salary ranging between $15,000 and $18,000. This was the first time we really talked about a full-time staff person. John Ahlfeld had been filling in up until this time. Representative Noah Wenger was working hard to develop language that would be acceptable to the House and still meet the needs of our Preserve Board. We moved that we would accept and support Noah Wenger's office, whatever direction they took us. These were only hopes at this time.

Our January 15, 1982, meeting was quite productive. It was the first time we had our staff assistant, David Watts, present. We met him and we were favorably impressed with him. Also, John Ahlfeld mentioned that there are now twenty townships that have effective agricultural zoning in Lancaster County. That was a big plus because I always felt that zoning is an important step to farmland preservation. Last but not least, Tom Johnston, my good friend from the Conservation District, distributed copies to the Board of Prime Farmland Study, done by Gerald Heistand and his sister Debra, with monies allocated for the purpose from the Conservation District. It could be said that this was the first ever printed paper or pamphlet on farmland preservation in Lancaster County. I still have copies of that information for reference purposes.

Our February 5, 1982, meeting was also productive. Jim Thomas distributed the revised sample deed restriction that he prepared. It was that good that we approved it unanimously. Now we had a document we can take out to our farmers who are interested in preserving their farmland. Also at this meeting, a motion was made and supportive action was taken to meet with the farmer representatives from Chester, Berks, Cumberland, York, and Lebanon Counties to talk about farmland preservation. Everyone was somewhat interested and they wanted to find out what we were doing. We were glad to share some of our problems and some of our accomplishments.

At our March 26, 1982, meeting we had a special guest, Robert Gray, policy development person for the American Farmland Trust. He talked about his experiences with American Farmland Trust, his experiences in Maryland where he lives, and he gave us a lot of good information. We were glad to have him there. What he told us was useful down the road. Not such good news—the Bill that we were trying to pass, 1499, was just about dead, we were told. It would not pass that year and probably would never pass. But at least we gave it our best shot. We would keep trying.

Since we were getting almost nowhere with enabling legislation to allow us to move ahead with a deed restriction program in Lancaster County, I searched for some way we could find that would allow us to move ahead, because we were just talking, not accomplishing much. We didn't have legal authorization to go ahead and do what we wanted to do. Somehow I found out about John Carson and his early involvement with Pennsylvania Act 442. He was an environmental consultant from Bucks County. I invited him to the May 7, 1982, meeting. He talked about the history of the Act. It was passed in 1968; there was no opposition to that particular bill. The purpose of the bill was to build conservation flood prevention impoundments, to get the easement for the flood prevention construction. He thought it was something we might be able to use. So we looked at it some more.

After talking to quite a number of people, I suggested at our July 2, 1982, meeting that the Board proceed to implement deed restriction program under Act 442, a bill already passed. Aaron Stauffer moved and Mr. Whipple seconded the motion, and it was voted unanimously that if no action is taken on House Bill 1449 by April 1, 1983, the Preserve Board will proceed to implement deed restriction program under 442. That was good news to me. It was the intention of the Board that Mr. Huber recommend to the other County Commissioners to budget the use of the revolving fund to purchase farmland in agricultural preserve areas. Deed restrictions would be placed on farmland purchased and would then be resold if necessary.

Following are some goals I suggested that we set, or at least think about, at our July 1982 meeting:
1. If no action is taken on 449 by April 1, 1983, we will go with 442 to implement our deed restriction program.
2. Place at least $500,000 in 1983 budget to be used as a resolving fund to purchase farmland with desirable quality and in a favorable location. A deed restriction would have to be on the land, and the land would then be sold to an interested farmer.

It was very gratifying to me to hear Preserve Board member Bill Forrey explain that one reason why professional developers have generally supported Agricultural Preserve Board's effort is because they put a builder and developer on the Board. He said that people depended on him to provide input to the Board's actions. So with Bill Forrey as an effective watchdog, the builders have not fought the deed restriction program because it was voluntary and had a twenty-five-year period limit. He said it was important that a trade-off exists between the county and developers in that the County Comprehensive Plan has set aside 100,000 acres of suitable land for development. Mr. Forrey said that the shelter industry was important to the quality of life as were farmland and food, which go hand-in-hand. I believed there was ample room for growth designated in the County Land Use and Comprehensive Plan.

The Background on the Second Most Important Meeting I Ever Attended

On September 10, 1982, Douglas Wheeler, then President of the American Farmland Trust, met with our Lancaster County Farmland Preservation Board. He complimented us on the progress we had made in spite of the lack of legislative support at the state level. He thought we were on the right track with our deed restriction program. However, he pointed out that we should be cautious about promising federal tax credits that might accrue to interested landowners for the donation of qualified conservation easement. The key word is qualified contribution. It was not at all clear that active farmland would qualify under the present ruling. Open space does qualify.

My question to Doug Wheeler was, "Why hasn't someone attempted to make fertile, active farmland qualify as a donation?" He did not have an answer.

The next day I called my congressman, Bob Walker, to discuss the matter. We set up a meeting. As briefly as possible, I described the problem and suggested he set up a meeting in his Lancaster office where we could meet with the right people in order to develop a ruling that would allow farmland mapped in our County Comprehensive Plan to remain in agriculture, provided the use of such land in perpetuity would be farming. The use of this land would be restricted by a legal covenant. The donation of such land should be eligible for federal tax credit.

Without hesitation, Bob Walker said he would do it. However, he pointed out the meeting would be much better attended by the right people if we held it in the House of Representative's Rayburn Building. Bob Walker assured me he would help set up the meeting and get the right people to the meeting.

I have attached a list of those who attended the December 1, 1982, meeting. Bob Walker did a great job of getting the right people from government there.

County Commissioner Jim Huber was our lead person. Our solicitor James Thomas accompanied us. He did not charge us for his time. Preserve Board member William Forrey, who was also serving as president of the

Home Builders of Lancaster County, persuaded someone or several individuals to provide us, at no charge, a great, roomy, twelve-passenger van for our trip to Washington, D.C.

Our December 2, 1982, meeting was easily the second most important meeting I ever attended. We were listened to. Our request was granted. The benefits of our efforts will be realized for many generations to come in Lancaster County and all over these United States.

Jim Huber and I were asked to testify again in Washington on September 14, 1983.

The following September 14, 1983, news release is an excellent ending to this very important series of events.

September 14, 1983

From: Lancaster County Agricultural Preserve Board
        50 North Duke Street, P. O. Box 3480
        Lancaster, PA 17603
        299-8355
        Alan R. Musselman, Administrator

FOR IMMEDIATE RELEASE

FARM SAVING TAX BENEFITS

FUNK AND HUBER TO THE IRS

Three years and many urgings after the U.S. Congress put forth the Tax Treatment Act of 1980, the Internal Revenue Service is finally ready to put final touches on some wordy regulations that will help preserve farmland in Lancaster County. Today farmland preservation and conservation organizations from across the nation are testifying on Constitution Avenue to the IRS. Among them will be Amos Funk and County Commissioner James Huber who will be there to deliver to IRS Lancaster County's support with some minor suggestions for amendment.

"What we've looked for is some firm assurance that the IRS will treat donated deed restrictions to Lancaster County's Agricultural Preserve Board as deductions from Federal income tax." (Huber)

"It looks like this (the regulations) will do it. We will be ready to assure Lancaster County farmers of some significant tax advantages for individually making a commitment to farm preservation." (Funk)

"Along with local leadership and widespread caring in Lancaster County about the future of our farmland, the IRS tax deduction incentive should inspire folks to get down to brass tacks in farm saving.

"There is quite a bit of interest and in deed restrictions. . . . I expect to be kept busy with the details of accepting and securing deed restrictions." (Musselman, Administrator)

The published regulations follow an advance trip to talk with Washington staffers by Funk, Huber, and company last spring with some good results.

ROBERT S. WALKER
16TH DISTRICT, PENNSYLVANIA

COMMITTEES:
GOVERNMENT OPERATIONS
SCIENCE AND TECHNOLOGY

STAFF IN CHARGE:
MARTHA C. MORRISON
WASHINGTON OFFICE
MARC T. PHILLIPS
DISTRICT OFFICES

Congress of the United States
House of Representatives
Washington, D.C. 20515

Those Attending December 2nd Meeting

Lancaster County Agricultural Preserve Board

James E. Huber
James H. Thomas/
Amos H. Funk
Aaron Z. Stauffer
Paul B. Whipple
Robert A. Schoch
Clifford B. Huffman
William H. Forrey
Michael Pflieger

American Farmland Trust

Douglas P. Wheeler
Douglas R. Horne
Edward Thompson
Robert J. Gray
Chris Allen

Other Representation

Senator Heinz's - Steve Perry
Senator Specter's - Laura Doty
Governor Thornburgh - Chip Foley
National Association of Counties
Hal D. Hiemstra
Chris Vaughn, Department of the Treasury
John Harman, Internal Revenue Service, and Malcolm Funn

Congressman Walker
Don Eberly

Congressman Jeffords

Penrose Hallowell

On October 1, 1982, action was taken when the Board unanimously approved that money be budgeted for 1983 to hire a second staff person to make incentive payments under the first year of the three-year deed restriction program. In addition to discussion, Mr. Skromme indicated he had reservations about the county borrowing money to make incentive payments for deed restrictions. Mr. Ahlfeld said that he could make a note that the alternative would be to budget $750,000 to require a deed restriction outright on 3,000 acres at $250 per acre. I expressed concern about accepting deed restrictions outside the agricultural preserves. I thought it would alienate developers. In addition, I thought that mixing farms and urban dwellers never was a good idea and would cause a lot of problems down the road. Opposition was not shared by everyone on the Board. Larry Skromme felt it was all right to take them if they were donated, and so did Phyllis Whitesell. But no action was taken. It was not a confrontation. It was just a difference of thinking among those of us on the Board. I think that is what these kinds of organizations are all about. I also expressed an opinion it should be a Board policy to obtain approval from officials of each respective municipality in agricultural boundaries before offering a deed restriction to those municipalities. The Board was asked for comments and issued a general consensus that it would not be Board policy to require municipalities' approval; however, any concerns that municipal officials have should be considered by the Board.

At the January 7, 1983, meeting John Ahlfeld reported that the Personnel Committee met on December 15 and decided to advertise for a Board administrative position, using the position described as approved at the Board meeting. The job will be available after April 1, 1983, and the salary will be negotiable between $12,000 and $20,000, based on the background and qualifications. Here again, we were told by the County Commissioners that the salary level for county personnel is usually determined by the number of people who are supervised. Here we are in the Preserve Board; we have one staff person, and that's it in addition to the work that John Ahlfeld has been doing over and above his work as director of the Planning Commission. We were in a rather difficult position of getting a qualified person because there is only one person to supervise, possibly two with a secretary. So we had to do the best we could.

During our January 3, 1983, Agricultural Preserve Board meeting our solicitor Jim Thomas presented a letter based on the IRS code relating to Lancaster County. In the letter Thomas questioned whether the donated deed restriction would qualify as a conservation contribution, since it would make it difficult to prove that the restriction would yield significant public benefit as required by code attachment G. Nothing was easy. We just had to keep plugging. Later we got a correct interpretation of the law. Productive agricultural land that was donated was eligible for tax reduction purposes, as is the case with art, etc.

At the May 6, 1983, meeting, I announced that the Personnel Committee had chosen Alan R. Musselman, former Executive Director of Maryland Agricultural Preservation Foundation, for the administrative position. After reviewing Musselman's background, Mrs. Whitesell moved and Mr. Whipple seconded, and it was very unanimously recommended to the County Commissioners that Alan Musselman be hired as the administrator at an annual salary of $20,000.

Alan Musselman—First Executive Director of the Agricultural Preserve Board

At our June 3, 1983, meeting, Alan Musselman was present and spoke to the group. He noted that the important principle of real estate is location and that the market studies seem to have pulled market data from a number of different sources. He said he doubted that a farm in a strong agricultural preserve area would remain on the market for a long period of time. I pointed out that the purpose of the study was to point out the potential problems of purchasing farms for deed restriction and resale, and that the study had served that purpose. Mr. Huber added that the study served the purpose of pointing out the potential problems, and that the Board must address these.

At our June 1, 1983, meeting, Alan Musselman reported on the subject of IRS proposed rules for qualifying conservation contributions. In his remarks he pointed out that the regulation dealing with deductibility of easement donations was published on May 23, 1983, in the *Federal Register*. Since 1980 there has been a great deal of uncertainty about federal income tax deductibility of easements on deed restricted donations. The uncertainty has resulted in reluctance on the part of interested landowners to either seek expensive private letter rulings or to risk the donations being treated as a gift or for tax purposes. These proposed rules were intended to clarify the 1980 law. An example of deductibility, example five on page 2.2.945, was tied very well to Lancaster County circumstances. In fact, the example obviously was influenced by the Lancaster County representatives' visit to IRS. I think the meeting that ten of us took to Washington was one of the most important meetings that I have ever been part of. This got the IRS to change their position and allow agricultural deductions. The Amish and Mennonites can use a tax deduction, but they don't want to get involved with government; that was a strong incentive for many of them.

On September 15, 1983, Jim Huber, Alan Musselman, and I went to Washington to make a presentation at the hearing held in Washington, D.C. I presented testimony on behalf of the Board, attempting to push for a favorable ruling. Although it sure takes a while to get things done in Washington, we did our best and waited to see what would happen.

At our October 7, 1983, meeting, the Preserve Board made our first effort to develop guidelines to determine the priority in which deed restrictions would be accepted, based on the quality of the land, the nearness to development, the quality of the soils, and nearness to sewer and water. This was a first effort and was changed as we went along. We made a good start.

During this meeting we also amended the bylaws as recommended by Attorney Jim Thomas. After considerable discussion, the Board approved a budget request to the County Commissioners in the amount of $500,000, $250,000 for deed restriction acquisition at $250 per acre, and $250,000 to reserve the purchase of farms for the purpose of placing deed restrictions and the resale. We didn't know what the County Commissioners would do. So far they hadn't nearly met our goal, but we would see.

The total expenditure for the Preserve Board in 1983 was $133,924. Looking at the minutes of 1983, it looked like the budget was pretty puny for 1984.

At our November 4, 1983, meeting, we again restated our request for $500,000 for 1984. We'd see what happens. During this meeting we updated our document for the granting of easements and changed the language to bring it up to date and include what we learned as a result of doing.

Esta and I Donated a Deed Restriction on our Farm

On December 9, 1983, my wife Esta and I placed a twenty-five-year donated deed restriction of our eighty-nine-acre Marticville farm donated to the county.

We on the Preserve Board were working hard to encourage township supervisors to designate within their township or a group of townships 1,000 acres or more of contiguous good agricultural land that might be preserved in perpetuity in agriculture. We have a potential designation of four preserve areas. One of them, encompassing over 34,000 acres including Ephrata Township, is already approved by the needed township supervisors that are included in the Preserve area, which is encouraging. Little by little we were making some progress, but it was slow and difficult. We had to do a lot of talking to get where we wanted to be, but it was worth it, so we kept trying.

At our January 13, 1984, meeting the Preserve Board revised the farm ranking system to better meet the needs that we envisioned in the future, and we also had a second draft of the deed acquisition proposal and the guidelines contained therein. Since we were starting from scratch, we had to change as we found the need to change and hopefully make our whole program better as a result of these changes.

On January 25, 1984, our first staff person, Mr. David C. Watts, sent his resignation to the Preserve Board, telling us he was planning to take another position on February 8. He had served us well and we wished him the best in the future.

Our First Field Trip

On Friday, April 27, 1984, the Preserve Board took their first field trip to a specific location to observe the farms and the amount of preservation there and the potential. This is something we continued and I think it is still being done till the present time, 1998.

Karen Freeman was hired to replace David Watts on April 6, 1984.

Donations of twenty-five-year deed restrictions were starting to come in now. As of May 1, 1984, we had four. On June 1, 1984, we had six applications for sale of easements. It's a warm feeling when you finally get results from much effort put forth to get people interested, and to try to explain the program to have people donate easements, and also ask for the sale of easements. We were on our way.

Applications came in for application sale in July 1984.

At our Preserve Board meeting on October 5, 1984, we were still battling the problem of anticipated need and actual expenditure of dollars. It was difficult to have them coincide because of the new type of legal work necessary, and we had to develop new guidelines and new methods of doing things. Commissioner Huber pointed out that we've asked for $500,000, yet in 1984 we only spent $53,000 to acquire easements. It was a problem for the Commissioners, but notwithstanding, at this meeting the Preserve Board went on record as requesting a budget of $450,000. It was approved unanimously.

During the period 1980 to 1988, sixty-four farms containing 5,665 acres have been protected by the Preserve Board with conservation easements.

By 1988 things had gotten quite a bit better for the Preserve Board. The passage of Act 149 made available $1.9 million from state funds available to the Lancaster Board. The County Commissioners also increased their allocation from $350,000 in 1988 to $500,000 in 1989.

However, pressure for development was increasing more rapidly than funding for conservation easement purchases. During the most recent three-year period, 1986 to 1988, according to the Lancaster County Planning Commission data the number of farmland acres approved for development in the county averaged 6,654 acres annually, compared to an average annual farmland loss of 2,500 during the twenty-six-year period 1960 to 1985. These figures represent an increased loss of farmland during 1986 to 1988 of over 266%. The Preserve Board appreciated the 45% increase in county funding and the $1.9 million in state funding. This gave us a big boost.

Alan Musselman's Resignation; Appointment of Karen Weiss and Thomas Daniels

Alan Musselman resigned on May 10, 1988, as executive director of the Lancaster County Agricultural Preserve Board to take a similar position with the Lancaster Farmland Trust. He contributed greatly to the growth and success of our Preserve Board during his nearly five years as executive director. He guided us through some difficult times. His experience in Maryland as state executive director of their Farmland Preserve Plan was most helpful. His adjustment from a large state program with at least a moderate amount of money to our much smaller Lancaster County Farmland Preservation Program with much less money, at least in the early days, was greatly appreciated.

Many of the suggestions and recommendations made by Alan Musselman were later adopted by the Preserve Board and now, although changed and modified to meet new conditions, are still used in 1998.

Karen Weiss was named acting director following Alan's resignation.

In the spring of 1989 I was a member of the Search Committee to find an individual to fill the position of Executive Director of the Lancaster County Preserve Board.

When Tom Daniels applied for the position, he was an Associate Professor of Regional and Community Planning at Kansas State University. Tom expressed a strong interest in farmland preservation. This interest came through very clearly to those of us who served on the Search Committee. Tom Daniels proved to be a very good choice. Over the years many people contributed to the success of Lancaster County's farmland preservation efforts. Tom Daniels' outstanding talents as an administrator contributed greatly to that success.

Tom announced his resignation as executive director on May 29, 1998. Tom, you gave us nine good years. You will be missed. We wish you well in your new position at the State University of New York.

My 1990 Letter to the County Commissioners

March 8, 1990

Lancaster County Board of Commissioners
50 North Duke Street, P. O. Box 3480
Lancaster, PA 17603-1881

Dear Commissioners,

    The year 1989 brought several major changes to the Agricultural Preserve Board and the operation of the Board's Conservation Easement Purchase Program.

    Tom Daniels became the Director of the Agricultural Preserve Board on May 15, 1989, and Karen Weiss stepped down as Acting Director to return to her position of Farmland Preservation Specialist. Karen performed admirably in the year she served as Acting Director.

    Jane Balmer joined the Board in January, and Bill Forrey announced his resignation, effective December 31, 1989. Richard Hurst was named to replace Bill as the representative of the building industry on the Board.

    The County received $2,433,838 from the State of Pennsylvania in 1989 for the purchase of conservation easements. This is the first annual grant made available to the county under Act 149 of 1988.

    Combined with the $500,000 allocated by the County for 1989, a total of over $2.9 million was available for acquiring easements.

    Based on 1989 experience, the cost of conservation easements is expected to be about $1,300 per acre in 1990.

    It is important to note, however, that pressure for development remains strong in Lancaster County. Many more acres are being developed than preserved each year.

    The Board appreciated the 50% increase in conservation easement funding, from $500,000 in 1989 to $750,000 in 1990, from the County. The increased funding will enable the County to purchase additional conservation easements.

Sincerely,

Amos H. Funk
Chairman

AHF/baf

My 1991 Letter to the County Commissioners

March 1, 1991

Lancaster County Board of Commissioners
50 North Duke Street, P. O. Box 3480
Lancaster, PA 17603

Dear Commissioners,

The Agricultural Preserve Board made progress on several fronts in 1990, and experienced a number of personnel changes.

Bill Achor replaced Karen Weiss as Farmland Preservation Specialist. Karen had been with the Preserve Board for three years, and had also served as Acting Director. Richard Hurst replaced Bill Forrey as the representative of the building industry on the Board. Also, Bob Brenneman replaced Jim Huber as the member of the Commissioners on the Board.

The Preserve Board and the County Commissioners entered into a cooperative agreement with the Lancaster Farmland Trust. This agreement will enable the County and the Farmland Trust to coordinate efforts in the acquisition on farmland easements, and should result in more effective farmland protection.

The Board's Conservation Easement Acquisition Program received a record 72 applications on 7,600 acres in 1990—an indication of the strong interest in easement sale among landowners.

The Preserve Board finalized ten perpetual conservation easements in 1990, and has received 14 signed contracts of sale from landowners. The cost of the conservation easements averaged about $2,000 an acre.

The County received $1,992,177 from the State of Pennsylvania in 1990 for the purchase of conservation easements. Lancaster County allocated $750,000 for easement purchases in 1990, the largest amount of any county in the commonwealth.

The Preserve Board commends the Commissioners on adopting the Parks and Open Space Funding Action Plan which includes $10 million for the purchase of agricultural conservation easements by the year 2000. The Board applauds the sale of $5 million in bonds, and is grateful for the $1,250,000 for easement purchases in 1991—an increase of $500,000 over the 1990 amount. Not only will this increased funding enable the County to purchase more easements, but also will enable the County to receive more in matching funds from the state.

The Agricultural Preserve Board looks forward to continued progress in 1991.

Sincerely,

Amos H. Funk
Chairman

My 1992 Letter to the County Commissioners

February 1, 1992

Lancaster County Board of Commissioners
50 North Duke Street, P. O. Box 3480
Lancaster, PA 17603

Dear Commissioners,

    The Agricultural Preserve Board made progress on several fronts in 1991.

    The Board's Conservation Easement Acquisition Program received a record 94 applications on 7,762 acres in 1991—an indication of the strong interest in easement sale among landowners.

    The Preserve Board finalized a one-year record of 35 perpetual conservation easements on 3,391 acres in 1991, and has received an additional seven signed contracts of sale from landowners. The cost of the conservation easements averaged about $1,700 an acre. The Preserve Board has now preserved 110 farms and just under 10,000 acres.

    The Preserve Board and the Lancaster Farmland Trust preserved a farm through a request and reimbursement procedure in which the Preserve Board requested the Trust to acquire an easement in an urgent situation and the County then purchased the easement from the Trust. This is the first such cooperative effort between the two organizations since an agreement was signed in August of 1990.

    The County received $1,967,027 from the State of Pennsylvania in 1991 for the purchase of conservation easements. Lancaster County allocated $1,250,000 for easement purchase in 1991, the largest amount of any county in the Commonwealth.

    The Agricultural Preserve Board looks forward to continued progress in 1992.

Sincerely,

Amos H. Funk
Chairman

Amos Funk's Resignation From the Agricultural Preserve Board

This picture taken by Marty Heisey, and the story on my resignation from the Preserve Board, written by Andrea S. Brown, appeared in the December 11, 1992, issue of the *Lancaster New Era*. The picture and story are used with the permission of the *Lancaster New Era*. Thank you, *Lancaster New Era*.

Amos Funk, 'father of farm preservation,' leaves ag panel

by Andrea S. Brown
New Era Staff Writer

Amos Funk wanted to be known simply as a Lancaster County vegetable farmer, but today he was honored as the father of farmland preservation.

"It's the most important thing in my life," Funk said today, before chairing his last meeting as chairman of the county's Agricultural Preserve Board.

"In Lancaster County, our land and our people are so special, and we can't preserve one without preserving the other."

Now, the board is faced with an enormous task: "How do you replace a legend?" asks director Thomas Daniels.

Funk, 81, is retiring from the board he helped create in 1980. Since then, it has gained easements on 12,600 acres of farmland.

I gave it 100 percent when I could, and I can't give it 100 percent anymore, so I thought I'd better step down," he explained.

Amos Funk prepares for his final meeting as chairman of the Agricultural Preserve Board today. He has served since the board was created in 1980.

He will, however, remain a lifetime trustee of the private Lancaster Farmland Trust, through which he will continue to be an advocate for his twin passions: preservation and conservation of the county's prime farmland.

At today's meeting, Daniels presented Funk with a Lancaster County-shaped plaque calling him the father of farmland preservation. Members of the board, two county commissioners and Alan Musselman of the trust praised his focus and dedication.

Funk has an easement on his 89-acre farm near Marticville and has been practicing erosion control there for decades. Since the 1960s, he has been working on farmland preservation at the state level, and he was the prime force behind the county's creation of the Agricultural Preservation Task Force in 1978.

He has won some of the most prestigious local and national preservation awards, including the 1984 National Outstanding Conservation Award, the 1990 Theodore Roosevelt Conservation Award, and the 1991 George C. Delp Award.

The board planned to throw a surprise reception for him this morning at 11:30.

Funk chaired his final board meeting in his usual style, leaning back in his chair and soliciting a wide range of opinions, giving each member of the board and those in the audience an opportunity to speak.

He praised state and local officials who helped to create the system through which farmers who agree to preserve their land are compensated. Now, he said, that notion is widely accepted, but when he first started pushing for it, he remembered one township official calling him a communist.

"It has always been challenging," he said with a smile. "Until recently it was difficult to get people to believe that this was as important as I thought it was. It gives me a great deal of satisfaction to see that folks see that this is the way to go."

County commissioner Terry Kauffman, who also sits on the Agricultural Preserve Board, said Funk's contribution was greater than the thousands of acres of land that have been saved. "It's an attitude, a philosophy. It's 422,000 people in this county who believe."

Musselman added, "Amos has made a tremendous difference in this county. Now there are many activists and many advocates."

Funk, looking spry as ever, vowed to work for state tax reform—shifting the tax burden from property taxes to income or sales taxes—"with the energy I have left."

"I think it's very important for farmers not to be overburdened by tax, particularly those who have preserved their farms," he said.

Also in his "retirement," he said, "I'm going to concentrate on Esta," his wife.

Members of the board had telling memories of Funk. Edward C. Goodhart III remembered riding his bicycle across Funk's fields when he was 8 or 9. Funk chased him off, but not before telling that the tires would create ruts that would allow sediment to run off.

"You've been a tremendous leader," said board member Richard Hurst.

And another board member wanted to know just one thing: "If I need advice, can I call you like I always have?"

Funk promised he could.

1992

The Board's Conservation Easement Acquisition Program received fifty-nine applications on 5,290 acres in 1992—an indication of the strong interest in easement sale among landowners.

The Preserve Board finalized twenty-three perpetual conservation easements on 2,270 acres in 1992, and has received an additional ten signed contracts of sale from landowners. The cost of the conservation easements averaged about $1,802 an acre. The Preserve Board has now preserved 133 farms and over 12,200 acres.

The county received $2,183,445 from the state of Pennsylvania in 1992 for the purchase of conservation easements. Lancaster County allocated $650,000 for easement purchases in 1992.

1993

The Board's Conservation Easement Acquisition Program received thirty-one applications on 2,927 acres in 1993—an indication of the continuing strong interest in easement sale among landowners.

The Preserve Board finalized twenty-one perpetual conservation easements on 1,657 acres in 1993, and has received an additional eleven signed contracts of sale from landowners. The cost of the conservation easements averaged about $2,180 an acre. The Preserve Board has now preserved 154 farms and over 13,900 acres.

The county received $3,180,000 from the state of Pennsylvania in 1993 for the purchase of conservation easements. Lancaster County allocated $845,000 for easement purchases in 1993.

1994

The Agricultural Preserve Board's Conservation Easement Acquisition Program received twenty-five applications on 2,778 acres in 1994—an indication of the continuing strong interest in easement sale among landowners.

The Preserve Board finalized seventeen perpetual conservation easements on 1,845.85 acres in 1994, and has received an additional five signed contracts of sale from landowners. The cost of the conservation easements averaged about $1,900 an acre. The Preserve Board has now preserved 170 farms and over 15,600 acres.

The county received $2,097,719 from the state of Pennsylvania in 1994 for the purchase of conservation easements. Lancaster County allocated $950,000 for easement purchases in 1994.

1994 Farm Sales Analysis Shows Increase in Farmland Prices

The 1994 Farm Sales Analysis, completed in March of 1995, shows that farmland in the farming regions of the county averaged $6,046 per acre, a 21% increase over the 1993 level of $4,964. A total of 6,851 acres changed hands; and 112 arms-length transactions were used in the study. The Northern region of the county had the highest price per acre of $7,214; followed by the Western region at $5,981 per acre; the Eastern region with $5,721 per acre; the Southern region with $5,487 per acre; and the Southwestern region at $4,930 per acre.

In the metropolitan around Lancaster City, six farms sold for $16,078 an acre. In other growth areas, one farm sold for development at $35,327 an acre.

Five farms preserved for agriculture by a conservation easement sold for an average of $5,678 an acre, an indication that land preserved for farming retains a strong agricultural value. Copies of the 1994 Farm Sales Analysis are available from the Agricultural Preserve Board.

March 1997 Preserve Board

The Agricultural Preserve Board made very good progress in 1997.

The Board's Conservation Easement Acquisition Program received forty applications on 4,488 acres in 1997—an indication of the continuing strong interest in easement sale among landowners.

The Preserve Board finalized twenty-five perpetual conservation easements on 1,929 acres in 1997, and has received an additional twenty signed contracts of sale from landowners. The cost of the conservation easements averaged about $1,943 an acre. The Preserve Board has now preserved 235 farms and over 20,700 acres.

The county received $3,509,808 from the state of Pennsylvania in 1997 for the purchase of conservation easements. Lancaster County allocated record $1,500,000 for easement purchases in 1997.

Effective Agricultural Zoning

Townships in Lancaster County have been using agricultural zoning to protect farmland resources since the mid-1970s. At the end of 1997, effective agricultural zoning was found in thirty-nine of the county's forty-one townships and covering over 320,000 acres, or more than half the entire county.

The primary purpose of the agricultural zoning district is to protect agricultural land uses and activities from conflicts with non-farm uses and activities, and to maintain agricultural land in large blocks. To achieve this goal, most townships allow only one building lot per twenty-five acres to be subdivided off the farm. Some townships, however, allow only one building lot per fifty acres to be subdivided off the farm.

Fall 1997

Over 24,000 Acres Now Preserved

The Agricultural Preserve Board and the Lancaster Farmland Trust have reached the mark of 24,000 acres preserved in Lancaster County. The Preserve Board has preserved 19,900 acres and 224 farms, and the Trust has preserved 4,300 acres and 65 farms. By the end of 1997, the two groups hope to have over 25,000 acres preserved.

Lancaster County ranks first among Pennsylvania counties in acres preserved, and fourth among counties nationwide.

My Ten Years with the Lancaster Farmland Trust

The preservation of Lancaster County's best agricultural land, located a reasonable distance from major highways, sewer lines, and ongoing developments, got a great boost when our county commissioners appointed a nine-member Agricultural Preserve Board in February 1980.

As we developed guidelines and procedures to preserve Lancaster County's farmland, after several years we became aware that there was one segment of Lancaster County's agricultural population that we were not reaching. We were not effectively reaching many Amish and various groups of Mennonites that make up our "plain sect" farmers. These farmers are very reluctant and often refuse to be involved with government at any level, even at the county level.

Marilyn Lewis, a longtime supporter of resource conservation and farmland preservation, suggested to me a number of times that something should be done to assist plain sect farmers, like a number of Amish neighbors living near her home in Strasburg, to preserve their farms for farming. I discussed this matter with a number of people including my friend Robert Campbell, then owner of the *Lancaster Farming* newspaper. He was very encouraging. I discussed this proposal with several other interested people. They, too, were encouraging. This information was then taken back to Marilyn Lewis. Marilyn further encouraged me by suggesting she might be able to get a small amount of money to get us started, from a foundation she was connected with.

I then discussed the matter with Alan Musselman, director of the Lancaster County Agricultural Preserve Board. He was also encouraging. He correctly pointed out, "We have a big job to do here in Lancaster County; we need all the help we can get."

As I recall, sometime later Marilyn Lewis, Alan Musselman, Robert Campbell, and I met somewhere in the courthouse. The purpose of the meeting was to decide on our next step. We talked about money. Robert Campbell, with his commercial connections, agreed to attempt to raise some money. Since it was agreed, in the beginning at least, we would not have a large program, we would not need much staff time. Since I was president of the Preserve Board, I should be able to persuade the county commissioners to let Alan Musselman spend a little time away from his duties as director of the Preserve Board and spend a little time with this new, non-governmental group.

Two additional decisions were made at this meeting. We decided to name the new group Friends of Agricultural Land Preservation, and we decided to have our first meeting, a dinner meeting, at which time we would officially organize. We would elect officers and directors. Bylaws will come later. The date for the dinner meeting was November 13, 1985, at 7:00 p.m. at the Olde Hickory Inn, Oregon Pike, Lancaster.

Part of a speech I made at the First Dinner Meeting of the Friends of Farmland Preservation

In the 1950s we were concerned with the loss of soil by rain-induced erosion. In the late 1960s we developed a new concern: We became concerned about the loss of entire farms or parts of farms when they were taken out of production for industrial or residential development.

Because of my interest and concern in this area, in December 1967 I was appointed by former Governor Shafer to an eighteen-member committee and given the charge to develop a plan to "preserve Pennsylvania's agricultural land."

After two years of work, we presented our report and recommendations to the governor. He and others complimented us on the report and described it as a good report. Unfortunately, to date, few of the recommendations have been implemented. Although this is disappointing to me, I learned a great deal from this experience.

In February 1980 the county commissioners took a very important and far reaching action. They appointed the Lancaster County Agricultural Preserve Board to prepare and implement a deed restriction plan to preserve the 278,000 acres of prime farmland designated to remain in agriculture in the county comprehensive plan.

Now, on this night of November 13, 1985, we are taking another important and far reaching action. In an effort to broaden our support base, we are organizing the Friends of Agricultural Land Preservation. This is envisioned as a public/private partnership to assist in financing and implementing our plan to preserve the prime farmland in Lancaster County.

Again I say, welcome to the first annual meeting of the Friends of Agricultural Land Preservation. This new organization which I assure you was not proposed just to bring into being another organization, but instead is envisioned as a very important support for the Lancaster County Agricultural Preserve Board. It is planned that the Friends of Agricultural Land Preservation will have their own officers elected at the annual meeting. The organization will have the necessary by-laws—quite simple at first, with further by-law refinement as the organization grows.

The organizational purpose is to promote the preservation of agricultural land in Lancaster County. Again, I would like to emphasize the point, the Friends of Agricultural Land Preservation might be referred to as an important support arm for the Agricultural Preserve Board.

This support can be financial support which will be used to help us with our deed restriction incentive payment program. Since our Friends program was initiated on September 5, 1985, $6,940 has been raised. This is very encouraging.

For those who feel they cannot support us financially beyond the $10 membership fee, we would welcome support in membership solicitation.

It would be helpful if we had a Friend in Agricultural Land Preservation on the Planning Commission and Board of Supervisors of each of the forty-one townships and on the Planning Commissions and governing bodies of the eighteen boroughs in the county.

Assisting in implementing the county comprehensive plan to preserve 278,000 acres of best agricultural land for agricultural use and attempting to guide growth toward the 100,000 acres designated for development near major roads, sewer, and water lines is a big job.

Seventeen townships in Lancaster County have not designated agricultural-zoned districts in their townships. Too many townships and boroughs have zoning ordinances that disallow desirable denser development. These municipalities should be persuaded to change these ordinances.

Our goal should be to not allow more than 1,000 acres of farmland per year to be used to accommodate the 4,000+ annual population and related growth in the county.

We need at least 1,000 Friends of Agricultural Land Preservation to assist us in getting this big job done.

The annual meeting held on November 13, 1985, was pretty well attended for our first meeting. Gerald Heistand, one of the staff people of our conservation district and a Mennonite preacher, asked the invocation on the meal (we had a family-style dinner). Following the dinner I spoke and my remarks are already on record. Alan Musselman, director of the Preserve Board, spoke of some things a friend of agricultural land preservation might do to assist the Preserve Board in their efforts. Richard Brown, Director of the Lancaster Environmental Action Council, talked about some of his environmental concerns and how the new organization might fit in to help them attain their goals. Chairman of the County Commissioners Jim Huber spoke about how he feels about the addition of a new group, these Friends of the Lancaster County Land Preservation, and spoke very favorably and encouraged us.

Earl Cramer, past president of the Home Builders Association, spoke for the shelter industry. I didn't know what to expect from Earl, but he was supportive. He outlined some concerns he and his industry had about what we should do and what we shouldn't do, at least in their opinion. It was helpful to get their point of view, and I think it made an important contribution.

We also had a short presentation from Leon Good, a Warwick Township dairy farmer. He outlined how difficult it was for him to finally own a farm, and he didn't have a family that could get him started as many young farmers do, but he made it. He loved to farm and it was an interesting story. Our principal speaker was Ralph Grosse, President of American Farmland Trust, headquartered in Washington, D.C. He spoke from the national point of view about what's happening nationally and it was pretty general that most of the development pressures occur on the best land, and most of the best land is around the cities and towns where development has already started. So the key was to develop completely—100% or as near as possible—in the cities where there is transportation and the service lines, and do what we can to prevent sprawl growth out into the farming area. In addition, to have more dense housing in the area where the services are available: transportation, electric, police and fire protection, etc.

The last two speakers were Larry Skromme and Phyllis Whitesell, both members of the Preserve Board. They spoke about how they feel about the new organization and how indeed they felt favorably about how we can work together for our mutual good.

Following that we did have an election of officers, and the president of the new organization was James Jolly, a history professor at Millersville State University and an ardent friend of all agricultural preservation. Jeanne Sonntag, whose husband was with RCA and always has been interested in the environment, and an active member of the League of Women Voters, was elected vice president. Secretary was Barbara Skelly. Barbara and her husband Bill are members of the Methodist Church in Millersville and neighbors living in Long Lane. Finance chairman was Robert Campbell, owner of the *Lancaster Farming*, a weekly newspaper magazine dedicated and directed toward giving farmers helpful information they can use. The three directors, in addition to those four officers, were Eric Probst, an auctioneer who did a lot of work with farms, selling farms and other properties; Marilyn Lewis, about whom I spoke earlier, who is always interested in environmental improvement and farmland preservation; I was elected as a director also. Put on just one more hat.

The first regular meeting of the Friends of Agricultural Land Preservation Board was held on December 10, 1985. We started at 1:30 p.m. Those in attendance were James Jolly, President; Jeanne Sonntag, Vice president; Barbara Skelly, Secretary; Robert Campbell, Treasurer and Finance Chairman; Eric Probst; Marilyn Lewis; and Amos Funk. Also present was Alan Musselman, whom we borrowed from the Preserve Board, and Karen Freemen and Stephanie Schnowman, Secretary of the Preserve Board. Apparently we borrowed her, too.

After the introductions were made, Alan Musselman discussed the need for and the plans for a fund raising breakfast to be held on December 14 and 15, Saturday and Sunday, from 8:00 a.m. to 12:00 p.m. at the family-style restaurant that is owned by the Skiadas brothers. What they have done is to arrange for interested sponsors to donate food for the breakfast, and they donated the labor. The Friends of Agricultural Land Preservation Board will get some of the proceeds. All of the profits were to go to Friends. So I guess profits would mean that any food that has to be bought was subtracted from the total sale of the breakfast. As I remember, the Skiadas family did not take any money out for the use of their own help or their facility. A most helpful volunteer effort.

A rough draft of the proposed bylaws were distributed and, as usual, there were problems. Marilyn Lewis, who knew quite a few attorneys, said she would try to get somebody to work free for our new organization to save some legal fees. I spoke about the mission of the organization as I saw it, and I mentioned that my goal was to have 1,000 members to provide support for the Preserve Board and our total efforts for preserving farmland in the county. Alan said his duties involve unsolicited contributions coming from the Farm Preservation office. A lot of our people here want to do something; they don't know what to do and they want to help as much as possible. As of November 10, 1985, about a month before our meeting, there was over $10,500 donated to help us with our new organization and we didn't even have a fund raising campaign. Alan also distributed copies of the annual report of the Lancaster County Agricultural Preservation Board, and in that report some new maps were made. The report noted thirty-three farms with preservation deed restrictions plus three large tracts of land which have been approved for agricultural preserve by the Lancaster County commissioners. Thirty-three farms are not a lot out of our total farms, but it was a start.

I mentioned that at present government funding, we will be provided with only enough money for eight farms a year with the Preserve Board. More money is needed because Ag Board has already had to turn down farmers who wish to receive the allotted $250 per acre, which is a bargain— a steal really. We have found out in 1998 that the cost of development rights are much higher than $250 per acre. Yet we did not have enough money back in 1985 to purchase offered farms at $250 per acre, but that's the way it goes. It takes a while to get started. Bob Campbell, finance chairman, spoke about the private corporation fund raising which was aimed for February and March of 1986. Marilyn Lewis suggested the possibility of volunteer contributions of a small amount of money of those who rent a motel. That idea did not go too far because it looks like a tax. At least we thought about it and talked to people about it.

Jim Thomas advised us that all contributions to Friends of Farmland Preservation are considered tax deductible. This was a big help. That was the end of our activity at that particular meeting. Our next meeting of Friends of Farmland Preservation was held March 20, 1986. Again the meeting started at 1:30. We met at the County Planning Commission room in the Lancaster County Courthouse on the sixth floor. In attendance were James Jolly, President; Jeanne Sonntag, Vice President; Barbara Skelly, Secretary, Robert Campbell, Finance Chairman; Eric Probst; Stewart Herr; and Tom Strause. Staff members from the Preserve Board gave us some help and Karen Freeman was also there. James Jolly thought that we should get more involvement and more commitments from the township supervisors because, in Pennsylvania's township form of government, the townships have the last word in zoning decisions, etc. The county might advise, but the townships are the ones that have the final decision. So it is important that we get the interest and participation of the township supervisors.

Alan Musselman said that they will put a little blurb in the quarterly newspaper about the combined effort of the Ag Preserve Board and Friends as being proposed, and things that can happen. Jim Jolly pointed out that we should have more financial and membership support from government officials. He pointed out that only Commissioner Jim Huber and one borough official, Jim Jolly, is a member of the Friends of Agricultural Land

Preservation. Jim is a member of the borough council in Millersville near where I live.

The July 10 meeting of the Friends of Agricultural Land Preservation was held in the Lancaster County Planning Commission, sixth floor of the County Courthouse. Members present were James Jolly, President; Barbara Skelly, Secretary; Eric Probst; and Amos Funk. The poorest attendance we have had so far—I guess there was a reason for it. Jim Jolly called attention to the update of the bylaw changes. It was decided every member on the board of directors of Friends shall have a full-time, three-year office, and two members shall be elected each year at the annual dinner. In order to begin a staggered system, the members who were currently involved were chosen by lot. It was determined that Bob Campbell would be serving a three-year term; Marilyn Lewis a two-year term; Jeanne Sonntag would be a one-year term, as would Barbara Skelly. Jim Jolly had a two-year term, Eric Probst, a two-year term. The 1985-86 term which the present directors have served will not be counted. There will be election of new directors in the fall of 1986. The first election of two directors will occur at the annual meeting in 1987.

The second annual dinner meeting will be held November 13, 1986, at Miller's Smorgasbord at 7:00 p.m. The price of the tickets was set at $10 and Miller's will be donating half of the price of a ticket to the Friends organization. This was tremendous cooperation and support by Miller's Smorgasbord and I am sure everyone appreciated it and expressed their appreciation. Alan Musselman reported that at present there are 153 members of the Friends and over $24,000 in contributions to the Deed Restriction Fund.

The next meeting of the Friends Board was held on October 3, 1986, in the courthouse. Present were James Jolly, Barbara Skelly, Eric Probst, Lou Shoemaker (Director of Development, Financial Committee), Tom Strouse, Howard Manning, Stewart Herr, and Dave Yoder. At this meeting we talked about the 501C3 status for making our group, the Agricultural Land Preservation Board, eligible for any contributions to be deducted as a charitable contribution. We knew we had to do quite a bit of work and letter writing and appealing, so we decided at least we'd go ahead and take the first step with that. We announced that at the directors meeting. A number of us got together, and we developed a program for the annual meeting. We attempted to make it shorter than in other years, because it got a bit long.

The first meeting we held in 1987 was on Tuesday, January 13, again on the sixth floor of the courthouse. President James Jolly, Barbara Skelly,

Amos Funk, Marilyn Lewis, Daniel Herr, Eric Probst, and staffer Alan Musselman; Karen Weiss Director of Development was also there. Jim Jolly called the meeting to order at 3:10. Jim Jolly brought up the question whether we could consider raising the number of the Board of Directors to nine instead of seven. He felt it would allow for a broader base than the present seven. Alan Musselman felt if we did decide to increase the number of the Board, we should then list one person who has made commitments to farmland preservation by donation or deed restriction. Marilyn Lewis felt that the Board could be expanded to twelve and still have a workable number. I suggested that we appoint a small committee to study the idea. It was then decided to put this idea on a future agenda and have it studied with a recommendation for the annual dinner meeting in November of 1987.

Alan Musselman reported there are presently four agricultural preserves established totaling 48,000 acres. Fifty-five farms have preservation deed restrictions placed on them as a result of the work of the Farmland Preservation Board. I asked Stan Herr if he would be willing to come to the next meeting with the idea of how to form a membership committee to handle renewal notices and how to expand membership. He agreed to do this. He said he would be happy to contact Ed Saggart to ask if he would be willing to put our membership list in their computers. The Friends organization would be willing to pay for the paper and supplies. Ideas were brainstormed on how to increase membership. It was suggested the mailing list for the Bar Association and Medical Association can be sought and the purchase of these mailing lists will be worth consideration. Our membership goal set over a year ago was 1,000. We are presently at 23% of that goal. Alan discussed budget, talked about 501C3 status. He is considering an annual report, but decided there should be a separate annual report for the Preserve Board and the Friends organization, but they should comprise one printed package which can then be widely distributed. We took action favoring this concept.

The next meeting of the Friends of Agricultural Land Preservation was held March 30, 1987, at 3:15 p.m. Members present were James Jolly, President; Daniel Herr, Vice President; Barbara Skelly, Secretary; Eric Probst; Marilyn Lewis; Amos Funk; Bob Campbell, Finance Chairman; staff: Alan Musselman, Karen Weiss. Call to order was done by Jim Jolly. As we thought ahead and thought about a future mission activity, Alan Musselman distributed a pack of information compiled by the staff of the Ag Preserve Board which analyzed farm sales for 1986. This complete valuable report will not be released to the public and press until it is fully documented. When this is complete, it will be printed and distributed, particularly to township supervisors and people in the financial community of farm credit and banking. It is hoped it will counteract much of the adverse publicity which has occurred in the past year since it proves the facts and figures show that farmland value in preserved areas does not decrease in value as compared to surrounding area. The question was what can we as the Friends organization do in the future. I responded that with more of the same. As an organization, we still have not met our goal for membership that we set at 1,000. There is much potential that has not yet been realized.

The next meeting of the Friends of Agricultural Land Preservation was held on June 3, 1987, at 3:30 p.m. at the courthouse in the usual room. Present were James Jolly, Daniel Herr, Barbara Skelly, Amos Funk, and Marilyn Lewis. Staff was Alan Musselman, Director, and Karen Weiss, Program Specialist. A number of things were discussed. The May contribution distributed to each Board member showing a total of $45,611 is now in the treasury. The November dinner meeting was set to be held on Thursday, November 12, restaurant location not yet determined. We at least set a date for the meeting.

A special meeting of the Friends of Farmland Preservation was held on August 12, 1987, following a Finance Committee meeting in order to act upon two pieces of business pending for immediate attention. The following members of the Board of Directors were in attendance: Jim Jolly, Barbara Skelly, Marilyn Lewis, and Amos Funk. The Board of Directors approved the following action: Upon the recommendation of the Finance Committee, the Friends of Agricultural Land Preservation agreed that the sum of $6,000 be paid to Alan Musselman in appreciation for his services rendered to the organization. The sum of $1,000 will be donated to the "vote yes" referendum committee for use in a statewide campaign to insure passage of the farmland preservation referendum which will appear on the ballot on November 3, 1987.

The next meeting of the Friends of Agricultural Land Preservation was held on Tuesday, September 28, 1987, at 3:30 at the usual courthouse conference room. Present were James Jolly; Daniel Herr; Barbara Skelly; Amos Funk; Marilyn Lewis; Eric Probst; Bob Campbell, Chairman of the Finance Committee; Alan Musselman, Director; and Karen Weiss. Stuart Herr and Linda Cohoe, members of the Finance Committee, were also in attendance. The finalization of plans for the third annual dinner meeting to be held November 5, 1987, to be held at the Good and Plenty Restaurant, were made. We decided the price would be $10 a ticket, of which $4 would be contributed to Friends organization. Mr. Lapp agreed to that. It is remarkable how these different restaurant owners want to help preserve farmland.

One reason I guess is because tourists come to see farmland, and it will help attract people who want to come to eat. It's great, anyhow, that they want to do it. Another matter that was talked about at this meeting was another Farmland Preservation breakfast. Pete Skiadas at the Family Style Restaurant may do it again.

We discussed the bylaws again and decided to increase the Board of Directors from seven to eleven or fifteen, with a quorum being determined by a single majority. That is to avoid not having a quorum at a meeting. Campbell-Lewis made a motion that Amos Funk be a permanent member of the Friends of Farmland Preservation in recognition of his status as a founding father of Friends organization. I appreciated this very much, and thanked him, but it wasn't necessary. Since that is how he felt, so be it.

Also happening at this meeting was Dan Herr told the Board he had recently been notified that the original approval was granted the 501C3 status for the Friends of Agricultural Land Preservation from its inception till December 1989. If we need more help, Dan, as an attorney, will take care of any letter exchanges that have to be done. Alan Musselman explained that through the action of the Ag Preserve Board, the county now owns the Neff farm and purchase-resale option. We didn't do many of those; we talked about it, we thought the Farm Land Preservation Board would be a good idea, but this is an example where, at the sale, I remember Eric Probst was the auctioneer, and it was done. I don't know how effective it is, but at least the county owns it now; we will give it a try.

The next meeting of the Friends of Agricultural Land Preservation took place on May 19, 1988, at the courthouse in the usual conference room. Members present were Daniel Herr, Eric Probst, Vice President Barbara Skelly, Secretary Stewart Herr, Finance Chairman Ruby Bollinger, Ron Brubaker, Amos Funk, Jim Jolly, Tom Strause, Linda Coho, Marilyn Lewis, and Doug Weidman. Staff present was Alan Musselman, Executive Director; Karen Weiss, Acting Director of Ag Preserve Board; Dan Herr, President of the Board of Friends of Agricultural Land, an attorney and now president, and a good man for sure. We talked about a lot about different things and different suggestions. We really didn't take much action at this meeting, but most of these meetings were needed in case action had to be taken or ideas finalized.

The second meeting in the year 1988 was held on June 10 at the regular location. In attendance were Dan Herr, President; Eric Probst, Vice President; Stewart Herr, Finance Chairman; Marilyn Lewis; Ruby Bollinger; Amos Funk; Ron Burkholder; Doug Weidman; Linda Coho; and Earl

Newcomer. Staff in attendance were Alan Musselman and Karen Weiss, Acting Director of Ag Preserve Board.

The May 10, 1988, meeting was held in the usual room at the courthouse. In attendance were Daniel Herr, Barbara Skelly, George Herr, Finance Chairman Jim Jolly, Ron Burkholder, Amos Funk, Ruby Bollinger, Linda Coho, Tim Strause, Earl Newcomer, Jeff Frey, Doug Weidman, and Marilyn Lewis. President Herr indicated that in the light of events of the past few days, the regular agenda of the meeting was being expanded. He asked Al Musselman to explain the sequence of events that led to his written resignation as director of Agricultural Land Preservation Board, which he submitted to the county commissioners May 10, 1988, at 12:45 p.m.

Mr. Musselman spoke at some length about his concerns and the meeting with Commissioner Brad Fisher and Bob Brenneman on Friday. He answered questions from various Board members, and discussion then centered around what the Board's response would be to its members, the public, and the press. It was decided a statement would be drafted at the end of the meeting.

Dan Herr asked if all Board members had received a copy in the mail of the brainstorming meeting held Wednesday, April 27, 1988. After a brief discussion, the Board unanimously approved the Funk-Weidman motion to adopt the guidelines proposed and the action and plan organized under the three headings: mission of Friends, organization, and methods. On a Lewis-Jolly motion, the Board unanimously approved withdrawal of all private source funds of the Friends of Agricultural Land Preserve that are presently being held in the county bank account. These private source funds are to be placed in private interest-bearing accounts and arranged by Stewart Herr, Finance Chairman; and Bob Campbell, past Finance Chairman. Stewart Herr and Bob Campbell are instructed to meet with county commissioners in person as soon as it can be arranged to make the request for the transfer of funds. Mr. Musselman was then asked to leave the Board meeting for a short period of time. On a motion by Funk-Herr, the Board offered Alan Musselman a full-time staff position as Director of the Friends of Agricultural Land Preservation for a period of six months.

The above motion was amended by Stewart Herr-Coho to read: Alan Musselman is offered a one-year contract as full-time director of the Friends of Agricultural Land Preservation with a sum of $4,000/month provided toward salary, fringe benefits, secretarial help, office space, and other administrative expenses as needed. Employment will be effective at termination of employment as director of Agricultural Preserve Board. This contract will be reviewed at the end of one year. Both the amendment and the motion were unanimously approved by the Board of Directors of Friends. Mr. Musselman was requested to return to the room and the approved motion was read to him. He accepted the full-time staff position as Director of Friends, and expressed his gratitude for their show of support. Mr. Herr asked him as his first duty to prepare a proposed budget of expenditures for the year. On a Funk-Skelly motion the Board approved the appointment of Dan Herr and Marilyn Lewis to be spokespersons for the press conference following the conclusion of the meeting. The following press release was drafted:

> *We fully support Alan Musselman and as an expression of that support, we are offering Alan a job as full-time Director of Friends organization for the next year. His job will be to further the goals and preservation of farming in Lancaster County, and foremost concern of the Friends Board is preservation of farmland in Lancaster County. Friends organization is calling upon fighting factions in the community to cooperate, work for planned growth, and save farmland. We would like to see an expression of support from the county commissioners, and we would like to have them take a firm stand in favor of farmland preservation by committing more money, the sum of $1,000,000 a year in resources, time, and effort.*
>
> *This press release was approved by the Board of Directors.*

At the request of the county commissioners, a special meeting was held on May 19, 1988, at the regular courthouse conference room. Commissioners Bob Brenneman and Brad Fisher requested to be able to attend today's meeting to speak to the Board about the concern the two commissioners had. They came to the meeting about 3:30 and each spoke approximately five minutes and then answered questions for about forty minutes. Both commissioners expressed concern over information charges that were reported, they felt, incorrectly in the press. They indicated to the Board that they had simply asked Alan Musselman to explain on Friday afternoon, May 6, what the check for $6,000 from Friends organization to him was for. They said they felt they were will within their rights to ask questions. They still have not received a documented list of services he performed for the Friends.

Dan Herr assured the commissioners that Alan performed quite a number of tasks for the Friends, and his list of services would be sent to them in the near future. Both commissioners said they had supported farmland preservation in the past and were committed to doing so in the future. Dan Herr explained to the commissioners that the Friends board had always worked very closely with the Ag Preserve Board and have always held their meetings at the courthouse. Friends would like to continue to meet at the courthouse. He asked the county commissioners to please notify him if there is a need to change this arrangement.

Marilyn Lewis suggested that Board meet with the three county commissioners annually, perhaps close to the annual meeting, to chart for them progress that has been made toward preserving farmland that year, to outline for them our goals for the coming year, and to hear from them any problems or concerns they may have. Commissioners Fisher and Brenneman agreed that this would be a good idea and suggested that perhaps a meeting could occur twice a year. Dan Herr and Alan Musselman thanked the commissioners for coming to the meeting and expressed the Board's desire to work cooperatively with the county in moving forward to the future to preserve farmland.

Dan Herr of the Executive Committee expressed his concern for the assistance in completing the reorganization that was talked about in the brainstorming session a few weeks ago. He felt that the best way to do this would be perform an on-going Executive Committee made up of officers and friends of the Board, plus a few others who have interest, energy, and time to devote to tasks. The purpose of the Executive Committee would be to meet more frequently in a monthly meeting in order to work on the job description for Alan, and set up work committees to form guidelines on how these committees were to function under the organization. The following people agreed to serve on the Executive Committee: Past President Jim Jolly; President Dan Herr; Vice President Eric Probst; Secretary Barb Skelly; Executive Director Alan Musselman, non-voting member; Doug Weidman; Marilyn Lewis; Amos Funk; and Linda Coho. On a motion by Strauss-Lewis, the Board approved the formation of the Executive Committee and empowered them to meet and make executive decisions concerning the organization.

Regarding the preliminary budget, Alan Musselman distributed a paper showing three possible budget structures. Each had a number of variations and budget ranges depending on the direction Friends wished to pursue. Alan felt the most staggering cost in the future should be paid from the funds of foundation grants and possible support from the American

Farmland Trust. It was decided that newly formed Executive Committee should work on this item and explore the wisdom of a possible merger with the land organization. Dan Herr recommended that a job description for the Executive Director of Friends be drawn up along with a job contract, and that would be a top priority item referred to the Executive Committee.

Since we no longer can use an office for both purposes, it was necessary to find an office for Alan Musselman to put his material and to work from with a telephone. Doug Weidman agreed to check on some possible office locations, as did several other people at the meeting. On Funk-Coho motion, the Board approved holding its regular meeting on the third Tuesday of each month from 3 to 5 p.m. at the meeting room on the sixth floor of the courthouse. The Friends Board expressed concern about the future of Ag Preserve Board and wants to be on record as supporting the Ag Preserve Board and its staff as separate and autonomous from the Planning Commission.

The next meeting of the Friends of Agricultural Land Preservation Board met on June 10, 1988. Those in attendance were Dan Herr, President; Eric Probst, Vice President; Stewart Herr, Finance Chairman; Marilyn Lewis; Ruby Bollinger; Amos Funk; Ron Burkholder; Doug Weidman; Linda Coho; Earl Newcomer. Staff were Alan Musselman and Karen Weiss, Acting Director of the Agricultural Preserve Board. Alan explained that the job would be a challenge here and he wished to stay. President Herr explained that the most important order of business was concerning the budget and a firm salary structure of our Executive Director Alan Musselman.

Alan Musselman had received a job offer from Sam Norris in Chester County, his preservation group, and Alan explained that the job would be a challenge here and he wished to stay in Lancaster County. However, he was given a firm offer in another area yesterday, and so he was considering accepting the job for many reasons. The new job offer includes a very good salary, which means financial security for a three-year period for his family, and also comes with a promise of stability and political support. There was much frank and open discussion by the Board members concerning this job offer to Alan Musselman. The salary was tentatively set by Friends for Executive Director. The Board then went into executive session to discuss details of the salary and contract. At this point in the discussion, both Alan and Karen left the meeting. In a motion by Dan Herr-Funk and approved by the Board, details were set forth to be offered to Alan Musselman. It was agreed that his contract would be put into writing by President Herr on Monday. Alan Musselman was asked to return to the meeting and Dan Herr explained to him the contract drawn up by the Board. Alan asked if he could have the weekend to think about the contract proposal from Friends Board and would make a decision by Monday, June 13.

On Monday, June 13, 1988, Alan Musselman announced that he will remain in Lancaster County as the Executive Director of the Friends of Agricultural Land Preservation. Needless to say, everyone was happy with his decision.

Under the leadership of President Daniel Herr, with Alan Musselman guiding our staff, we made considerable progress in 1988.

In August 1988, the name of our organization was changed to the Lancaster Farmland Trust. Quite an improvement in my estimation.

In June 1988, Karen Weiss joined the staff of the Trust. She continues to provide excellent staff assistance as this is being written in 1998.

Karen Weiss

Karen Weiss has many talents. She is an excellent salesperson for farmland preservation, and she also does rather well in selling conservation farming. Perhaps the area in which I am most pleasantly surprised in Karen's work is her ability to work successfully with our Amish and other plain sect farmers. We appreciate her efforts.

A Record Farm Sale in 1990

In March 1990, a farm on which an agricultural-use-only easement was placed sold for a record high price, to date at least. The sale price was $6,967 dollars per acre. The farm was sold by Harriet B. Herr.

The old record was set in 1986. The selling price on this preserved farm was $4,343 per acre.

The above validates our position that a permanently preserved farm does not lose its value, especially when farming is a strong and vital occupation.

Alan Musselman Reports

In Executive Director Alan Musselman's report contained in the Lancaster Farmland Trust's April 1992 *Newsletter*, he pointed out that "Lancaster County's population is now close to 420,000, and we accommodate more than five million tourists per year."

Alan continues, "First natives and then visitors have recognized the special place this landscape represents in America and we have begun to retain it. Receipts of over $800 million come from our farms. From Maine to Florida, no place comes close."

From a very meager beginning, organized by several of us to meet what we thought was an urgent need, the Farmland Trust was born. From the start we have had excellent leadership: Presidents James Jolly, Daniel Herr, Darwin Boyd, Phyllis Whitesell, and presently in 1998, John Swartz. These presidents of the Lancaster Farmland Trust have all been great leaders. All of them have had excellent supportive officers and Boards of Trustees to assist them.

We have come from almost no staff to a very effective staff. There have been changes, but we kept moving ahead.

One of the trustees of the Farmland Trust has been especially kind to me. I am speaking of my good friend Dr. Kenneth Messner. At one of the Board meetings I was unable to attend, Ken Messner advanced an idea. He was successful in having his proposal adopted by the Board.

Amos Funk Farmland Trust

Ken's proposal was to set up The Amos Funk Farmland Endowment Trust. In addition, he started the fund with a $1,000 gift. Naturally, I was very pleased and grateful. However, the thing that makes this action so meaningful is that Ken Messner had the vision to set an Endowment Trust Fund for farmland preservation that would gain so much support. In the few short years since The Amos Funk Farmland Trust Endowment Fund was started, there is now in 1998 more than $650,000 in the fund. It would seem many people are interested in farmland preservation and they want to help. Many thanks to all of them.

Ken Messner and his wife, Sandy, donated a permanent conservation easement on the farm on which they live. Their story appeared in the April 1992 Lancaster Trust's *Newsletter.*

---

250 Years of Family Heritage
A Farmstead Legacy

We recently donated a permanent conservation easement on our farm in Rapho Township, and we asked to share our thoughts about our decision to place a permanent easement on our farm with Lancaster Farmland Trust.

We feel that agriculture has been (and still is) providing the economic backbone and social fabric of life in Lancaster County. Agriculture has been the leading industry for Lancaster since colonial times, providing us with a standard of living that is difficult to match anywhere else. It is unfortunate that arable land has not been recognized as an irreplaceable resource in many parts of this country, and that so much has been needlessly and permanently lost. We want to avoid that mistake in Lancaster County.

Lancaster County has been called a "living national treasure" by our Lancaster Farmland Trust Board of Trustees president, Darvin Boyd. This concept became personally evident to us when we recently celebrated the 250th anniversary of the arrival of our family in Lancaster. We noted this event by organizing a country-wide family reunion. Nearly 400 people attended with over twenty states represented. The major reason for some attendees to travel over 2,000 miles was to experience their heritage and discover their roots. The soil of Lancaster County nourished those roots in the 1700s, just as it continues to nourish us today. That simple truth became evident to us and to those who attended that family reunion.

As a result, we feel an obligation to protect this nourishing land of Lancaster County, as it has provided so much for us. Our children deserve no less, but we realize that if efforts are not made to preserve agriculture through permanent farm preservation, that nutrient system will be destroyed. Thus we look upon a permanent conservation easement as the best investment for our farm. There is no more reliable way to assure the presence of agriculture in Lancaster County for the next generations.

Ken and Sandy Messner

The Myer Homestead, 1759, the birthplace of Abram R. Myer, grandfather of my wife Esta Myer Funk, was permanently protected by the use of a donated conservation easement in 1994. The story as it appeared in the December 1994 Lancaster Farmland Trust's *Newsletter*, follows.

"The Myer Homestead, 1759"
Hess Family Leaves a Legacy
A National Bicentennial Farm

One exceptional piece of the patchwork quilt of farms in Eastern Lancaster County spreads gracefully north of East Eby Road in Upper Leacock Township. The owners, members of the Hess family, grew up on the farm but now are involved in their own careers and live in different parts of the country. Omar and Elvin live here; brother and sisters Robert, Allegra, Margaret, and Dorothy live in Ft. Wayne, Ind.; W. Chicago, Ill.; Ontario,

Can.; and Claremont, Calif., respectively. The family's roots are in Lancaster County, however, and more particularly in the Myer Homestead.

Last spring the family gathered around the table at the Trust and came to a strong, unanimous decision, "preserve the family farm." Plans were being made to sell the farm, but not until a conservation easement was completed and recorded in the land records with the Trust in stewardship. This 65-acre dairy farm has a special "feel." Trout glide in a stone-walled spring race emanating from beneath one of two historic homes on the farm. It's a quiet, tranquil place amidst predominantly Old Order Amish farms. The soil is Lancaster County's deep, fertile best. Visitors frequent the ancient Myer Cemetery, now adopted by the Amish community and perched on a slight adjoining knoll.

Now, a conservation easement has been finalized and recorded, and the farm was sold at a small public sale in November to a nearby Amish neighbor at a "rather significant price."

The Hess family is considering a permanent historic placard for the farm. Their commitment has led to other interest in preservation among the neighbors.

Alan Musselman guided our organization through some difficult years. His assistance was greatly appreciated over those years. Alan Musselman resigned his position as Executive Director in the spring of 1996. He explained that he plans to do private consulting work.

**Amos Funk Joins Phyllis Whitesell and Others
In our Thanks to Alan Musselman**

When Alan Musselman resigned his position as Executive Director of Lancaster Farmland Trust, Phyllis Whitesell, president of the Trust, wrote a letter of appreciation. As an individual who worked with and benefited from my association with Alan from the first day he arrived in Lancaster County, I fully concur with the thoughts Phyllis expressed.

I am grateful to both Phyllis and Alan for their most helpful assistance in our efforts to preserve farmland in Lancaster County.

A Letter of Thanks and Appreciation to Alan Musselman

I have known Alan since 1980 when he was hired as the first executive director of the Lancaster County Agricultural Preserve Board, of which I was a member. He was the director of the Preserve Board before coming to the LFT as its first executive director. I have observed Alan as a director of both organizations: the Preserve Board is Lancaster County's public program for farmland preservation, and the LFT is a private land trust, which has grown under Alan's leadership to more than 2000 members.

As the first director of both organizations, Alan has been a passionate spokesman for agricultural preservation in Lancaster County. His communication skills to the business and agricultural communities are excellent, and he is able to explain complex technical concepts of land preservation in understandable terms. Citizens of Lancaster County clearly identify Alan Musselman with farmland preservation.

Alan is interested in issues beyond the immediate charges of the LFT and has been active on boards of other conservation organizations in the community. I am aware that he has served on the boards of both the Historic Preservation Trust and the Lancaster County Conservancy, and he was an organizing member of the Lancaster Environmental Alliance.

He follows governmental action that affects farmland preservation. Following Lancaster County's 1995 property reassessment, the first since 1960, farmers were distressed about their increased assessments. Alan worked hard in organizing efforts to help farmers enroll in Pennsylvania's "Clean and Green" program, a preferential assessment program for farmers.

As Executive Director of the LFT, Alan has managed a staff of three and a budget last year of $234,000. He is developing computer skills following the Trust's purchase of a new computer system that includes Windows '95.

Alan Musselman is a committed preservationist and a crusader for farmland preservation. I believe that his greatest strengths are in initiating and mobilizing support for such an effort. He leaves the LFT strong in terms of membership and financial support and with a dedicated board and staff.

Sincerely,

Phyllis C. Whitesell

Thomas D. Stouffer

After considerable search, a Lancaster County native, an ex-Marine, Colonel Thomas D. Stouffer, was chosen as the next Executive Director of the Lancaster Farmland Trust. He is doing a great job. We wish him well.

The fact that Tom is a native Lancasterian, graduating from Elizabethtown High School, may be the reason he cares so deeply about Lancaster County's farmland. I an convinced Tom really cares!

Tom is proving that he is a good administrator. He can solve problems. He has suggested new and innovative approaches to encourage farmers to preserve farmland. We are very glad he is on our team!

Lancaster Farmland Trust Membership

On November 13, 1985, I publicly set a membership goal for the Friends of Agricultural Land Preservation of 1,000 members. Membership growth was slow but steady. By January 1990 the organization had 464 members.

Not satisfied with the level of membership growth, the Board of trustees endorsed a new, exciting, all-out plan to get new members. It worked! By September 1990 membership passed 1,000. What an effective campaign!

Now at the end of 1997, the membership is fast approaching 1,500 members.

Lancaster Farmland Trust Funding

On November 13, 1985, donations to the Friends of Agricultural Land Preservation totaled a bit over $7,000. During the past year, 1997, contributions to the Lancaster Farmland Trust for all purposes exceeded $800,000. What a gratifying increase!

Lancaster Farmland Trust Farms Preserved

We had a dream in 1985 to form a non-governmental organization to preserve farmland. Progress was slow in the early years. Trust in the organization by our plain sect farm families was difficult to build. All of us were heartened by the response in 1997. The seventeen farms preserved, with the assistance of the Trust in 1997, brought the total number of farms preserved through the Trust to eighty farms. These farms comprise over 5,000 acres of Lancaster County's fertile farmland preserved in perpetuity. Of the seventeen farms preserved in 1997, ten were preserved with donated conservation easements. That means the trust did not make any cash payments to the owners. Those families chose full eligibility for federal income tax deductions.

The other seven families chose to receive small cash payments for preserving their farms. The average payment in 1997 was $300 per acre.

THE PENNSYLVANIA ASSOCIATION OF CONSERVATION DISTRICT DIRECTORS

The first enabling legislation authorizing counties to form conservation districts within their boundaries was passed in 1937. Lancaster County's Conservation District, encompassing part of the county, was organized in 1938. Five other counties in Pennsylvania also organized conservation districts encompassing only part of their counties before 1945. The acceptance of conservation district organization was slower in Pennsylvania than in many other states. Many feared the beginning of land control.

The districts established in parts of six counties in those early days were Lancaster, Clarion, Franklin, Northumberland, Indiana, and York. The first two counties to establish conservation districts encompassing the entire county were Potter and Fulton. These districts were established in 1945. In 1950, the counties of Lancaster, Cambria, and Perry established conservation districts including the entire county.

The Pennsylvania Association of Conservation District Directors was organized in 1950. Clayton Jester from Adams County was the first president of the Association. By 1950, there were conservation districts encompassing the entire county in twenty-seven counties. The most recent county to establish a district was Forrest in 1972. This brought the total number of conservation districts in Pennsylvania to sixty-six. Only Philadelphia County has not established a conservation district as of the year 1998.

The first president of the Pennsylvania Association of Conservation District Directors (PACDD) that I remember well was the fourth president, elected in 1956. His name was Stanley Hamilton from Tioga County. The Tioga County Conservation District had been very helpful as a result of their cooperation with U.S. Soil Conservation Service and other agencies, in the building of a number of important water impoundments in Tioga County. These water impoundments were used for flood control, water supply, and recreation. Stanley Hamilton was very effective in pointing out the value of districts to anyone who would listen, including the chairman of the Tioga

County Commissioners. What did I learn from Stanley Hamilton? First, provide the best leadership you can to have your conservation district do something positive to help the economy of your county. Be sure to let others know what you are doing. It is especially important that you impress your county commissioners. This is where a lot of your funding comes from.

The fifth president of PACDD was Edward Fisher from Potter County. Edward Fisher was a busy man; he was a county commissioner, chairman of the conservation district, and in 1957 was elected president of PACDD. Ed Fisher proved to be not only a good leader of PACDD, but also a great promoter of Potter County. He insisted Potter County was God's gift to hunters. Not only were the deer in abundance, but wild turkeys were everywhere. He used as proof the abundance of "turkey dust." It, too, was everywhere!

My good friend Henry Hackman was the sixth president of PACDD. Henry served two one-year terms in 1958 and 1959. Henry was a schoolteacher, farmer, and had a deep concern for the wise use of our natural resources. Henry made an important contribution to PACDD.

I was elected president of PACDD in 1963. As I look back to that year, it is very likely that I learned more than I contributed. I learned about the workings of the National Association of Conservation District Directors (NACD), an organization made up of more than 3,000 local districts like Lancaster County. As I observed the procedures that took place in arriving at positions taken and resolutions passed, I discovered that most of the leadership came from those state associations that had elected individuals to represent their states at the national level, who had at least five years' experience. They did not change executive council members every year as we did in Pennsylvania and many other states. My conclusion was: We paid dues to the National Association; however, we were not getting good representation.

I got considerable satisfaction out of the fact that when I voiced my concern at the next quarterly meeting of PACDD, the idea received reasonable support. The following year, the decision to have the NACD Executive Council member serve a multi-year term was adopted and is still in place.

The nineteenth president of PACDD was another very good friend of mine from Lancaster County, Aaron Stauffer. Aaron was elected in 1972 and 1973. His election established a record no other Pennsylvania county has yet equaled. Over the years, three PACDD presidents came from the Lancaster County Conservation District. As I think back and attempt to reflect on the leadership of these three PACDD presidents from Lancaster County, we all led in different ways. My hope is that we led well!

My Twenty-Four Years
With the Pennsylvania Conservation Commission

Another organization closely related to conservation districts is the Pennsylvania Conservation Commission. In the early days of the Commission, the chairman was designated by law to be the Pennsylvania Secretary of Agriculture. Later Maurice Goddard, Secretary of Forests and Waters, served as commission chairman. Later the law was changed.

The commission chairman shall be the Secretary of the Department of Environmental Resources. Now, as of 1998, the chairmanship rotates between the Secretary of Environmental Resources and the Secretary of Agriculture.

I was first appointed to serve as a farmer member of the commission in 1963. I was nominated by Governor William Scranton, and later confirmed by the Senate. I had the honor of being nominated by four Pennsylvania governors and, in each instance, I was confirmed by the Senate. I had the good fortune to serve twenty-four years as a member of the Pennsylvania State Conservation Commission, and was elected vice chairman a number of years.

In addition to the Pennsylvania Secretaries of Agriculture and Environmental Resources, the membership of the Commission includes the State Conservationist of the Soil Conservation Service, Dean of Penn State's College of Agriculture, Penn State's Director of Extension, five farmer Commission members, and one urban Commission member.

I have always felt this group was very important to the sixty-six conservation districts in Pennsylvania and to their district directors.

As I envisioned the mission of the Conservation Commission, it was to suggest, but not demand, the direction district directors should consider following in their own counties. It was always important to guide but not push the directors, as an attempt was made to solve problems that were so different in various parts of the state. Just as the problems were different, solutions were different. It took me a while, living in Lancaster County, with our special problems of development, manure, and soil erosion, to fully appreciate the serious problems of those folks living in coal producing counties. Their problems, were also very real.

In the early days of the Commission, most of the money and staff time was allocated to building water impoundments to prevent flooding, to provide an adequate water supply, and to provide recreation and the resulting recreational income to an area.

Later the emphasis was changed to promote cleaner water, and still later the Chesapeake Bay Compact was signed into law. With this federal legislation came a great amount of new monies to be used to install recommended conservation practices on those soils that drain into the Chesapeake Bay.

These extra dollars provided additional cost share dollars to establish recommended practices on farmers' land. In addition, monies were also provided to hire staff to sell farmers on the idea and to assist SCS in applying the practices on the land.

Wisely, the Pennsylvania Soil Conservation Commission was chosen to implement the program in our state. A great many good things have been accomplished. Much remains to be done.

In 1995 I decided not to have my name placed in nomination for another term on the Commission. I left a lot of friends and many fond memories of my time serving as a Pennsylvania Conservation Commission member.

THE PENN STATE
AGRICULTURAL ADVISORY COUNCIL

Former Dean of Penn State School of Agriculture, Dr. Russel Larson, appointed an Advisory Council to the School of Agriculture. As the name suggests, the charge to the Council was to bring problems and concerns of Pennsylvania's agricultural industries to the attention of the university. The goal, hopefully, was that by working together, solutions might be found.

Each member of the Advisory Council represented a different segment of the many agricultural industries in Pennsylvania. It was generally agreed this cooperative effort between Penn State University and the representatives of Pennsylvania's agricultural industries was successful. Problems were solved. Concerns were alleviated. I had the privilege of serving as president of the Penn State Advisory Council from 1972 to 1976.

My Appointment
To The Advisory Committee of the U.S. Soil Conservation Service

In the year 1974, I was honored by U.S. Secretary of Agriculture Earl L. Butz when he appointed me to an eighteen-member National Committee to serve as an advisory group to the U.S. Soil Conservation Service.

I have included the list of names to illustrate how working with and listening to these outstanding individuals and others like them, my outlook was broadened and hopefully decisions I made were arrived at more intelligently.

Members of Public Advisory Committee on Soil and Water Conservation

Chairman - Robert W. Long, Assistant Secretary of Agriculture for Conservation, Research, and Education.

Alternate Chairman - Kenneth E. Grant, Administrator, Soil Conservation Service.

Secretary - R.M. Davis, Assistant Administrator, Soil Conservation Service.

Members:
  Lyle W. Bauer - farmer and Vice President of NACD, Harper, Kansas.
  Howard F. Bier - farmer and Director of Bank of Hazelton, Hazelton, North Dakota.
  Frank G. Eubank, Jr. - real estate developer, McLean, Virginia.
  Michael F. Frost - farmer, President and part-owner of Southwestern Fruit & Vegetable Company, McAllen, Texas.
  Amos Funk - farmer and President of Pennsylvania State Agricultural Advisory Council, Millersville, Pennsylvania.
  Leonard Graumann - member of Greet County Conservation District, and member of Oklahoma Conservation Commission, Granite, Oklahoma.

Frederick C. Gross - civil engineer for Waialua Sugar Company, and Director of West Oahu Soil and Water Conservation District, Waialua, Hawaii.

Dr. David A. Hamilton - Dean of the School of Agriculture and Home Economics, Tennessee State University, Nashville, Tennessee.

Arturo Jaramillio - Conservation District Supervisor and RC&D Project Steering Committee Member, Chimayo, New Mexico.

John A. McAllister - owner of beef cattle and tree farm, and Chairman of Soil and Water Conservation District, Mt. Carmel, South Carolina.

Dr. Richard S. Schleusener - Vice President and Dean of Engineering, South Dakota School of Mines and Technology, Rapid City, South Dakota.

Jerome E. Specht - member service director and a cooperative electric association and former county agent, Buffalo, Minnesota.

George C. Stubbert - Director, State Water Resources Board; member, Soil Conservation Society of America, Roseburg, Oregon.

Mrs. Rebecca Tompkins - cherry grower, and Chairman of the Michigan Commission of Agriculture, Traverse City, Michigan.

Mrs. Jerri Wagner - Co-owner of Miller Valley Builders Supply; past Director of Arizona Safety Council, Prescott, Arizona.

Mrs. Lois Weeth - farmer, native plant specialist for Western Fresno County, Coalinga, California.

Robert D. Whitmore - farmer and member of Washington State Soil and Water Conservation Committee, Fullman, Washington.

Harold H. Wilson - farmer and Regional Chairman of National Association of Conservation Districts, Peru, Indiana.

Failure to Adequately Tell the Important Story of Agriculture

Too often northeast United States agriculture is written off as unimportant or soon to be lost to development of all kinds. In my 1982 presentation to Conservation District Directors representing the twelve northeastern states at a meeting held in Connecticut, I attempted to refute that premise. My remarks follow:

Soil erosion is a serious problem in most districts in our area. What makes the problem more challenging is the fact that we have to correct the problem with less money and quite likely fewer people—at least fewer Soil Conservation Service people, the principal source of technical assistance ever since districts were created.

As I look at it, one of the chief reasons we in the northeast are being shortchanged at the federal level, with technical assistance and with adequate funding, is the fact that we have not told our story very well.

Too many people write off the northeast as just an area of little agricultural value and simply a growing metropolitan area that will soon be entirely planted to houses and other development. As all of you know, this is far from the truth. While it is true that many areas here in the northeast are under intense development pressure, we still have a great amount of farmland left.

Although those of you who have attended the northeast area meetings held in Delaware and West Virginia have heard me make some comparisons to show how much prime and important farmland we have remaining in the northeast, I think the numbers need to be repeated because I feel we in this area have a lot going for us and we need to look diligently for cost-effective methods to prevent further erosion of the fragile six inches or perhaps even less of topsoil, so necessary if we in the northeast are to continue to be a viable producer of agricultural crops and products. Just how do we compare to other states and other regions?

It is interesting to note that acre for acre, the northeastern states have a higher percentage of prime farm areas than their western counterparts.

Some facts revealed by the National Agricultural Land Study are worthy of emphasis.

Pennsylvania has more prime farmland than Oregon and Washington combined while New York has nearly as much as those two states. Maryland and New Jersey each have more acres of important farmland than found in Montana, Arizona, Nevada, Utah, or New Mexico.

Maryland and New Jersey have nearly as much important farmland as Florida, in spite of the fact that Florida has three times more total acres than Maryland and New Jersey.

Massachusetts, with only 8,500 square miles of land, has as much important farmland as New Mexico with over 121,000 square miles of land, a land area fourteen times as great as Massachusetts, and yet Massachusetts has more acres of important farmland.

California with over 158,000 square miles of land and 7.8 million acres of important farmland is considered one of our great agricultural states, yet five of the smaller northeastern states—Maryland, Delaware, New Jersey, Connecticut, and Rhode Island—plus Virginia, with just about half the total land area, have the same amount of important farmland as California.

The four states of West Virginia, Vermont, New Hampshire, and Maine have a combined acreage of prime farmland greater than the combined prime farmland acres of the states of Arizona, Nevada, New Mexico, and Utah, and yet these western states have a combined cropland acreage, not prime farmland, more than two times as great as the combined cropland acreage of West Virginia, Vermont, New Hampshire, and Maine.

The point that needs to be made is that we still have a lot of prime farmland here in the northeast. We need to protect it and keep it producing food, fiber, and perhaps energy, too.

Presentations
I Have Made

In my effort to promote interest in preserving farmland and protecting our soil and other natural resources, I attempted to share my thoughts and experiences on how to work toward achieving these desired goals by speaking to the listed groups that invited me to speak to them from 1966 to 1990.

The Paradise Rotary

The following remarks made on April 10, 1966, represent the first presentation I made to any group on the subject of soil conservation and farmland preservation.

When Mr. Heberlig asked me to speak to you, I reminded him that Christ Lapp had also asked me to fill a spot in your meeting schedule sometime in March. Gentlemen, thank you for the double invitation! You certainly have an active program committee. Whether or not you have a wise program committee will be determined about fifteen minutes from now when I will have finished my presentation.

As some of you know, I have spent all of my life on our family farm, formerly owned by my father and my grandfather. Lancaster County has been good to my family and me. This is the reason I am concerned about what happens in and to our county. This is the reason that for the past twenty-one years I have tried to give what leadership I could to the efforts of our Lancaster County Soil and Water Conservation District in an attempt to promote the conservation and wise use of the natural resources of our county. This is also the reason I have consented to speak to you today on the value of agriculture to Lancaster County now and in the future.

We live in a great county, outstanding in many ways. Let us look at what we have going for us as far as agriculture is concerned.

There are 604,000 acres of land in Lancaster County. Today 440,000 acres were used for agricultural production; 354,000 acres, or nearly 76% of all the land used for agricultural production, was Class I, II, or III land. This is compared to 41% in Berks, 37% in Dauphin, 68% in Chester, and 56% in Lebanon Counties. In addition to having the greatest amount of the most productive land in the state, Lancaster County is blessed with favorable rainfall and a long growing season, 180 frost-free days compared to 120 in Mercer County, State College, and in Tioga County. In addition, Lancaster County has more irrigatable land than any other county in the state. Using the U.S. Soil Conservation guidelines of a fifty-foot lift from the water source and the land to be irrigated being within a half-mile from the water source, Lancaster County has 36,000 acres of land that can be irrigated efficiently as compared to 1,500 acres in Lebanon, 6,000 acres in Chester, 5,000 in Berks, 20,000 in York, and 4,800 in Dauphin Counties.

What you may not know, however, is the average farmer spends 80% of his gross sales for production input. This represents a sizable boost to the economy of our county and might be most easily remembered if we would say the expenditure by Lancaster County farmers for feed, fertilizer, seed, etc., is $1 million every forty-seven days.

In addition, as a result of agriculture being present in Lancaster County, there are many agricultural supporting activities such as seed, feed, fertilizer, farm supply houses, farm equipment dealers, food processing plants, veterinarians, livestock sales and auctions, and others. There is ample evidence to indicate that the raw product value of agricultural production is increased at least ten times through agribusiness activities in an area. Applying this formula to Lancaster County, we would find that in addition to the 100 million agricultural raw product value, agricultural supporting industries located in our county contribute over a billion dollars annually to the economy of our county. Phrasing it a bit differently, in a manner that may be easier to remember, the value of our farm production added to the value of agribusiness located in our county and applied on a per-day basis, we would come up with a very impressive million dollars per day—the amount added to the economy of Lancaster County as a result of agriculture being present in 1965.

Then, too, I would call your attention to the $400 million real estate value of agribusiness in our county. I believe you would agree with me, the contribution of agribusiness to the total tax base cannot be ignored or taken lightly. I would remind you, however, that as agriculture leaves an area, so do must of the industries that support agriculture.

It is difficult to put a value on the quality of a freshly pulled ear of sweet corn or on the delightfully different taste of a cantaloupe allowed to ripen on the vine or a tree ripened peach. These taste treats are made possible only when fruits and vegetables are grown on farms located in our county. They are impossible to enjoy when these items are hauled sixty to 100 or more miles to market.

Now let us talk about the value of agriculture in Lancaster County in the future. Here the picture becomes less clear. According to census figures, Lancaster County lost annually approximately 3,000 acres of agricultural land to non-agriculture use from 1954 to 1964. Population in the county increased approximately 4,000 persons per year.

Population projections to the year 2000 indicate annual population increase in Lancaster County may reach 6,000 persons. Today, new land uses are being observed that were unthought of in 1954: the Muddy Run Project, PP&L Bainbridge land acquisition, and the mysterious land purchase at Washington Borough. The much needed accelerated highway construction program will also make sizable inroads into our present farmland. With these new uses in mind, it is entirely possible that unless we do something about it, we may lose annually as much as 4,500 acres of farmland.

In 1964 we had 468,000 acres of farmland in Lancaster County. By the year 1990 we would lose 25% of these acres and one-half of our 1964 agricultural land acreage would change to non-agricultural use by the year 2020. In addition, if present land use patterns are followed, most of the best farmland will be gone.

One very knowledgeable person told me within the past month that on the basis of current trends, 200,000 acres may be removed from agricultural production in Lancaster County during the next twenty-five years. I hope this does not happen. It this would happen, it is quite likely the $2.5 million daily addition to the county's economy by agribusiness would be reduced at least to half. These questions might be asked: Will the new uses contribute as much or a greater value to the Lancaster County economy? Will the taxes received pay for the services demanded? What kind of new people will be coming into our county? How will a 50% reduction in farmland affect the very important tourist industry in our county?

I think it is most important to consider the long-term effects of what we are doing or failing to do in regard to the use of our land resource. Are the alternatives being explored?

Cost of Strip Mining

At a meeting of Governor Shafer's Committee for the Preservation of Land for Agriculture, John K. Tabor, former Secretary of Labor and Industry for Pennsylvania, told us that early in Governor Scranton's administration, a study was made to estimate the cost of repairing the devastation caused by unregulated strip mining in our state, and the cost of reducing the acid mine pollution of our streams to a tolerable level. The resulting answer was most shocking. The estimated cost of such an effort was found to be equal to the total value of all the coal removed from all the mines in our state. The irony in this situation is the restoration would be paid for by the public instead of the companies who mined the coal. I would say here is an excellent example of progress in reverse. Any county or any state must continue to grow in terms of population (and this means new homes), new industry, new highways, etc. The plea I would make at this time is for more orderly growth, less urban sprawl, and more professional planning.

Perhaps the most relevant argument for the preservation of agricultural land at this point in local history is that such a program would provide a valuable tool for guiding intensive types of development and land use in a more realistic manner. Present development patterns constitute not only a hazard to valuable farmland, but place a financial burden upon local government in the form of streets, water and sewage facilities, police and fire protection, and other public services. More realistic use of our land resource would result in multiple benefits. This, then, establishes the need for consideration far beyond farmland alone when developing a preservation program.

I would also recommend that an effort be made to use our less productive land for development and attempt to keep our most productive land in agriculture. This is not a new idea. I mention it only in an effort to attach new meaning to the thought. Farmers can stay in business longer even at today's low prices on our better soils. If these soils are kept open for fifty or more years, there may be far more important uses develop for these agricultural lands not even thought of at this time. Agricultural land can be converted easily and cheaply to these new uses. Land covered with asphalt and concrete may be too costly to convert to these new uses.

Farms Threatened by Urban Growth

This September 1, 1966, interview with Sam Christensen appearing in the Lancaster New Era *newspaper was the first major newspaper story on my thoughts regarding farmland preservation. The story is used with the permission of the* Lancaster New Era.

Farms Threatened By Urban Growth

Amos H. Funk Outlines Proposal To 'Save' County's Agriculture

by Sam Christensen, *New Era* Staff Writer

A growing blight of urbanization will desolate Lancaster County's rapidly disappearing open farmlands unless county and state governments act now, a leading Millersville farmer and conservationist warned today.

Amos H. Funk, a member of the Pennsylvania Soil Conservation Commission, appealed to all government levels "to brush aside volumes of paper work and get to work on a practical and long range program" to make sure that in 1980 the county will still be the state's "garden spot."

In an interview at his 240-acre fruit and vegetable farm, one mile southwest of Millersville, Funk unfolded a four-point program which he will detail at the September meeting of the Conservation Commission.

Funk will propose that:

KEY TRACTS

- Key tracts be earmarked for preservation by the County Planning Commission and Soil Conservation District, which would draw up a comprehensive development plan, subject to review by citizens and civic groups.

- Development rights on these key farms be purchased by the County with the help of funds from the State and Federal Government.

- County school tax assessments be kept at their existing "reasonable" rates as proposed in a bill before the State Senate by State Senator Richard Snyder, for Lancaster County, 13th District.

- Lands set aside for recreation and highway use be restricted to the low grade, class three and four farm tracts.

ROOM

"No one likes to live in a crowded area," Funk said, summarizing the purpose of his program, "we all like to have a little room around."

In addition to livability, the program aims to keep the County's economy balanced between agriculture and industry and to preserve the area as a tourist attraction.

Taking a brief break from his farm chores, Funk described his ideas, seated in a swing on the front porch of his white frame farmhouse.

Pointing to a well on the front lawn, Funk declared, "Now, there's a good example of urban blight right there in front of us."

MILE AWAY

In the old days, Funk said he could pump all the water he needed for his irrigation right from that well, but now with developments coming in and tapping the same water source, "I've got to pump my water a mile away from the Conestoga Stream."

"There's nothing more definite than what happens to your own place," mused Funk.

Across Slackwater Road which runs in front of his home, Funk pointed to the 100-acre Wyble farm which was recently sold for $1,500 an acre to Builder A.B. Mellinger.

"If zoning changes go through, that could mean 100 acres of houses and apartments where there used to be beautiful open space," Funk said.

Pulling out a speech he had recently delivered to the local Rotary, Funk cited facts and figures.

"Projections to the year 1980 place our county population at 425,000. Nearly 150,000 more persons will be living in our county than were living here in 1960."

Funk read on: "To accommodate these additional people, projections show we may lose 110,000 acres of agricultural land to provide houses, schools, churches, new industry, and roads."

"In other words," commented Funk, stuffing his speech back into a folder, "for every 100 increase in population, 75 acres of land now in farms will be removed from agricultural production."

"Getting behind the statistics," Funk continued, "you see the expanding non-agricultural section demanding and getting more land. In many cases agriculture is outbid for the use of land. Medium size farms like the one across the street have been sold for as much as a million dollars."

SOLUTION

And what's the solution to these long term problems? Funk pointed to the provision in his proposed program which calls for long range planning and the purchase of development rights.

Together, the Lancaster County Planning Commission and the soil conservation district, after review by responsible citizens, should earmark key tracts that would not interfere with the county's industrial development, Funk offered.

"Then, you assess the development value of these key tracts, pay the price with the help of Federal and State funds, and so the County becomes the owner of these development rights in the legal form of easements."

Using easements, Funk explained, the farmer continues holding title as owner and continues farming and paying taxes. But he can't sell to a developer, because that right would belong to the County which had already paid the farmer.

"Everyone likes a little gravy and the farmer should not be penalized to keep the county nice for everyone."

NO VIOLATION

"So I don't see why farmers would object to this—I think they would be for it; it's not a violation of the free enterprise system," Funk concluded.

Funk commended a bill recently introduced in the State Senate by Richard Snyder, State Senator from the 13th District. The bill proposes that the State preserve the existing farm tax structure which assesses farms on the basis of present not potential use.

"I was talking with a fruit grower in Delaware County last week," Funk said. "He pays 100 mills at 25 per cent assessment school tax. He will not remain agriculturally competitive at those tax rates very long."

In conclusion, Funk urged countians "not to down grade the economic power of agriculture. Many of our surpluses are disappearing. Great population pressures are building up at home and abroad."

With that note, Funk jumped up from his swing seat, and concluded the interview with an intent glance at his irrigation pumping system in a nearby field. It was high time to get back to work!

Lancaster Exchange Club

My good friend and fellow church member at Grace Methodist Church in Millersville invited me to speak to his Lancaster Exchange Club in August 1968. There were some very important people in the club I was addressing. I did my best to be effective.

Thank you, Sam Campbell. Thanks also to the Lancaster Exchange Club for inviting me here to discuss a matter that has concerned me for some time. I have not talked about this concern too freely because I feel there are relatively few people in our county or in our state who are disturbed by the loss of our prime farmland.

As a matter of fact, there are a number of very knowledgeable people who feel the loss of farmland is not a cause for alarm. For example, my good friend Abe Bucher, veteran farm consultant, said in an interview published in the *Intelligencer Journal* June 17, 1968, and I quote: "In my opinion, I believe we have plenty of land for agriculture."

Now, Mr. Bucher is a very respected gentleman with a solid background in agriculture. However, I cannot agree with him or anyone else who takes this point of view. I would also disagree with those who say, yes, it is a problem, but there is nothing we can do about it.

Let me first speak to the point that there is enough land for agriculture. According to census figures from the years 1954-1964, Lancaster County lost more than 31,000 acres of agricultural land to non-agricultural use, or an average of a little better than 3,000 acres per year.

When we look at population figures as of 1966, we find our population in Lancaster County is increasing approximately 4,000 persons per year. There seems to be little doubt that in our county at least, the loss of agricultural land is directly related to population increase. Land is needed not only to provide homes, but for schools, hospitals, industrial sites, etc.

When we relate the history of agricultural land loss with population increase, we find that for every 4,000 population increase, we lose 3,000 acres of farmland. Putting it differently, for every 100 increase in population in Lancaster County, we lose 75 acres of farmland.

I think we would all have to agree that up to this time this trend has caused no serious economic or aesthetic problems. Our county is economically quite healthy. Lancaster County is still a beautiful county. In fact, U.S. Secretary of the Interior Stewart Udall, when he appeared at Hershey as banquet speaker during Governor Scranton's Conference on Natural Beauty in 1967, made this statement: "If I were asked to name a beautiful countryside east of the Mississippi River, I would pick Lancaster County." I would raise the question here today: Can we keep it beautiful? I think we can if we try!

Just what kind of an economic impact does agriculture have on an area? We know our county's total agriculture production is over $100 million each year. However, this does not represent the total contribution of agriculture. Let me illustrate with some Pennsylvania figures. In 1967 Pennsylvania's 77,000 farmers produced nearly 937 million dollars' worth of products (remember Lancaster County produced over 100 million). Most farmers spend approximately 80% of their gross income for current inputs. Pennsylvania farmers contribute to the economy of our state about $750 million annually, or $2 million daily. However, agriculture's contribution does not stop there. According to a recent study, the raw product value might be multiplied by as much as 2.6 times by agriculturally supported activities such as seed, feed, fertilizer, farm supply and equipment dealers, food processing plants, veterinarians, livestock auction sales, and others. When this 2.6 multiplier is applied to Pennsylvania agriculture, the total income generated by farming may be $3.4 billion annually.

Farmers pay real estate taxes. Some of us think they are quite high. Now, you have at least one farmer in your Exchange Club. The Honorable Abram Snyder is not only a farmer, but also a former county commissioner. I believe he will agree that farmers pay their share of real estate taxes.

Several weeks ago my neighbor, County Commissioner Abram Dombach, took Commissioner Chairman Ben Weaver on a tour of farms in Manor Township. Several farmers in particular were observed. Upon getting back to the courthouse, they looked up the property taxes paid by these individuals. Ben Weaver's comment was simply, "I do not see how they can pay this level of property taxes with farm prices generally so low."

I was not invited to speak to you on the question of whether the farmer pays his share of property tax. The point I would like to make is taxes on farm real estate are quite sizable. Again, I do not have any data on Lancaster County, but Pennsylvania farmers pay annually $38.8 million in real estate taxes. This represents over 4% of their gross income.

The same study referred to earlier indicates that industries and services supporting agriculture pay annual property taxes 5.3 times as great as the farmer. In Pennsylvania this would be $205 million. Therefore, $243 million may be added to county, township, and borough tax rolls as a result of agriculture being present in Pennsylvania in 1965, the year the study was conducted.

As briefly as I could, I attempted to outline the contribution agriculture makes to open space and its multiple contribution to the economy of an area.

We need land for houses, industrial sites and all related uses. My plea is for greater planning in the use of our land resource, which would result in far wiser land use.

In Pennsylvania and particularly here in Lancaster County, we should create an agricultural climate that would encourage and make it possible for any farmer who wants to farm to continue to farm. High taxes, as a result of high assessments, should not force a man off his farm. However, some farmers are just waiting for the right offer to sell for development. The increase in land value has been a major source of farm income for the past twenty to thirty years.

There are plans advanced in a dozen or more states to protect those farmers who want to farm and yet not provide a tax shelter for the land speculator. I have read most of them and talked to men in many of the states where they are being tried. The plan I like best is the one made possible by California's Land Conservation Act of 1965. I would favor a similar act for Pennsylvania, and I will attempt to do all I can to include this as one of the recommendations to Governor Shafer from our committee.

As I see it, this Act will provide part of the answer to the preservation of agricultural land. The voluntary feature of the California Act is what gives it great appeal. However, it is also one of the weaknesses of the Act.

Experience in New Jersey's attempt to provide tax relief to its farmers revealed that few farmers in northern New Jersey near the metropolitan centers took advantage of the special agricultural assessments allowed by their act. They wanted to be free to sell their farm when the right offer was made. In central New Jersey a greater number availed themselves of the advantages of the Act. However, it was in south Jersey where the greatest participation was realized.

If we are to provide permanent open space near our boroughs and the city of Lancaster, I feel key tracts will have to be earmarked by the Lancaster County Planning Commission, and an all-out effort be made to preserve these key tracts.

Pennsylvania Power and Light Conference on the Environment

This presentation was made on March 22, 1972, during Pennsylvania Power and Light's Conference on the Environment. In my presentation I outlined some of our early efforts to preserve farmland in Lancaster County.

I wish to thank Arch Knisely and Richard Green for inviting me this evening. I would also like to commend Mr. Gerald Faber and those who worked with him for scheduling and planning this meeting.

It is important to the folks at PP&L to tell the public about their environmental concerns. It is more important to be told what they are doing about these concerns. It is also important for a large company like PP&L to discuss publicly to what degree they can and will support the general planning concept as outlined in Sketch Plan II.

Folks at PP&L have discussed the proposed 16,160 acres of industrial park development areas with the Lancaster County Planning Commission staff. Some new areas were proposed by them. I believe this is what John Ahlfeld and his staff want: review of Sketch Plan II, improve it, and then support the general concept as outlined in the document. I believe PP&L is nearly ready to give it such support.

In December of 1967, I received a letter from former Governor Shafer requesting me to serve on an eighteen-man committee to study the problem of the loss of agriculture land in the state. Governor Shafer called attention to the fact that since 1950, Pennsylvania has lost three million acres or 20% of its total agricultural land. The governor also pointed out that if farmland diversion remains unchecked, food shortages may occur in thirty or forty years.

The committee was further charged with the responsibility of making recommendations that would preserve agricultural land. Now, when you get a letter from the governor requesting you to participate in an activity in which you are intensely interested, you say yes!

Twenty-four months, an equal number of regular meetings, plus ten special committee meetings. Later, a report was presented to Governor Shafer. During the presentation ceremonies, I appealed to the governor to implement at least some of the recommendations contained in the report at the earliest possible date.

What has former Governor Shafer and present Governor Shapp done about the report on the Preservation of Agricultural Land? The answer is: just about nothing.

In August 1971, nearly two years later, I called Irving Hand, former Director of the State Planning Board and asked if the state had developed a land use plan for Pennsylvania (a recommendation it was felt should have highest priority). His answer was no. He assured me it is being considered, but no plan as such has been developed.

He suggested I call the Department of Agriculture. Secretary McCale was unavailable when I called and I was referred to Jim Patton, former president of the National Farmers Union and one of Secretary McCale's top advisors. His answer to my question was, "No, there is no plan but we are thinking about the problem." In fact, he pointed out, Governor Shapp has scheduled a national land use conference to be held in Pennsylvania in early summer. Great, just what we need, another meeting, possibly the appointment of another committee to prepare another report, to gather dust just like ours did!

There is in circulation in Lancaster County another report that I hope gets much better treatment. I refer to Sketch Plan II prepared by the Lancaster County Planning Commission. With proper support, this document could well become the blueprint for future development in Lancaster County.

If the guidelines set forth in Sketch Plan II were followed, we can continue to have the excellent mix of agriculture, industry, and people that has made this county great.

The main thrust of this report is a recommendation for a shift toward a higher concentration of residential land use rather than scattered development. Today, 60% of present residential acreage is classified as low density. Medium density comprises 35% of the total. High density development makes up 5% of the total residential acreage. Sketch Plan II recommends equal areas of low and medium residential density comprising 45% each and doubling high density development to approximately 10% of total residential development.

Provided in the plan are 16,160 acres of industrial park areas. These areas are so located that undue pressures will not be exerted on areas recommended for agricultural production.

If these industrial and residential land use goals could be approached or attained, the 200,000 projected increase in population in the county by the year 2000 could be housed on less than 25,000 acres of land.

Past land use patterns from 1954 to 1970 reveal that, for each 100 increase in population, seventy-five to 100 acres of agricultural land were removed from production. Land transition from agriculture to other uses under Sketch Plan II proposals would set aside approximately 237,000 acres of our best Lancaster County agricultural land for farming and open space.

Today we are not making good use of our land resource in Lancaster County. Land, unlike people or even fish, does not breed. We have in our county only 604,000 acres of land. Today there are about 450,000 acres of undeveloped land remaining in the county. Even under the guidelines set forth in Sketch Plan II we may have less than 300,000 acres of open space, including agriculture, by the year 2000. This, of course, represents a reduction of 33% in twenty years.

Many people decry the disappearance of farmland. Sketch Plan II in my opinion offers the best solution to date, to give direction to future development and growth in Lancaster County.

Is Lancaster County's agriculture worth saving? Lancaster County, the Garden Spot of America, is a tribute that has been earned by farmers of this great county since its early settlement.

I hope the citizens of Lancaster County will support our efforts to preserve our productive farmland and strive to have a desirable balance between agriculture, people, and industry.

I will conclude my remarks by quoting from the Second Annual Message of Governor William T. Cahill to the New Jersey Legislature on January 11, 1972.

"We do indeed seek more industry in New Jersey to sustain a growing economy, but we must be selective as to the kind and its location. We are in urgent need of more dwellings for our citizens, but we do not want them constructed on unsewered filled-in coastal marshland. To accommodate those residents who seek apartments, we need more high rise buildings, but we ought not to construct them in the flood plains of our streams and rivers. We welcome commerce in our state, but we do not want its arrival to consume our farmland, ushering the vital agricultural industry into oblivion."

The development ethic which served us so well when the frontiers were limitless and clean air and water were here in abundance can no longer be our only guidance. Balance is the key.

An increasing number of people are joining the group that has for its slogan, "We have to try to do better."

Testimony on House Bill 1056

I was asked to testify before the Agricultural Committee of the Pennsylvania House of Representatives on May 5, 1972. I supported the passage of House Bill 1056. My testimony of support follows:

My name is Amos Funk. I live in Millersville, Pennsylvania. I am a vegetable grower with a farm market sales outlet.

Although I was named chairman of a special committee representing the Pennsylvania Association of Conservation District, Inc., to prepare a policy statement on House Bill 1056, my testimony does not reflect a consensus of thought of this group and, therefore, is not a policy statement. This situation exists because of the many points of view regarding the proposed legislation held by the district directors and the shortness of time in which to develop an acceptable statement.

Therefore, my statement reflects the thinking of some of the directors of the Association and my own thoughts on legislation to allow preferential taxation on land, including agricultural land, agricultural preserves, forest lands, and open space.

Pressures on agricultural land in many of Pennsylvania's urbanizing counties is very great and much of our best agricultural land is being lost to non-agricultural uses. For this reason I commend Chairman Kennedy and the committee for acting so rapidly.

For example, in Lancaster County we are losing 8,000 acres of agricultural land to non-agricultural uses each year. This is double the rate of transfer during the years 1954 to 1964, when 4,000 acres were removed from agricultural production each year.

We have in Lancaster County approximately 440,000 acres of land in agricultural production, representing ownership by about 5,500 farmers. If the present rate of loss of agricultural land continues, all of our farmland in Lancaster County will disappear in fifty years.

This is what will happen if we continue down the scattered development road we are now following. This loss of prime agricultural land should not take place and would not occur if a plan called Sketch Plan II, prepared by the Lancaster County Planning Commission, were followed. This plan would put the proposed 200,000 projected population for the county by the year 2000 in 25,000 acres of land instead of 200,000 acres of land required under current development patterns. Over 16,000 acres of industrial park area are provided for in the plan; and, finally, the plan provides for the retention of 250,00 acres of prime agricultural land set aside as agricultural preserves. These preserves contain all Class I, II, and III land.

However, this is just a plan, and like most plans it is of little value until implemented. I think a bill patterned similar to House Bill 1056 would assist greatly in implementing this and other similar plans that exist throughout the Commonwealth.

In other areas of Pennsylvania, loss of farmland may be greater and in some areas, far less. However, in nearly all instances the best and most productive land is being developed.

Some farmers want to sell. By one stroke of the pen they can make more money than by farming for ten to twenty years. However, too many farmers recently have found it necessary to sell because of exorbitant property taxes.

Legislation is needed to create an agricultural climate in Pennsylvania that will enable farmers who want to farm, to continue to do so. There is also a need to allow farmers the right to sell if they so desire.

New York Agricultural Districts

The New York law allows for an individual farmer to enroll in a contract procedure as well as a group of farmers enrolling as an agricultural district. Seventeen districts comprising over 287,000 acres have been certified in the state of New York to date. It is reported 200 towns are considering the formation of districts.

I would like to see the agricultural district concept included in Pennsylvania's law because it will retain a greater amount of land in agriculture and open space for a longer period of time. The penalty provisions of the New York law bear out that premise. Additional reasons for me favoring agricultural districts are:

1. Farmers living in predominantly agricultural districts are more easily serviced by feed stores, implement dealers, etc.
2. District boundaries would tend to discourage construction of sewer and water lines within those boundaries.
3. Highway construction should be routed around agricultural districts.

4. Anyone building homes near an agricultural district should be aware of the likely presence of manure smells, the noise of farm tractors, and trucks spreading lime and fertilizer.

The definition of prime agricultural land in House Bill 1056 is adequate. Other suggestions concerning House Bill 1056 are as follows:

1. Legislation should provide that each county must participate in the program and offer preferential taxation to landowners to qualify under the law.
2. Any tax rollback in case of violation or termination of a contract should be a period of eight to ten years.

Taxes and Farmland Preservation

Throughout the years Pennsylvania's taxing policy has treated land as if it were the problem. People create the problems, not the land. Taxes are generated to create people services such as education, sanitation needs, roads, fire and police protection.

Legislation is needed to tax land on its use, not market value, in order that farmers who want to farm may continue to do so and not be forced off the land by exorbitant property taxes.

I think it is about time we declare a new "land ethic." It is time we treat land as a non-renewable resource rather than solely as an economic unit. The value of land for open space, agriculture, recreation, and environment protection can outweigh its highest and best use as determined by market value.

Who pays for this effort to shift a major portion of the tax from the land to keep it open? A good question, and one that state legislatures have chosen to ignore. But it is obvious if a bill based on this new land ethic is adopted in the future, people will be taxed and not the land. Those receiving the benefit of education, roads, sewers, fire and police protection will pay for the services, and I think it is about time. We all recognize that commercial and industrial properties pay more in real estate taxes than they take from the community in services and benefits, while residential properties as a whole don't begin to be self-supporting.

When it comes to land, however, you have a property class which requires minimal services from the community. The agricultural taxes received by the municipality from farm real estate broadens the municipality's tax base without providing services to the farm community.

In other words, landowners traditionally subsidize homeowners. The only change brought about by a bill assessing land on its use rather than market value would be a reduction in the amount of subsidy to the homeowners.

Thank you for permitting me to testify.

The Pennsylvania Forum
Hershey, Pennsylvania

This presentation to the Pennsylvania Forum was made on April 30, 1975. I attempted to call attention to the importance of farmer involvement in land use planning. Mention is made of my early involvement in soil conservation in 1939, and finally, some of my thoughts on farmland preservation. My presentation follows:

I must admit I was a bit surprised, although very pleased, when Dr. Fox invited me to participate in this conference. I was surprised because quite often active farmers are not invited to participate in conferences such as this one. I was pleased because agriculture has and can continue to make a vital contribution not only to the economy of Pennsylvania, but to the quality of life for many Pennsylvanians.

Input from farmers should be sought in the development of land use planning at all levels of government. This is important because farmers own most of the land, the use of which is to be regulated.

In Maryland, farm input was not sought in the development of land use legislation in that state. The proposed bill was in the first reading before farm and agribusiness groups became fully aware that there were things in the bill that would be difficult for farmers to live with. A successful lobbying effort weakened the bill to such an extent that in the opinion of many, the act is not too effective. This is unfortunate because farmers need good land use legislation more than any other group. However, few will admit it.

Many farmers decry the use of prime farmland for development and think something should be done about it. However, for many of them, doing something about it does not include a township official, a county commissioner, or some bureaucrat from Harrisburg or Washington, telling him what he can or cannot do with his land. This makes the preservation of prime farmland difficult. The effort is opposed by the very people who are trying to be helped.

In Suffolk County, New York, where disappearance of prime agricultural land has been so acute that the County Legislature has made available $60 million in the county's capital budget to buy the development rights of some of the farmland, County Executive John V.N. Klein reports that farmers in the county vigorously opposed this seemingly very generous plan. In order to have farmers respond positively, a sixteen-member Suffolk County

Agricultural Advisory Committee was appointed. A plan to preserve the farmland in the county was developed by these sixteen farmers. This plan was accepted by the County Legislature in March 1974 and later won an award from the National Association of County Officials. Interestingly, too, opposition to the plan from farmers virtually disappeared.

I trust I have made my point concerning farmer involvement in the development of land use legislation.

As a third-generation farmer living on our home farm in Millersville, I am proud to be a Pennsylvanian. I think we have a great state and I think agriculture has contributed to that greatness. However, the future of agriculture in many parts of our state is unsure.

Farmers are faced with an increasing number of challenges that are causing a rapid decline in the number of farms in our state. Between 1910 to 1974, there was over a 300% reduction in farm numbers, from 220,000 farms to 71,000 farms. Similarly, the amount of land in farms decreased from 18.6 million acres in 1910 to 8.9 million acres in 1969.

At this point I would like to discuss some things that are happening in Lancaster County. I chose Lancaster because it is my home and I know more about it. I am certain some of the same changes are taking place in many other counties of the state, perhaps even more rapidly.

I first became involved in resource management in 1939 when we requested the United States Soil Conservation Service to prepare a conservation plan for our home farm. This was an effort to control soil and water loss through a combination of recommended practices.

In 1950 a Conservation District was formed in our County. I was asked to serve on the original board and I am still serving.

I have been concerned about the loss of agricultural land to non-agricultural uses for some time now. My concern increased as more of the depressing numbers became apparent.

I was discussing this concern with a friend of mine who owns a plane. He suggested we take a plane ride and observe the great amount of farmland remaining in the county. Of course, his inference was that I was over-concerned. Having flown over our county, his meaning was clear. However, when a closer look is taken at twelve farms immediately surrounding our home farm, we find four farms are farmed by the owners; one is lived on by the owner and rented to a neighbor to be farmed; the other seven are owned by developers and on most of them, some development has already taken place. Only four of them are farmer owned, farmer operated. Although at present crops are being grown on the other eight farms, development is their future use, not farming!

Fortunately, thanks to the Amish and Mennonite farmers in our county, the situation around our farm is not entirely typical for the county. In Paradise Township in 1930, there were 122 farms, of which ten were Amish-owned. In 1974 there were 114 farms, of which seventy-three were Amish-owned. Non-Amish purchased only four farms sold at public auction in the past ten years.

While it is true the Amish and Mennonite farmers are holding on to their land, of the 432,000 acres of land now in agricultural production in our county, we are losing 8,000 per year to non-agricultural use. This is double the rate of transfer from 1954 to 1964, when 4,000 acres annually changed to non-agricultural use.

I have a grandson who is presently thirteen years old. He insists he wants to be a farmer. If this desire on his part persists and he buys a farm and hangs on to it until he is my age (sixty-three), he could quite likely be one of the last fifty farmers left in Lancaster County, if our present development patterns continue.

I am glad to report we are doing something about it! Our Lancaster County Planning Commission has prepared a comprehensive plan that provides land for the projected increase in population to the year 2000: 12% to 17% of land for expected industrial growth, and retaining 277,000 acres of our best farmland. These agricultural areas for preservation are properly mapped and plans for their protection are provided. Several townships, including Manor Township in which I live, have announced plans to direct growth away from the prime farmland. The problem is, how do we implement these plans? To have a plan is great; to implement the plan represents a successful achievement!

As an illustration of the lack of plan implementation, I call your attention to what happened in Santa Clara County, California. Here was a rich agricultural count like many located in our state. Because of its location and vigorous promotion by the Chamber of Commerce and other leaders, 800,000 people moved into the valley in twenty years. Karl Belser, Director of Santa Clara County Planning Commission from 1950 to 1965, had a plan for the development of the valley. His plan would have allowed for an eventual population of 900,000 people in tight urban development in the foothills and on the less fertile areas of the valley. The plan would have left much of the valley floor, the rich agricultural land, free for agriculture. Karl Belser's plan was not followed.

So far, my remarks were directed to the need for land for food production. Land does much more than produce food. Agricultural land provides open space, tax producing open space. Forty-seven percent of all forested land is located on farms. Farmer-owned land supports 80 to 85% of all the harvested game in the nation. Agricultural land is needed for ground water recharge.

Research at Penn State has proven the sewage effluent from the 50,000 residents of the State College area can safely be sprayed on a properly prepared 400-acre site at the rate of two inches per week, fifty-two weeks per year, with no harmful effects. The effluent is pumped four miles and distributed through a sprinkler irrigation system at a cost of thirteen cents per 1,000 gallons. Forage grown on the sprayed area yields phenomenally and can safely be fed to cattle. Sewage sludge, not high in heavy metals and shredded garbage, can safely be applied to soil, thus achieving increased yields and improved soil conditions.

Although the highest and best use of land at present may not be agriculture use in the near future, a much higher value may be placed on land reserved for agricultural use.

At last, we in Pennsylvania have made a start in land use. The Clean and Green Amendment, Act 319, and the Flood Plain Control legislature, now under consideration, are examples of positive legislative action.

It would seem to me at this time, we have most of the information needed to develop effective land use legislation for Pennsylvania. My plea this afternoon: Let's get on with it!

Millersville Lions Club

In my May 27, 1975, presentation to members of the Millersville Lions Club, I called attention to efforts to regulate the use of land. Attention was drawn to what is happening elsewhere. Eight points to ponder were also suggested.

The provision of The Clean Streams Law represents for the first time in Pennsylvania's history, a major attempt by the legislature to regulate the use of land. A farmer may no longer farm up and down the hill in large unbroken fields. By so doing, it is quite likely the sediment loss from his farm would exceed acceptable levels, and he would be prosecuted. After July 1, 1977, the voluntary decision will be gone. The farmer must have, and carry out, a conservation plan for his farm.

Because of increasing pressure nationally, as well as at lower levels of government, I am certain there will be more regulation concerning the use of land in the future. My concern is, will the legislation be good legislation? Can we live with it?

I would hope farmers and farm organizations are given ample opportunity to provide input into any land use proposal at all levels of government because farmers own most of the land, the use of which is to be regulated.

In Maryland, farm input was not sought in the development of land use legislation in that state. The proposed bill was in the first reading in the House before farm and agribusiness groups became fully aware that there were things in the bill that would be difficult for farmers to live with. A successful lobbying effort weakened the bill to such an extent that in the opinion of many, the act is not too effective. This is unfortunate because farmers need good land use legislation more than any other group. However, few will admit it.

Many farmers decry the use of prime farmland for development and think something should be done about it. However, for many of them, doing something about it does not include a township official, a county commissioner, or some bureaucrat from Harrisburg or Washington, telling him what he can or cannot do with his land.

It disturbs me when I am told we do not have to be concerned about the loss of farmland. The assumption is, food can be produced in other areas. The question might be asked: What other areas?

A preliminary report published November 1972 by the Stanislaus Area Association of Governments in California on environmental resource management, devoted to agriculture, states: "Current estimates show that in California, 400 acres of farmland are being converted to other uses every day, including 100 acres of prime agricultural land." This amounts to over 134,000 acres per year compared to 100,000 acres per year in early 1960. It is projected that if this rate of conversion continues to increase, over 75% of the state's farmland will be gone by the year 2000.

California is an important agricultural state. In 1974, cash receipts from marketing agricultural crops amounted to $8.5 billion, 9% of the nation's total production. B. Dale Ball, Michigan's Commissioner of Agriculture, reports that the state's present eleven million acres of agricultural land could be reduced to 2.5 million acres by the year 2000 if present land use trends continue. Mr. Ball insists that Michigan needs 8 million acres of agricultural land to meet their future needs.

In Pennsylvania, between 1910 and 1974, there was over a 300% reduction in farm numbers from 220,000 farms to 71,000 farms. Similarly, the amount of land in farms decreased from 18.6 million acres in 1910 to 8.9 million acres in 1969 (52% reduction).

New Jersey lost 600,000 acres of farmland in twenty-five years, more than half of its present acreage of 1.1 million acres.

In New York the situation was similar to Pennsylvania until their legislature passed their Agricultural District Law, a law Sherm Hill and I worked for, instead of Act 319, which is essentially a tax relief law. Pennsylvania Act 319 will help. However, it is far from the final answer in developing a good land use plan for Pennsylvania. To me, it just makes good sense for each state to do what it can to direct growth away from prime agricultural land and retain as much of their good land in agriculture as possible, and it should be done soon!

In summary:
1. The Clean Streams Law might be considered the first major land use regulation in our state's history.
2. Additional land use legislature is bound to come. Let's do all we can to see it is good legislation. Let's get involved.
3. Farmers own most of the land, the use of which is to be regulated. They better get involved.
4. The rate of conversion of agricultural land to non-agricultural uses is at an all-time high.
5. Lancaster County ranks eighteenth in the nation in the value of agricultural products sold, nearly $385 million in 1974.
6. Most states are losing agricultural land at an alarming rate so it is a bit dangerous to say food can be grown somewhere else.
7. The solution to the problem is not easy, or quite likely it would have already been accomplished.

This interesting photograph is intended to demonstrate the possible conflict between farmland preservation advocate Amos Funk and the very well-known and quite successful builder, E.G. Stoltzfus. This was the cover picture of the January/February 1989 issue of the *Lancaster County* magazine. Then editor Deborah H. Shenk took the picture and was responsible for obtaining the position of papers reflecting both sides of the farmland retention vs. home building issue.

In my opinion, proper balance was achieved. Differences were aired. Progress was made.

Permission to use the cover photograph was granted by the *Lancaster County* magazine.

The Greater Lancaster Board of Realtors

My presentation to the Greater Lancaster Board of Realtors on March 16, 1977, at the Host Town in Lancaster, was quite a challenge. However, since I have always thought it is important to develop the greatest degree of understanding possible with all groups, I accepted their invitation to speak to them. In my opinion, at least, the results were very satisfactory. Greater understanding was achieved.

As I thought about what I might say to you, I could not help but think about the very great differences there may be between what many of you feel is best for Lancaster County, and what I feel is best for our county.

These possible differences were first demonstrated to me during the period of time I served on the Land Use Committee of the Lancaster Chamber of Commerce, chaired by Paul Diller. Two members of that committee, Manny Murry and Ray Sydansk, took positions directly opposite from me. These men are no lightweights; they have been most successful, and what they have to say should be listened to very carefully.

Rather than discussing these differences, I would prefer to find areas where we may have common concerns, and hopefully find solutions in some of the problem areas.

I am certainly not against the building of new homes in our county. I am aware of the fact that to reach the housing goal needed by 1980, more than 3,000 units will have to be built each year. However, I would hope they are not sprawled over our best farmland, and that hopefully, some way may be found to put more housing units on each acre. The P.R.D. concept makes sense to me; land is used more efficiently.

In 1974, the USDA Economic Research Service released a report stating that only 1.5% of the total U.S. land area is occupied by urban development. The inference was plain. There is no need to be concerned about the loss of prime agricultural land. The report did not mention that one-third of U.S. land area is public land, owned by the U.S. Government. Another one-third is forested, the greater part of which is owned by federal and state governments. It would have been more realistic if they would have used the percentage of crop land now in urban use. After all, crop land is where most of the development takes place. The percentage of 1.5% is not very meaningful to anyone living in Suffolk County, New York, where approximately 80% of the total land area is urbanized. It surely does not apply to New

Jersey, where 35% of the land area is urbanized, or even here in Lancaster County, where 22% of our land area is now urbanized.

Senior County Agent Max Smith, in his paper prepared for the Lancaster Tomorrow Committee on which I serve, using U.S. Bureau of the Census data, shows that between 1954 and 1964 an average of 3,088 acres changed annually from agricultural to non-agricultural use in Lancaster County. However, in the five-year period from 1964 to 1969, 41,226 acres were lost from agricultural production, averaging out to be an annual loss of 8,245 acres.

In my view, the outstanding example of effective land use planning in the nation today is the New York Agricultural District Law. This act, passed in June 1971, has enrolled 3,838,114 acres in the program. This represents 25% of the state's farmland and involves forty-four counties. This is the kind of an act I wish Pennsylvania would have passed instead of 319. I tried to persuade the chairman of the Agriculture Committee in the House to push for an Ag District Bill. Sherman Hill and several other legislators lent their support, but we were not successful. Act 319 is satisfactory, but it doesn't go far enough.

Under the New York act, farmers voluntarily joined together under certain guidelines to form agricultural districts comprising areas of 500 to 73,000 acres. In addition to tax relief, farmers receive other benefits, such as protection from complaints concerning manure odors, excessive noise, and dust. Farmers make a commitment to remain in the district for at least eight years, with a penalty for early withdrawal.

Very often more drastic action has to be taken as urbanizing pressures become greater in a given area. Usually, this more drastic action carries with it a higher price tag if agricultural land is to be preserved. In Suffolk County, New York, of the original 677,000 acres in the county, only 60,000 still remain in agricultural production. The county legislature approved a plan to include $60 million in the 1974 to 1976 capital budget to purchase development rights for at least 9,000 acres. The development rights of a property is the difference between the value for farming and the value for development. This is pretty much a voluntary program. Each property owner sends in a sealed bid containing his version of the development rights value. All exorbitant bids are rejected.

I have been told that although this program was ready to go, politics raised its ugly head and caused some problems, as is often the case. The county legislature, predominantly Republican, has approved this plan. However, in the most recent election, the legislature changed to predominantly

Democratic. In addition, some of the Democrats did not like the county executive, also a Republican, and the county legislature refused to authorize the sale of the thirty-year municipal bonds needed to fund the program. As a result, things are in a state of limbo up there.

I thought New Jersey had a plan that would work. Under their state's open space plan, real estate dollars transferred for farmland preservation in New Jersey would have amounted to $22 million.

I thought this was a great program. Especially since Secretary Alampi insisted the transfer tax would adequately provide for the financing. Adequate financing is always a stumbling block to an effort like this.

However, this program didn't fly, either. Again, politics entered the picture. Governor Calhill was not re-elected. Governor Byrne is now New Jersey's chief executive. Passage of a state income tax law for New Jersey received priority consideration and New Jersey's agricultural open space plan was put on the back burner.

What about Lancaster County? We have already made some progress. Our Lancaster County Conservation District in 1971 developed long-range goals for the county. One of these goals was to preserve a reasonable amount of our best farmland for agricultural production. In order to do this, we made a map showing blocks of at least 4,000 acres of our best soils in areas where urbanizing pressures were slight to moderate. The total area in the map comprises 314,000 acres.

I am happy to report the County Planning Commission used this map as a guide. Revisions were made and in their comprehensive plan "directions," the planning commission designated 237,000 acres of that best land for agriculture and open space.

Now these plans are fine. They needed to be prepared, but very little worthwhile will happen unless plans are implemented.

I think it would be most helpful if each township in our county would review these maps and attempt to determine how much agricultural and open space land they would like set aside and where it should be located. A public meeting should be held to get public reaction and hopefully public support.

In addition, I would hope an act similar to the New York District law might be passed by the Pennsylvania legislature. I believe a lot of farmers in our county would request inclusion in such a district program, especially after the county is reassessed. Although, as a result of recently passed legislation, Pennsylvania farmers are now provided with some benefits contained in the New York law, such as those proved in Act 319. There are enough other advantages to encourage enrollment.

Later, I hope it will be feasible to buy the development rights from as many of our Lancaster County farmers as are willing to participate. As I view it, this is the fair and sure way to insure a permanent agriculture for Lancaster County and provide a source of food, fiber, and environmental open space.

To those who would simply zone an area agricultural and deprive a farmer of the appreciated value of his land, I would say you are being unfair. To many farmers, the appreciated value of their land is the only pension they have. Farmers are reluctant to give that up. Actually, the best crop a farmer has is his real estate. Farmers are entitled to the purchase of their development right.

Now, where do home builders fit into this plan? I am not sure. I do know that many realtors favored the original New Jersey plan to reserve a million acres for agricultural production. Since considerable land would have been removed from the real estate market, the land that developers owned would become more valuable.

In Suffolk County, where 43% of the land being farmed is owned by developers, quite a number of those offering the sale of their development rights to the county were developers. Apparently some of them wanted to get their money out in order to put it to other uses.

Possibly the most important point I would make today is that we have in our county only a finite amount of land. No one has found a way to create more land. Land does not breed. Let us use it wisely.

Agriculture, even at very high land prices, has continued to "hang in there." With the combination of intensive livestock and poultry programs and very productive soils, our farmers are producing more than $1,000 from each acre in crop production without irrigation.

If we use our land wisely, perhaps our grandchildren will point to our county with pride as a very desirable place to work and live. If we continue to make poor decisions, perhaps they will return someday and say, "This used to be a beautiful county before they spoiled it." The choice is ours; however, very little will happen unless we make it happen.

Funding Farmland Preservation Using Township Funds

In August 1977, because of the lack of interest at this time on the part of our Lancaster County legislators who represent us in Harrisburg, and because of the apparent absence of extra funds at the state level, I decided to explore the possibility of seeking funding for farmland preservation at the Manor Township level, in which I live. The results of this approach were not too encouraging, to say the least. However, once again I tried.

I surely support House Bill 111. However, Secretary Goddard remarked to a number of us that if last year's bill would have passed, it would be impossible to build a road, establish a park, or build a water impoundment. The language of the bill, as I read it, states that before land can be condemned, the alternatives must be carefully considered. Too many times in the past this has not been done.

Chances for favorable consideration by the Senate may be improved if the provisions of the bill were to apply only to farms enrolled in Act 319. I am quite sure the original intent of the bill was to protect all prime farmland. The original intent of the bill may be realized after most counties in our state complete reassessment. The way farmland is selling in Lancaster County, I believe the sign-up for Act 319 in our county after reassessment will nearly equal New Jersey's sign-up for Farmland Assessment Act, where by late 1973, 88% of the farms were enrolled in the program in that state.

In discussing this meeting with State Senator Noah Wenger, he suggested there may be time for me to share with you some thoughts I have on land use.

There is no need to waste the time of the committee discussing the problem. The loss of agricultural land to non-agricultural use is serious in many counties in our state. We are aware of the problem.

However, we are very short on solutions. Except for the $5 million pilot effort to buy development rights in Burlington County, New Jersey, and the attempt to initiate the "Transfer of Development Rights" concept in Buckingham Township in Bucks County, very little has been done except for the agricultural district programs in New York and California. These voluntary agricultural district programs like Act 319 and New Jersey's Farmland Assessment Act, are admitted to be only holding actions. As Chairman Paul Yarner knows, I favored the Ag District approach as a means to further strengthen Act 319. However, the legislature has already strengthened Act

319 by the exemption of sewer and water assessments for farmers. The Act protects farmers from prosecution for dust created during soil preparation. The enactment of House Bill 111 would further strengthen Act 319.

Recently I visited with our Manor Township Supervisors concerning the Barley Farm hearing. They suggested that as soon as the condemnation proceedings have been resolved, while interest is high, Manor Township should do something about the preservation of some of the best farmland in the township. They further suggested that if I had any ideas to accomplish this goal, they would listen.

As outlined in the current land use policy of the Pennsylvania Farmers Association, and the Pennsylvania Grange, the first step is to identify the area within a municipality that a local committee designates for retention in agricultural production.

Approximately 4,000 acres are recommended to be retained in agriculture in Manor Township. If the supervisors and the residents of the township so desire, this can be done.

One method to accomplish this goal is to zone it agriculture. However, to do this would be very unfair to the farmers in the agricultural zone.

To many farmers, the appreciated value of their land is the only pension they have. Farmers are reluctant to give that up. Actually, the best crop a farmer has is his real estate. Farmers are entitled to the purchase of the development rights of the land they own.

The Suffolk County, Long Island, and the New Jersey approach is to buy the development rights by accepting or rejecting sealed bids reflecting the owner's appraisal of the value of the development rights. Funding for this type of program is very difficult.

In order to get things in proper perspective, let's look at the township in which I live—Manor Township—in 1977.

Our assessed valuation is:	$16,000,000
4 mill township tax yields:	$64,000
1/2% wage tax in 1976:	$275,000
1% real estate transfer tax in 1976:	$50,693

(above used by school district)

1976 annual budget - approximately $700,000

Proposal

Buy development rights: .... 4,000 acres
    @ 1,000 per acre; cost $4,000,000
If purchase is divided over 15 years,
    Annual cost $266,660

If voters would permit $1,000,000 bond issue or note of indebtedness, interest alone at 6%: $90,000

13% of present budget

VERY DIFFICULT TO ACCOMPLISH

Another approach: Assure these farmers in the 4,000-acre agricultural zone that if and when the farm is sold, they will receive $2,000 per acre for the purchase of the development rights.

Lancaster County has approximately 420,000 acres in agricultural production. In 1976, 6,000 acres changed from agricultural to non-agricultural use. This represents 1 1/2% loss in agricultural land in the county. A 1 1/2% loss of the 4,000 acres agricultural reserve would mean that sixty acres would be sold annually.

60 acres x $2,000 (development rights) cost $120,000 (annual cost to buy development rights for Manor Township).

This amount could be raised by 1/4% increase in wage tax.

Another approach might be called the Aaron Stauffer approach. It represents his thinking. To me, it makes sense. Again, the agricultural zones need to be established. If Aaron's proposal is to be implemented, I feel sure enabling legislation would have to be passed. This enabling legislation would permit a municipality to reserve the option to place the last bid on a farm property at the time of transfer, at which time the municipality would sell the property, minus the development rights, to an interested buyer. The municipality would then own the development rights and the farm could be used only for farming.

Undoubtedly, these proposals will have to be refined. There are questions to which we do not have answers. However, answers must be found.

Although the Manor Township Supervisors have read this paper and have commented favorably on several thoughts expressed, they have had little time to study the proposals that have been made. For this reason, at this time, they cannot endorse or reject the proposals.

We may not be able to do much at the local level, but perhaps if the legislature helps with some enabling legislation, we can do a little. Doing a little is better than doing nothing.

I have not mentioned the state funding. From what I have been hearing, the state deficit will be large enough for the present fiscal year without any help from me.

Thanks for allowing me this time to share some ideas that may contribute a bit to our continuing effort to find an effective method to retain a reasonable amount of our productive agricultural land for farming.

Lancaster Tomorrow

My presentation to the Lancaster Tomorrow Committee was made May 10, 1978. I recognized Wesley Shope as the great salesman that he is. He convinced me that the Lancaster Tomorrow Committee can help Lancaster County's agriculture. If it is not apparent in my book by this time, please be assured I care deeply about the future of Lancaster County's agriculture. When Wesley Shope assured me that his Lancaster Tomorrow Committee could help, I decided to cooperate. My presentation follows:

When Wesley Shope came to the farm to visit me and requested that I become a member of the Lancaster Tomorrow Committee, I recall I asked, "What can I contribute to that effort? I know very little about what makes the City of Lancaster tick. I know about the city's reported problems. I surely don't have any solutions. In addition, how can what happens to the City of Lancaster affect good land-use decisions in the county, an area of considerable interest to me?"

Wes advised me that there is a relationship and suggested that if somehow we can persuade more people to retain their homes in the city, and possibly encourage some folks to move back to the city, the pressures on farmland in the townships will be reduced.

I admit I was skeptical, but good salesman that he is, Wes persuaded me to get involved. I am glad he did. I have met some interesting, effective people. It has been most rewarding. I am very impressed that Armstrong Corporation, National Central Bank, and others have invested so heavily in downtown Lancaster. Confidence in the revitalization of downtown is higher than at any time in my memory. Lancaster City today is much healthier than it was several years ago, and with the same positive leadership, quite likely it will be much healthier tomorrow.

How about Lancaster County? I think the county is in good shape today. We still have the desirable balance between agriculture, industry, and people that Tex Burnett talked about when he was president of the then Chamber of Commerce. However, I am not so sure about Lancaster County tomorrow.

Lancaster City's broad goals are rather well defined. Let's fill up the empty space downtown with shops and offices. Let us make the inter-city attractive and safe to attract more residents.

I am not so sure about the goals for the county. John Ahlfeld and his staff at the Planning Commission have set some very satisfactory goals for future growth for the county in the comprehensive plan "directions." My concern is, are we going to be able to implement the plan?

Are we going to be able to preserve 237,000 acres of our best agricultural land until the year 2000?

What are the goals of the Lancaster Association of Commerce and Industry for the county?

What are the goals of the Industrial Development Bureau, and the Pennsylvania Dutch Tourist Bureau? Most important of all, what are the goals of the township supervisors in the county?

I am encouraged by the position taken by Chairman Jack Buch and the supervisors and other officials in Earl Township. Their township has provided for the required amount of residential growth, and is dead set against additional building on the rich farmland in the township.

I am not so sure about another nearby township where officials requested the Lancaster County Planning Commission to approve the construction of a major sewer system with a trunk line going to the borough and, in addition, build five pumping stations, most of them located on rich undeveloped farmland. The Sewer and Water Advisory Committee on which I serve recommended to the Planning Commission that they approve the major trunk line to relieve the sewage disposal problem they now have, and disapprove the construction of those pumping stations.

I trust the Planning Commission will support our recommendation. I think it would be most helpful if each township would set a goal as to how much agricultural land they would like to retain in their township by the year 2000. This, then, would support the provisions of the County Plan "directions." Later, each township should indicate on a map where this farmland should be located.

Several news articles that appeared recently in our local papers shook me quite a bit. The first stated: Lancaster County, second in industrial growth rate in the state in 1977-78. New industrial operations that will provided 1,444 new jobs. To many people in the county, this is great news! To me, it may mean an increase in population of 4,000 or possibly more people. Depending on the housing development patterns that take place, this could mean the loss of 3,000 acres of agricultural land. In the past, we have had periods when seventy-five acres of agricultural land were taken out of production of each 100 increase in population.

Can Lancaster County be second in industrial grown in the state and still retain our position as the leading non-irrigated agricultural county in the nation? I doubt it.

Would any manufacturer reduce the size of a plant if that plant is twice as efficient as competing plants in the state? Lancaster County's soils are twice as efficient in productivity as the average soils used in agricultural production in the state; 76% of our soils fall in Class I, II, and III compared to 38% for the state.

Would any manufacturer reduce the size of his work force working in this more efficient plant if the workers have proven superior to other workers in the state? Our farmers are younger, hard-working, and frugal, yet many of them have to quit farming or leave the county because of the lack of land to farm.

Jerry Malloy assured me last year at the Lancaster Tomorrow Conference at F&M, that there is no major effort being made by the Association of Commerce and Industry to attract new industry. I have had similar assurances from the Industrial Development Bureau. I trust these policies are still in effect.

The fact remains, Lancaster County is a nice place to work and live. Stewart Udall, former Secretary of the Interior, speaking at Hershey some time ago, said that he if were to pick an ideal community east of the Mississippi in which to live, he would choose Lancaster County. This is our problem: our county is just too attractive. I am sure a lot of counties in the state wish they had this problem.

I am fearful that unless we guide development a lot more carefully, and hopefully slowdown the rate of growth, our county will not continue to be an attractive place to work and live. However, former Oregon Governor Tom McCall found out that it was counter-productive to say, "Come to visit us, but don't stay." Many people were curious to find out what was so special about Oregon, and population increased significantly.

I hope that we in Lancaster County can work together to have moderate growth and guide this growth away from our best farmland.

The Pennsylvania Dutch Tourist Bureau has apparently taken a different position than the Association of Commerce and Industry and the Industrial Development Bureau. This position was outlined in the second newspaper article that shook me. The Pennsylvania Dutch Tourist Bureau is increasing their advertising budget substantially. Their goal is to attract more tourists to further congest our now overcrowded highways, and cause more harassment to our Amish farmers. I am not sure how much more our Amish farmers can take.

I think the Tourist Bureau is wrong to engage in this promotional effort at this time. I hope they will be more moderate in their approach.

The reported expenditures in the county by tourists in 1975 was $108 million. This is a sizable amount of money. However, in 1974, according to the last census figures, farmers in the county spent $199 million on farm production expenses, a sum 54% greater than the income from tourism. Farmers in the county also stimulate the economy.

At the present time, legislation is being drafted in OSPD to permit the formation of agricultural districts with the promise by the state to buy the development rights from those farmers in the district who wish to sell.

Our Pennsylvania Association of Conservation Districts adopted a Land Use Policy after two years of hard work. We have some outstanding individuals on the Land Use Committee: Dr. Tom King, Director of Extension; Neal Buss, Deputy Secretary of Agriculture; Chuck Slaton, OSPD; and a good number of other dedicated people.

I understand the legislation being drafted contains many of the proposals contained in the Conservation District's Association Land Use Policy. There is a concerted effort being made to get broad based support for this legislation: the FFA, Grange, League of Women Voters at the state and local levels, Federated Women's Clubs. I sent a copy of our proposal to Phyllis Whitesell of the local League of Women Voters.

Our proposal designates .5% of the real estate transfer tax, amounting annually to $15 million to be used to buy the development rights in Pennsylvania. To those who say this $15 million would not go very far, I would say fifteen million is three times as much as New Jersey started with. Maryland plans to start with a four to four and one-half million and Massachusetts will start with a $5 million pilot effort.

To those who say the purchase of development rights will cost too much money, I would reply, yes, it will cost the residents of the county and our state tax dollars; however, there is no giveaway by the taxpayers. In fact, a considerable amount of money could be saved over the long haul if farmland is kept in agricultural production.

While it is readily agreed that industrial and most commercial development produces considerable excess of tax revenue over costs, a number of studies indicate that in residential development, educational and service costs, in many cases, are far greater than the revenues received in taxes.

As an example, I would like to cite a study conducted by Jane Rhinehard, Chief of Rural Services with the Pennsylvania Department of Agriculture. The study was conducted in Bradford County, Pennsylvania.

The study showed that the local school district studied saved $12,666 per year in service costs during the twelve-year study period for each 200-acre farm kept in agriculture. The study showed the school district involved would be $152,000 to the good over a twelve-year period by keeping a 200-acre farm in agriculture.

I trust the study initiated by the Land Use Committee of the Association of Commerce and Industry to be carried out by the U.S. Soil Conservation Service with the endorsement of the county commissioners at the Lancaster Conservation District will give us the kind of economic and soil association information that will enable us to make the proper land use decisions in order that Lancaster County can remain a nice place to work and live, not only for us, but our children and grandchildren as well.

Getting Greater Farmland Preservation Support From Lancaster County's State Legislators

It had come to my attention that not all legislators who represent Lancaster County were in favor of our county's farmland preservation program. If indeed this is true, it would be difficult to have our Lancaster County legislator support needed state legislation.

Again to develop understanding, a meeting was held May 5, 1978, at the county courthouse. Ninety percent of our legislators were present. I presented my remarks. Questions were asked and answered. I think the meeting accomplished the intended goal. My remarks follow:

I just finished reading a book written by Earl Nightingale. Part of the book was devoted to the importance of goal setting.

I can hear Aaron Stauffer saying to himself: "Amos, at your age, why should you be interested in goal setting?"

Well, there are a couple of goals I am interested in. If I were to ask each one of you today, what are your goals for Lancaster County by the year 2000 and even beyond, how would you respond? Have you thought about it? By the year 2000, how much land should remain in agriculture? What should be the population density? Where should the people be and where should the farms be? How many more industries should we have in the county by 2000?

My own goal is that we should only have enough additional industry to provide jobs for our young people.

During recent congressional hearings on the National Land Use Policy Act, a citizen of Monclova Township, Ohio, near Toledo, read the following statement and I quote: "Nowhere in the United States does a community tear down a thriving factory in order to put up developments or make room for more industry. Why, then, because four brick walls do not enclose our farmlands, would any community, county, or state want to encourage destruction of the farm factory with its proven record of successful contribution to our society?"

To my knowledge, no one here today is guilty of encouraging the destruction of farmland. To the contrary, the actions of the State Legislature and the county commissioners have been most helpful. At the state level, I would cite as examples Acts 515 and 319. The water and sewer hookup exemption for farmers and a number of other favorable actions have been taken by the legislature. The Lancaster County commissioners present and past have kept assessments on farms at reasonable levels. The light sign-up in Act 319 by our farmers is ample proof of that.

I suppose the greatest fault one could find with the state and local government is that there has been very little action taken to direct growth away from our best agricultural land. If I were a preacher, I might say the sin is one of omission, not commission.

John Ahlfeld and his staff have established some important goals for Lancaster County. I am referring to those goals set forth in Directions, a comprehensive plan for the county adopted by the Planning Commission and the county commissioners in 1975.

As most of you know, Directions has set as a goal the retention of 237,000 of our best farmland by the year 2000. This would allow more than 150,000 acres of land presently used for agricultural production to be used for other purposes. I trust this much will not be needed. In fact, if the recommended shift, as outlined in Directions, toward a higher concentration of residential land use rather than the current scattered development could be achieved, the projected 200,000 population increase by the year 2000 plus all expected industrial could be housed on less than 50,000 acres. Past development patterns reveal that for each 100 increase in population, seventy-five acres were removed from agricultural production.

As all of us know, Directions is a comprehensive plan. Very little that is desirable will happen if the plan is not implemented.

In Santa Clara County, California, Karl Belser, a director of their Planning Commission, had a plan for the development of their county. He recommended residential development be guided to the foothills in the county and allow the rich valley floor to remain in agricultural development.

Mr. Belser's plan was not followed. Instead, 800,000 people moved into Santa Clara Valley in twenty years. Commercial agriculture in the county has been destroyed. What has been the economic impact on the county? The cost of services demanded by the new residents has far exceeded the tax revenue to support those services and as a result, Santa Clara County has the highest per capita debt load of any county in California.

Is this our goal in Lancaster County? Sometimes I think this is the goal of some of the citizens of the county.

Since Lancaster County is such an important agricultural county, I think it would be most helpful and it would be very fitting if, after adequate review and appropriate changes in the Bill, members in the House representing all or part of Lancaster County became sponsors of the upcoming

Bill on Farmland Preservation. After all, the National Land Use Policy Act had fifty-two sponsors. I understand an attempt will be made to incorporate some of the provisions of Sam Morris's Bill on the creation of agricultural districts, in the new Bill.

Congressman Bob Walker called me to inform me that he is interested in the purchase of the development right concepts. He is considering a federal bill that would reward an individual with income or other tax credits if a gift of the development rights is made to the county.

It would seem to me that if we get started at the state level with some later help at the federal level, we may finally be able to permanently lock in some of our best agricultural land to agricultural production, and still retain it in private ownership and on the local tax rolls.

Speaking for Farmland Preservation

My good friend Dieter Kreig, then editor of the Lancaster Farming *newspaper, wrote a series of articles beginning on May 20, 1978. The title of the series was "Amos Funk Speaks for Land Preservation." The following pages selected from those articles were written by him for the* Lancaster Farming *newspaper. Permission to use the material was granted by the newspaper.*

Amos Funk does not seek publicity, and it should be noted right from the start that the well-known farmer-conservationist was not seen giving a speech beneath a tree. The picture, above, is really two photographs spliced together to show Amos Funk in the type of backdrop that he loves. The two go together like a horse and carriage—love and marriage. What Amos Funk was really doing when his picture was taken was to present testimony on behalf of the Barley Brothers, near Lancaster, who last year had 58 acres of their farmland condemned for a landfill. Many people helped to win that battle for the Barleys, and Amos Funk was one of the most influential of all. It should be noted, too, that he is a very modest man. The information about Mr. Funk that is contained in this edition of *Lancaster Farming* was gleaned from acquaintances of his. "Mr. Conservationist" had no more than a faint hint that a feature about his work would appear in this newspaper.

Amos Funk Speaks for Land Preservation

by DIETER KREIG

MILLERSVILLE - Amos Funk, a grandfatherly Lancaster Countian, has two titles by which he is known throughout southeastern Pennsylvania—farmer and conservationist. He's a man who has shown devout dedication to agriculture and outstanding soil stewardship throughout his life. A 1966 nominee for Master Farmer, he has won the respect and admiration of thousands who have gotten to know him personally or heard of his work at meetings or in print. To many, Amos Funk is "Mr. Conservationist." The Lancaster County Commissioners formally bestowed that title on him in 1967.

Despite his many achievements and constant dedication for the good of agriculture, Funk is a quiet and modest man. His manner can best be described as "grandfatherly."

Born in October of 1911 in the farmhouse which has been in his family for three generations, and his maternal grandmother's family for several generations before that, the amiable "Mr. Conservationist" grew up with farming. The family operation consists of three farms encompassing 270 acres and since 1963, Funk's Farm Market. Fruit and vegetables are the specialty.

Married in 1936 to the former Esta Myer of Oregon, north of Lancaster, Funk and his wife have shared in the work of their farm and community. "If there's something where he thinks he can help, he goes all out," Mrs. Funk said in a tone which revealed her admiration for the man she's been married to for 42 years. With their son, Fred, taking over more and more of the responsibilities, both have found more time for concerns and activities other than actual farming. Efforts to preserve farmland are just as strong as ever, however, and Amos Funk's voice is one to be heard in countless meetings on the subject. He has become so renowned and respected that his dedication and expertise has been sought by governors and college deans, among others.

A 1929 graduate of the old Manor Township High School, Funk had plans of going to Penn State, and he did. But with the advent of the Great Depression, "the money got all" and young Funk was unable to complete his college education. He had wanted a degree in agricultural economics and wasn't too sure of what his career plans were. As it turned out, he returned to the farm. According to many people in the area, it's the best thing that could have happened to agriculture in southeastern Pennsylvania.

"When you give that man a job to do, he gets it done," Mrs. Nancy Burkhart says of him fondly. She serves as treasurer of the Lancaster County Conservation District, a group with which Funk has been actively involved since 1950. He was chairman of the LCCD for 17 years and has been vice chairman since 1969.

A friend of all who have an interest in preserving farmland, Funk has made some special friends among those who have benefited profoundly from his conservation efforts. During February and March of 1977, for example, Funk worked tirelessly for the preservation of 58 acres of prime farmland which had been condemned by the Lancaster Area Refuse Authority for a landfill. John and Abram Barley, owners of the farm which was involved in the case, were able to save their land and continue normal farming operations as a result of hundreds of concerned citizens. Amos Funk was one of the leaders in that concerted effort.

Abram Barley told *Lancaster Farming* the following, in regards to Funk's work to save 58 acres of their farmland: "I could never appreciate enough what he did," he began. "He worked to get all kinds of details for our behalf and was instrumental in presenting testimony and numerous meetings, including talks in Harrisburg before the House Agriculture Committee. He just put an endless amount of time into the case and initiated a fund-raising campaign. These are just a few things—whenever you needed him, he was there. We have a lot of confidence in him and just couldn't praise him enough," Barley exclaimed.

"Amos is a man who is extremely honest—he makes sure that when he gets up to make a statement, it's truthful and accurate," he concluded.

Similar comments can be heard from others who know him. Funk has served on numerous committees and received nearly an equal number of awards.

The Lancaster County conservationist and farmer served as an advisor for agricultural land use to Governors William Scranton and Raymond Shafer and is a member of an agricultural advisory council at Penn State University. In addition, Funk is chairman of the National Association of Conservation Districts' research committee for the Northeast and a past president of the Pennsylvania Soil and Water Conservation District, Inc. The Lancaster Countian is also a past president of the Pennsylvania Vegetable Growers Association and the Conestoga Valley Association, of which he is a charter member.

The recipient of the Keystone Chapter Award from the Soil Conservation Society of America, and the first Manor Township citizen to receive the prestigious "Service to Mankind Award" from the Penn Manor Sertoma Club, Funk is also active in several private organizations. Whenever someone wants to discuss land use and conservation, Amos Funk is likely to be on the program.

Funk has received honors from the American Conservation Society, the Lancaster County Conservation District, and numerous other organizations—all because he believes wise land use is essential for the continued well-being of mankind.

My Presentation to the Lawrence County, Pennsylvania, Grange

March 29, 1979

Mr. and Mrs. Arthur Wilson
R.D.#3
Volant, PA 16156

Dear Art and Agnes or Agnes and Art:

    Aaron, Elva, Esta, and I plan to come out there May 10th to participate in your county Grange meeting to be held at New Williamson.

    We may need some help from you legislators in our effort to amend Act 442 to enable us to move forward with our Lancaster County Deed Restriction Program.

    Aaron and I are going down to Charles Wismer's Grange meeting at Trappe on April 5. I hope to discuss our Deed Restriction Program and share with them some of my thoughts on land use.

    I will do my best to present something of interest and hopefully suggest some ideas you may find helpful in Lawrence County.

    I have enclosed a copy of my biographical sketch as you suggested. I trust you will take care of our motel reservations. Aaron and I plan to check on the farm owned by Aaron's sister in Ohio on Friday morning. I am sure you folks can keep Esta and Elva busy for part of Friday.

Best regards,

Amos

New Wellington Grange

Thank you for inviting us to Lawrence County and, specifically, to New Wellington for your county meeting.

When Art and Agnes invited us to speak to you, I knew very little about Lawrence County. I have known and visited the Weinshenks when they had their greenhouse and vegetable growing operation. I knew Joe the best, his brother George, fairly well, and young Joe slightly. They were a great family.

Of course, we all know the Wilsons. Art served with distinction as President of the Pennsylvania Association of Conservation Districts, Inc. He continues to serve in various important positions in this association.

Agnes served not only as chairlady of the Ladies Auxiliary of the Pennsylvania Association of District Directors, but later served as chairlady of the Ladies Auxiliary of the Northeast Area, twelve states, of the National Association and, most recently, was elected treasurer of the entire National Association's Ladies Auxiliary, 3,000 districts. This is quite an honor and I am sure you are all proud of the Wilsons as we are proud to know them.

Thanks to Art Wilson, we have learned quite a bit about Lawrence County since our invitation to speak to you.

One of the background informational pieces Art sent me was entitled, "Overall Economic Development Program for Lawrence County," published in 1976. Mention was made of the unemployment rate and population outmigration as major problems. Our problem in Lancaster County is many people coming into the county and your problem is having too many leave. I suppose young people have to leave the county because of apparent lack of desirable job opportunities. This is a worrisome concern and I suppose a difficult problem to solve.

There is one statement in the report that bothers me. It is found on page 37 and I will quote from the report. "Farming has provided a small number of people with a livelihood and this should continue contingent upon National and State Agricultural Policies."

First, I am not sure what is meant by "contingent upon National and State Agricultural Policies." Second, there is a lack of emphasis on the value of agriculture in Lawrence County. Perhaps the writer does not think agriculture is important, although is stated "farming should continue."

According to the 1974 census, you still have 85,000 acres of land in farms representing nearly 30% of Lawrence County's total land area.

In another fact sheet Art sent me, it was pointed out that the most recent value your county's agricultural products is $13.1 million, with dairy as your principal agricultural enterprise.

Lawrence County has nineteen industrial plants that are engaged in the manufacture of "food and kindred products." These establishments provide employment for 282 people and have annual payrolls of over $2.3 million. The total value of their production was listed at $46.1 million.

As many of you know, the multiplier effect of having agriculture in an area is very real. It is important to save as much of our agricultural industry and our agricultural land as we can.

You have the same problems in Lawrence County as most counties have. Cities like New Castle, Elwood City, and many of the small towns and boroughs have been built on the best soils in the county. In the past, most building everywhere took place on the best land available.

The reason is, it is easier and cheaper to build on this land. However, this land is best for farming also. It is less erodable and more productive. Developers nearly always outbid the farmer because development provides greater immediate return than is received by the farmer for his crops or livestock. Prices farmers receive, although improving somewhat, have just not kept up with the price consumers pay for other cost-of-living items.

Quite recently, there are stirrings among members of the American Agricultural Movement and others to push for the formation of a "grain cartel" among grain-producing nations. Wouldn't it be great to tie the price of grain to the cost of oil? Quite likely, this one single step would do more to preserve farmland than anything else we could say or do. Back in 1973, one could buy a barrel of oil for a bushel of wheat. Now it takes four or five bushels to buy a barrel of oil. It just doesn't seem quite right.

State Grange Meeting at Trappe, Pennsylvania

My remarks to the Pennsylvania State Grange meeting at Trappe, Pennsylvania, were made on April 5, 1979, to one of the less friendly groups to whom I have spoken over the years. However, in an attempt to develop some understanding and support for our farmland preservation efforts, I made the following carefully worded presentation:

Usually after being introduced to an audience to whom you have been invited to speak, it is customary to thank the group for the invitation to appear. However, in regard to my appearance here tonight, I believe I should wait until I have finished my presentation and responded to questions before I express any thanks. I may be speaking to a very hostile audience. In fact, I feel as nervous as a long-tailed cat in a room full of rocking chairs.

How could I help but be apprehensive after reading the March 9th issue of Pennsylvania Farmer's Association publication, *Voice*, in which the Montgomery County Farmer's Association is circulating a petition opposing the proposed Land Use Plan prepared by the Delaware Valley Regional Planning Commission and the Montgomery County Planning Commission. The plan proposes that agricultural preservation areas would be established in upper townships in the county.

In addition, in a recent issue of *Land*, publisher John McIhinney quotes my good friend Charles Wismer, as follows: "I used to be for the preservation of agricultural land. If you want a farmer to stay, you have to give him a break on his products. If he can't make a profit, then we have to allow him to sell a little bit of land. The farmer has to be compensated." As to development rights, Charles Wismer asks, and again I quote: "Who is going to pay? I have an open mind. It would have to be on a local or regional basis."

I have known Charles Wismer for some time now. There are few people I hold in higher regard. He has done a lot for farmers in Pennsylvania, and I am sure his efforts are appreciated here in Montgomery County.

As Jim Davis will tell you, I accepted this invitation to appear here with some reluctance. Not only was I troubled by the already mentioned concerns, I am fully aware that Montgomery County is under very intense urban pressure.

From 1949 to 1974, Montgomery County lost 53% of its land in farms. During that same period, Lancaster County lost 20% of its area in farms.

According to the 1974 census, Montgomery County had a bit more than 19% of the county's land area remaining in farms. Lancaster County had 63% of its land area left in farms. I am sorry to report that Lancaster County has gained the dubious distinction of being the fastest developing county in the state. The average loss of farmland is 7,000 acres per year. We are beginning to experience the same problem you folks have had for years.

Before finally making up my mind to speak to you, I called a number of people I know in Montgomery County and asked what they hoped these meetings would accomplish. The first man I called was my friend, Frank Ebert, chairman of your Conservation District in the county. I have known and respected Frank for more than twelve years. It was not surprising to me when Frank informed me that he and Charles Wismer were members of the Planning Committee for this series of meetings.

I also called Francis McDonnell and Leroy Derstine to obtain their opinion as to the concern of members of their organization, the Montgomery County Farmer's Association, and why the petition was being circulated. I appreciate their concern.

As mentioned in the program handout, I am a farmer. I am the third-generation Funk to farm our home farm in Millersville. My father and grandfather were general farmers; each had a small dairy herd and operated a retail milk route in Millersville. After college, I worked for my dad, and gradually our emphasis was shifted to vegetables and fruit until in 1950, when my wife and I bought the home farm, we were growing all vegetables and fruit. We sold 75% of our products retail in the Lancaster farmers' markets and at area markets such as Root's Market in East Petersburg.

In 1963, our youngest son, Fred, came into the business. We then built our Farm Market. We expanded it a number of times, and now we sell retail at the Farm Market 90% of the production we grow on 244 acres.

In 1976 we sold the home farm and the business to Fred. He rents the other two farms. Now I work for Fred. I guess it could be said I have now come full circle: First I worked for my dad and now I work for my son.

I have included this bit of personal history to try to make the point that we are full-time farmers. We want to stay in the farming business.

The subject of this series of meetings, farmland preservation, is something nearly everyone is in favor of, but virtually on one wants to pay for. Understandably, the farmer does not want to pay for it. This is the reason most farmers oppose strict agricultural zoning. This type of zoning is viewed as substantially reducing the anticipated value of that land if the farmer is afforded an opportunity to sell for development.

Yet most farmers, where the use of Act 515 or 319 provides tax advantages, are asking that their properties be taxed on present use rather than potential use.

There is no great outcry by the public to spend tax dollars to preserve farmland. Most programs to purchase development rights of farmland have been initiated by public officials like John Klein, Phil Alampi of New Jersey, and Paul Silvers in Bucks County.

Purchase of development rights is an effort that is difficult and rather costly to implement. It is considered costly by today's standards. However, I feel there is insufficient information available to measure the cost of building everything solid in houses, etc. Purchase of development rights is one of the few programs that is fair to the farmer who owns the land.

Although zoning is an important short-range tool, there are few examples in the nation where local zoning has significantly reduced the conversion of prime farmland to non-farm use, over the long haul. Again, let me repeat, it is an important first step.

As an example of the inability of zoning to do the long-time job, I would like to call your attention to King County in the state of Washington, containing the city of Seattle.

King County has a land area of more than 1.3 million acres and a population of 1.4 million people. In 1945, King County had 165,000 acres of land in farms. By 1975, thirty years later, the county lost 58% of its farms and 33% of its agricultural land.

Lancaster County adopted our comprehensive plan in 1975. King County adopted its Comprehensive Plan in 1964. One of the stated purposes of King County's Comprehensive Plan was to protect certain agricultural lands.

In 1972, this goal was reinforced by the adoption of Ordinance 1096 which stated that Class II and III soils, presently being farmed, shall be preserved for current and anticipated needs in King County.

In 1974 Ordinance 1839 was adopted, reinforcing the concept of withholding certain lands from development to protect their inherent agricultural capacity. However, the erosion of King County's agricultural land base continued.

In December 1975, the County Council adopted a one-year moratorium on future development of agricultural land. In February 1977, another ordinance was passed extending the moratorium to August 1979. On September 11, 1978, the County Council voted to place Proposition 1 on the November ballot authorizing the sale of bonds in the amount of thirty-five million dollars to purchase the development rights to 40,000 acres of the best farmland in the county.

The cost to support this effort for a family owning a $50,000 home would have been $7.35 per year for twenty years. Proposition 1 failed by two-tenths of one percent to gain the sixty percent of the vote needed to pass.

Given the temper of the times, especially the anti-spending mood, it may be difficult to persuade urban and suburban voters to sanction expensive programs for saving farmland. However, I am not certain elected officials will be willing to pay the political costs involved in denying the farmers land value expectations.

The dilemma is a difficult one. How can the community satisfy the farmer's notion of equity and still keep the cost of retaining farmland at acceptable levels?

I believe the farmer will have to reduce his expectations a bit and the taxpayer will have to contribute a reasonable amount to save our farmland if it is to be done on a permanent basis.

New Jersey's pilot program was allocated $5 million to buy development rights in Burlington County. However, it was so difficult to implement the program, that after two years no development rights were purchased. Now the program is nearly dead. One of the problems is, instead of the original estimated cost of $1,000 per acre to acquire the development rights, the cost in this instance set by appraisers was $1,700 to $2,300 per acre. Here again, 46% of the farmland in Burlington County is owned by speculators.

Another problem that added to the dilemma in New Jersey was an assessment problem. New Jersey's present average assessment of farmland, participated in by 85% of New Jersey's farmers, is $350 to $400 per acre. The new assessment, done by qualified assessors under the New Jersey Purchasers of Development Rights Plan, valued agricultural land at $1,000 per acre. This increase in assessed valuation would have cost New Jersey farmers, if applied statewide, $19 million annually in extra taxes. Naturally, New Jersey farmers opposed this extra tax burden.

John Van Zant feels the county assessment offices would not have used the higher figure for tax purposes. However, our Lancaster County Chief Assessor insisted he would be bound by law to use the higher appraisal.

Again I would repeat, most meaningful land use proposals are difficult to implement. If it would have been easy, satisfactory solutions would have been developed a long time ago.

This entire procedure of preserving farmland would not be a problem if farming was more profitable. The pressure on government and by government during the past several administrations to provide cheap food to the citizens of this nation dramatically reduces the profitability of farming. Then, add to this problem, the maze of regulations farmers have to put up with; it is no wonder many farmers give up in disgust.

Professor John C. Keen, a planner at the University of Pennsylvania, puts it well when he is quoted in the February issue of the *Country Journal* as saying: "Too often the problem of preservation has been viewed as arising primarily from the inadequacy of land use controls in preventing the conversion of farmland to incompatible uses. But in fact, most farmers sell out because of insufficient net income and the declining attractiveness of farming as a way of life."

Governor Thornburgh has said: "To preserve farmland, we must first preserve the farmer."

One charge leveled against the plan to designate Agricultural Preserve Areas in Montgomery County is that the soil in those areas is too poor and taxes are too high for agriculture to prosper. There is no one better able to respond to this criticism than the farmers who have lived in these areas for a number of years.

It is no secret that in nearly every county of this state, development has and is continuing to take place on the best farmland. More than one-half of Pennsylvania's Class I and II soils have already been built upon. The reason is, it is easier and cheaper to develop on these better soils.

Quite likely in Montgomery County, unless strong measures are taken by county officials with the support of farmers, sprawl type of development will continue to take place in the designated preserve areas as suggested by the Planning Commission.

For the farmer nearing retirement, this may be desirable. For many farmers, the value of their land represents the total source of funds for their retirement income. Naturally, most farmers do not wish to see the size of that fund reduced by regulations at any level of government.

However, for the young farmer who wishes to continue farming, development near his farm could cause him serious problems, particularly if concentrated animal or fowl agriculture is a major part of his farming program.

Much is said about certain land use regulations interfering with individual rights. Let's consider a situation where there are three adjoining 100-acre farms that we might call Farms A, B, and C. Farms A and C are owned by young farmers who want to remain in farming. Farm B is owned by a man sixty-five years old with no children interested in farming; therefore, he wishes to sell out. Farmer B sells to a developer who proceeds to build 100 or more homes on the farm. Several years later, Farmer A wishes to build a large cage-layer house on his farm, and Farmer C wishes to build a large commercial hog-containment barn on his farm. Quite likely, the new home owners located on Farm B will not only object to the construction of these two animal and fowl facilities, they will circulate a petition and prevent Farmers A and C from carrying out these much needed additions to support their farming operations and enable them to pay the high interest rates and principle repayments needed to hold on to this very expensive farmland in southeastern Pennsylvania.

Private property rights are a many-sided issue and should be looked at from more than one point of view.

I believe before too many years have passed, farmers will have to make a relatively long-time commitment to retain their land in farming, or pay the tax and other costs of holding speculative land and continue to farm if they are able.

I say this because very little that is being done now significantly has reduced the conversion of farmland to non-farm use. Let's take a look at what is happening over the nation.

Pennsylvania has lost half of its land in farms since 1940. In the past eighteen months, our state has lost 51,000 acres of farmland to non-farm use. New Jersey on the average is losing one farm every three days. Remember, New Jersey has 85% of its farms enrolled in the preferential assessment program. Maryland is losing more than 46,000 acres of farmland annually. Iowa lost 25,000 acres in 1976.

It is apparent to me that neither currently-used preferential assessment programs nor zoning will do the long-time job.

The Wisconsin Legislature in 1974, after narrowly amending the uniformity taxation clause in their constitution, refused to adopt a preferential assessment act like our Act 319 or Act 515. Urban legislators said such an act would only give the farmers a simple tax break. The present Wisconsin act passed in 1977 requires farmers to have a conservation plan for the farm completed or in the process of completion.

Frank Ebert told me Montgomery County requires this also. You are to be commended.

In addition, in Wisconsin, to get state income tax credits which may go as high as $2,100 annually, your farm must be located in a county where the county has adopted an effective policy to preserve farmland. The stronger the agricultural preservation policy, the greater the payment.

In counties where there is no farmland preservation policy developed by 1982, farmers will not be eligible for any payment.

Another concern has been expressed by Neal Potter in a letter to the County Council in Montgomery County, Maryland. Mr. Potter is an urban member of that council. I think his comments are worthy of review.

He points out the Maryland farmland assessment law enacted in 1960 has had little effect on the rate of land conversion in Maryland. Remember, Maryland is losing an average of 46,000 acres a year to non-farm use.

Farmers living hear a newly-constructed shopping center or other such commercial establishment would have great difficulty paying taxes on land so located if market value of the land was used as a basis for assessment.

Without the farm use assessment, farmers may be forced to sell out. Quite likely, the farm would then be bought by a speculator. The tax break provided to the farmer carries with it no long-term commitment by the farmer to keep the land in agricultural production. Breaking the five-year contract in Maryland or eight-year contract in Pennsylvania under Act 319 carries with it a penalty usually paid by the developer at the time of sale and, therefore, is no real deterrent to land use change.

Mr. Potter feels a reform in farmland assessment laws is needed. Low assessments should be provided only for those farmers who are either in the rural zone or who are willing to commit their land to an agricultural district and sell the development rights to the county. He feels it is quite unreasonable to provide millions of dollars in subsidies for land speculators whether they be farmers or non-farmers with no long-term benefit to preserving agricultural land. This is especially true at a time all citizens are complaining about very heavy tax burdens at all levels of government.

I have been told about several farmers in Bucks County who insisted they would not sell their development rights for $3,000 per acre. This is their privilege. However, these same farmers are enrolled in Act 319. Since the tax penalty for breaking the contract required under Act 319 has proven to be no major deterent to selling for development, one wonders what purpose is really being served by the use of Act 319 and Act 515.

At best, the use of these acts has to be considered a holding action until a better means of preserving farmland gains the support of farmers and the public at large.

Much has been said and written about the need to protect personal property rights. However, one has to wonder about the rights of the non-farm citizens of this Commonwealth who voted for the Clean and Green Amendment by an overwhelming majority in order to preserve Pennsylvania's farmland. They agreed to pay tax dollars to save our farms and it is not happening. Remember, Pennsylvania lost 51,000 acres to non-farm use in the past eighteen months.

Perhaps if the recent improvement in the economic position of many farmers continues, it will prove to be a source of encouragement to many young farmers to make a long-term commitment, the only one that really counts, to remain in farming.

Perhaps, too, more farmers who really want to remain in farming will reduce their anticipated land values to levels that will make permanent preservation programs, such as the purchase of development rights and the deed restriction program we are proposing in Lancaster County less difficult to implement.

Hopefully, too, our urban neighbors will appreciate the value of having farms in the area and agree to provide adequate tax dollars to satisfy the farmer's expected reasonable equity he has in his land. After all, for many years now, real estate has been for most farmers their most valuable crop.

We still have quite a bit of good soil left in Lancaster County. I suppose this is the reason development pressures are getting greater.

I believe the deed restriction program we are developing in our county will permanently preserve a great amount of prime agricultural land. This is how it will work:

A Lancaster Agricultural Preserve Board will be created and funded by the Lancaster County Commissioners.

The goal is to retain permanently in agricultural production 278,000 acres of Lancaster County's prime agricultural land. This will allow more than 100,000 acres now being farmed to be used for development in the county. The areas in which these preserves would be located would follow as nearly as possible the agricultural areas in the Land Use and Transportation Plan as contained in the County Comprehensive Plan, Directions.

The County Agricultural Reserve Board, working with other agencies and groups, would further refine area boundaries and place them on easy-to-read maps. These maps should delineate farm boundaries.

Hearings will be held in various geographic areas of the county, not only to explain the program, but to allow public comment and questions. It is important for every property owner to know which properties are in or out of the preserve area. Special notification will be sent to each property owner in these preserves, possibly by certified letter.

The County Agricultural Preserve Board will only get involved in a property transaction when the owner of the property plans to dispose of or change the use of the land.

At no time will the Board interfere with the operation of the farm, such as choice of crops, choice of tenant, or methods of production.

In all cases, when a property is in a preserve area, notice must be given to the Board by a person planning to sell privately, by public auction, or otherwise transfer property. The Board will have thirty days to get involved or not to get involved in the transaction. In an agricultural preserve area, upon a sale of property without a deed restriction, it is important that suitable amendments to Act 442 be enacted to enable the Agricultural Preserve Board, after a sale has been concluded at a public or private sale, to take certain actions. The Board needs to have the option to match the sale price for the property.

I would like to emphasize here that the seller gets market price for the property. The Board is the buyer for the county. The Board would then resell the property with an agricultural deed restriction applied to the most recent owner or to a new buyer no later than 120 days after the Board purchased the property.

Any difference in price, and it is believed in many areas of the county this difference may not be great, will be made up by the county from a revolving fund.

The Board is not planning to hold any property longer than 120 days. Lancaster County is not going into the real estate business.

I would like to emphasize several points at this time. This is a voluntary program and does not violate the principles of the free enterprise system.

There is no limit to the price a property may be bid to under this program. There quite likely will be a limit the county can pay. The Board, acting for the county, will lose some farm properties. It is hoped there will not be too many farms lost.

Under the proposed program, a farm property owner could voluntarily place a deed restriction on a property in return for certain cash and/or tax incentives at the local, state, and federal level. My congressman, Bob Walker, is very interested in this part of the program. In fact, he is preparing legislation that will include Billy Haverstick's recent proposal. This could be very helpful in reducing capital gains not only for the initial owner, but for succeeding owners as well.

This deed restriction program will enable present farm owners to receive market prices for their land and, in the future, reduce to reasonable levels the appreciation of farmland in order that those of our children and our grandchildren who want to farm will not only have land to farm, but will have land to farm not subjected to steeply escalating values as a result of development pressures.

These Lancaster County Agricultural Preserve areas could take on the appearance of a green oasis in a desert of development in years to come! I am optimistic about the program. I know it can work! However, we need the support of the county government, the farm community, and the public to make it work. We can do it if we try!

Lancaster County Farmer's Union

On April 16, 1979, I made this presentation to members of the Lancaster County Farmer's Union. I was not sure how my remarks would be received. I attempted to share with them my thoughts on farmers' attitudes and concerns regarding farmland preservation.

Quite likely there are at least four groups of people in the audience tonight. The first group is perfectly satisfied the way things are. This group wants the free market system to work pretty much the way it is now. A farmer should be able to sell to whom he pleases and when he pleases and to the highest bidder.

The second group thinks we ought to save our farmland, but don't do anything that will interfere with our personal property rights. This group favors the purchase of development rights from voluntary sellers, but are not sure where the money should come from. This group is against zoning since zoning interferes with the right to sell.

The third group is in favor of farmland preservation and is interested in any good program that will accomplish this end. They are not anxious to have the value of their property reduced by zoning. However, they will accept zoning if necessary because zoning is not permanent. If you pursue the right technique, zoning can be changed.

This group has real concerns about their farms being included in the proposed agricultural preserves. They feel even though the Deed Restriction Program would allow for competitive bidding at a public sale, the level of bidding would be reduced because of the fact that farming shall be the predominant use and sales for development would not be so likely to occur.

Then there may be a fourth group present here. Quite likely they are few in number or even non-existent in this audience tonight. However, there are some in the county who have said, "We like your proposal. We like the idea of public bidding. Although we may get less than a developer would pay, we want to keep our farm in agriculture production."

One farmer owning quite a bit of land in State Senator Noah Wenger's legislative district said, "I am willing to take a price that is less than a developer would pay. I want to keep this land in agriculture." However, he asked Noah, "Isn't there some way if I do this, if I take this apparent loss on my land, I can get a reduction on my capital gains?" He has been working for two years with attorneys and apparently no one has suggested a satisfactory solution.

We believe after we have put this deed restriction program in place in Lancaster County, we will find legislative answers at the state and federal levels to many of these problems. Bob Walker's legislation will include Billy Haverstick's proposal and is the kind of capital gains help that is needed. This will help not only the present landowner but future owners with deed restricted land.

The third group to which I referred, and I believe this represents the largest group, says, "I am for the preservation of farmland. I don't want it to cost me anything personally." They don't say it quite this way, but this is what they mean. This group is particularly concerned about their farm property being included in the agricultural preserve area. They are sure the bidding at a public sale will not go as high as if a developer is involved.

I would say to this group, first, there is nothing to prevent a developer from paying $10,000 or more per acre for your farm. At this price, I am sure the county could not afford to get involved.

The second thing I would say to this group is, if you are really sincere about preserving Lancaster County agricultural land, must you have every last dollar that you can possibly ring out of that property? What has been your rate of return on investment per year using today's farming value, not development value, if there is a difference. Our farm in Martic Township with no development potential and no road frontage appreciated 22% per year for thirteen years. How much more than that does one need?

In addition, according to the December 1978 issue of the *Farm Index* in Wisconsin, where they initiated the Wisconsin Farmland Preservation Program in 1977, farmland values rose 18% compared to an average rise of 9% and (-4%) in Nebraska. Wisconsin's program is one of the strongest farmland preservation programs in the nation, yet farmland values in that state rose most sharply. No one knows for certain what will happen in those preserve areas. However, one farmer with a large acreage said it would be worth $1,000 per acre not to have so many cars traveling the roads over which he is trying to move his large equipment. Too many people also interferes with other farming activities. More and more, it is becoming evident to me that people and farming do not mix very well.

If we are ever going to permanently preserve farmland in Lancaster or any other county, I believe farmers will have to somewhat reduce their anticipated equity they feel they have in their land, and the public will have to use tax dollars to provide an incentive for the farmer to make a commitment to permanently keep the farm in agriculture. Government at all levels will have to provide additional incentives to farm without a lot of governmental regulations.

Hunterdon County, New Jersey

I was surprised and pleased when I received a request to speak to a group in Hunterdon County, New Jersey, on May 5, 1979. If I remember correctly, I believe it was Stephanie Stevens who put my wife Esta and me up for the night. She also prepared a great breakfast for us. It was a pleasure for me to speak to them. I trust they gleaned something worthwhile from my remarks. My presentation follows:

When Stephanie Stevens first called me to participate in this conference, I was most reluctant to do so. How could I come to New Jersey and tell you how great our Deed Restriction Proposal is when we can't even get it through our Pennsylvania Legislature. At this date, we expect it to be reported out of the House Legislative Reference Bureau by November 12, 1979.

Stephanie assured me that you folks would understand and that you would want to hear about our program in spite of Legislative problems.

Over the past several years, I have gotten a great deal of help in my efforts to save Lancaster County's farmland from your Secretary of Agriculture, Phillip Alampi, and more recently, from your Coordinator of Rural Resources, John Van Zandt.

In discussing my visit to your county with him, he stated in no uncertain terms, that Hunterdon County is a very important agricultural county and that somehow, some way, Hunterdon County's farmland must be preserved.

John sent me some material including some data from the most recent census from which I learned that Hunterdon County has 930 farms, comprising over 109,000 acres with crop and animal production amounting to over $22.5 million. I am sure sales are even higher today.

According to a USDA Economic Research Report, published in 1977, Hunterdon County ranks second in the state in the amount of acres in farms exceeded only by Burlington County. Hunterdon County ranks third in the state in the amount of cropland exceeded only by Burlington and Salem Counties.

According to a report issued by the New Jersey Rural Advisory Council, entitled "Agricultural Land Sales in New Jersey," during a one-year period from July 1, 1976, to June 30, 1977, Hunterdon County led all New Jersey counties in the number of parcels transferred and in total acreage transferred. All lands in the study were from farms of six acres in size and larger and only lands under the Farmland Assessment Act were included in the study.

Another interesting, if not significant, statistic was that 71% of the parcels transferred and 62% of the total acreage transferred in Hunterdon County were between six and forty acres in size.

Few grain and hay or dairy farmers can conduct a viable operation on this kind of limited acreage.

I feel those of you who are responsible for arranging this conference are to be congratulated. It is important to protect the farmland in Hunterdon County. It is even more important to preserve the agricultural industry in your county and certainly includes the farmer himself.

Farmers are being buffeted by all kinds of regulations and rules from state, local, and federal governments that make it much less attractive than it was fifteen or twenty years ago.

So what do we do about the problem? John Van Zandt and others have said, one of the very useful things that come out of the Burlington County Farm Preservation effort is that quite likely it will be necessary to use more than one technique even in a given area to preserve farmland.

This brings me to our Lancaster County's Deed Restriction Program.

A Deed Restriction Proposal

Most methods to preserve agricultural land are difficult to administer (example: Transfer of Development Rights), quite costly to implement (example: Purchase of Development Rights), or are very unfair to the farmer (example: Strict Agricultural Zoning).

Lancaster County has 63% of the county land area remaining in farms. 53% of that farmland falls into Class I and II soils.

Pennsylvania lost 55,000 acres of farmland to non-farm use in the past eighteen months. Nearly one-fifth of that loss occurred in Lancaster County.

Noah Wenger, Vice Chairman of the House Agricultural Committee, is drafting (may) legislation that will enable Lancaster County to pursue possibly as a pilot effort, a voluntary deed restriction program in the county. It is believed this program will work in Lancaster County and possibly other counties as well.

Following passage of enabling legislation, the "Deed Restriction Program" would be implemented as follows:

An Agricultural Preserve Board will be created and funded by the county commissioners. The goal is to follow the recommendations of the County Comprehensive Plan and retain permanently in agricultural production 278,000 acres of the county's prime agricultural land. This would allow

100,000 acres near major highways, water and sewer lines, now being farmed to be used for development in the county.

The County Agricultural Preserve Board, working with other agencies and groups, would refine area boundaries and place them on easy-to-read maps. These maps should delineate farm boundaries.

Hearings will be held in cooperation with township supervisors and township planning commissions. If before or during a hearing, strong opposition is expressed by farmers or the general public, to the designation of a preserve area within a township, it is unlikely that any deed restriction activity will take place in that area. Remember, this is a voluntary program!

The County Agricultural Preserve Board will only get involved in a property transaction when the owner plans to dispose of or change the use of the land.

At no time will the board interfere with the operation of the farm such as choice of crops, choice of tenant or methods of production.

In all cases, when a property is in a preserve area, notice must be given to the board, by a person planning to sell privately, at public auction, or otherwise transfer property. The board will have thirty days to get involved or not get involved in the transaction.

Legislation is needed to permit the county to offer, on a uniform basis, cash incentives to property owners who are willing to place a deed restriction on their farm designating the land for agricultural use only.

However, in an agricultural preserve area, upon the sale of property on which no deed restriction has been placed, it is important that the proposed legislation enable the Agricultural Preserve Board, after a sale has been concluded, at a public or private sale, to take certain actions. The board needs to have the option to increase the sales price and purchase the property for the county.

It should be emphasized that the seller gets market price for the property. The board is the buyer for the county. The board would then resell the property with an agricultural deed restriction applied to the most recent owner or a new buyer no later than 120 days after the board purchased the property.

Any difference in price, and it is believed in many areas of Lancaster County, this difference may not be great, will be made up by the county from a revolving fund.

This is a voluntary program and does not violate the principles of the free enterprise system.

There is no limit to the price a property may bid under this program. A developer could bid a property to $10,000 an acre. Quite likely, this would be too great an amount for the county to pay. The board, acting for the county, will lose some properties. It is hoped there will not be too many farms lost.

This problem of the possible total development of one or more 100-acre farms in an agricultural preserve area is a concern and a recognized weakness in the proposal. Since this is a voluntary program, there is no way this problem can be averted.

However, the township supervisors could prevent this problem, if they so desire, through proper zoning.

This deed restriction program will enable farm owners to receive market prices for their land and in the future, reduce to reasonable levels the appreciation of farmland in order that those of our children and our grandchildren who want to farm will not only have land to farm, but will have land to farm not subjected to steeply escalating values as a result of development pressures.

Because of the concentration of farm activity and the designation of the area as an agricultural preserve area, farmers will be insured of the "Right To Farm," a right being infringed upon in an increasing number of instances in the Commonwealth.

A 1980 Progress Report on Our Deed Restriction in Lancaster County

This is an early progress report on our attempt to preserve farmland in Lancaster County. County government involvement started November 15, 1978. It is gratifying to have continuing and increasing support from county government. However, there have been setbacks and disappointments along the way. This is life!

After years of discussion about the need to save Lancaster County's prime agricultural land, on November 15, 1978, the commissioners of Lancaster County took a giant step forward toward solving this problem. The commissioners appointed a fourteen-member task force and charged them to develop a plan to preserve the county's prime farmland. Later, the task force was expanded to fifteen members, to include William Forrey, representing the Home Builders of Lancaster County.

At that same November 15 meeting, John Barley presented a resolution adopted by the Lancaster County Farmer's Association requesting the county commissioners to develop a plan to preserve Lancaster County's prime farmland.

On February 27, 1979, the task force presented its report and recommendations to the County Commissioners.

Early in March, legislative recommendations implementing the recommendations of the Agricultural Preservation Task Force were presented to Representative Noah Wenger to prepare appropriate legislation.

On March 17, 1979, a seven-member Agricultural Preservation Legislative Coordinating Committee met with Agricultural Secretary Penrose Hallowell, three of his deputies, representatives of the Grange, Pennsylvania Farmers' Association, and several lobbyists for farm organizations.

On June 15, 1979, Mr. Edward Hussie, Chief Counsel to the Majority Leader of the House of Representatives, sent to Representative Wenger, the County Commissioners, and members of the County Preservation Legislative Coordinating Committee, copies of a preliminary draft of proposed legislation, an Agricultural Preserve Act.

Early in July 1979, the County Commissioners and the County Legislative Coordinating Committee, met to discuss the proposed draft. Rather extensive changes were made to the preliminary draft.

On September 10, 1979, another meeting was held with Secretary Hallowell and his deputies. The presence of a representative from the governor's office highlighted this meeting. All House members representing any part of Lancaster County were invited, The Pennsylvania Association of Township Supervisors, the Pennsylvania Association of County Commissioners, plus the Pennsylvania Farmers' Association and the Pennsylvania State Grange.

On September 21, 1979, a meeting was held in the Harrisburg office of the Pennsylvania Environmental Council seeking their legislative support. That same day, meetings were held in the Camp Hill offices of the Pennsylvania Association of Township Supervisors, and the Pennsylvania Farmers' Association in an effort to get their support for the revised Bill.

On September 24, 1979, the Legislative Coordinating Committee met with the County Commissioners to review proposed changes in the Bill suggested by the Pennsylvania Association of Township Supervisors Association.

On October 2, 1979, Representative Armstrong delivered the proposed Bill to the House Legislative Reference Bureau for their review and processing in preparation for introduction in the House.

November 14, 1979, House Bill 1983 was introduced by Gib Armstrong representing Pennsylvania 100 Legislative District in which I live. The Bill was signed by all House members who entirely or in part represent Lancaster County.

On October 8, 1979, the Lancaster County Farmer's Association at their fall annual policy development meeting, endorsed by a clear majority the enactment of legislation to enable Lancaster County to proceed with the implementation of the Deed Restriction Program.

Several provisions of House Bill 1983 are not consistent with current PFA policy on land use. For this reason, PFA has not been able to support House Bill 1983.

It is hoped that the Lancaster County Farmer's Association, working with PFA membership in other southeastern counties, through the policy development committees in each county, can broaden the present PFA policy on land use to include the procedures as outlined in House Bill 1983.

The County Commissioners will soon appoint an Agricultural Land Preservation Board. An interim plan to preserve the county's prime agricultural land will be initiated. This plan is not as effective as the procedures provided for under House Bill 1983, but it is a start.

Nov. 14, 1979, House Bill 1983 was introduced by Gib Armstrong, representing Pennsylvania 100 Legislative District in which I live. The bill was signed by all House members who entirely or in part represent Lancaster County. This number includes Earl Smith, who represents both Lancaster and Chester Counties. I am glad to report that Joe Pitts and Peter Vroon, representing Chester County, also signed the bill. We appreciate their help. It is a bit ironic that House Agricultural Committee Minority Chairman Paul Yarner signed the bill and Majority Chairman Reno Thomas would not go on the bill.

On December 4, we met with Reno Thomas, Chairman of House Agricultural Committee. In attendance from Lancaster County were newly elected since named Chairman of Lancaster County Commissioners, Jim Huber; Earl Newcomer, President, Lancaster County Farmer's Association; Representative Gib Armstrong; Aaron Stauffer; and myself. Charles Wismer, Master of Pennsylvania Grange, was also present.

Our meeting with Chairman Thomas was not very productive. He told us he didn't like the bill. It is not voluntary and quite likely the designation areas for agricultural use only concept would reduce the value of a property owner's land within a preserve area. These concerns were not new; we had heard them before from Representative Noah Wenger and others.

Chairman Reno Thomas gave us little hope that House Bill 1983 will come up for consideration soon. We are doing what we can to persuade him to change that position.

It has not been easy. We have not given up.

History of Our $250 Per Acre Development Right Offer

This handout was prepared to describe the early procedures used to arrive at our $250 per acre, purchase of development right plan.

We wanted to offer a larger payment per acre. Our program was new. We did not have the money. Instead of offering nothing, our preserve board offered something, $250 per acre. Our funds were used up quickly, even at this low offer we made a start!

Purchase of Development Rights and
Lancaster County's $250 Per Acre Payment Plan
Proposed by Amos Funk
Adopted by Preserve Board

Maryland's Purchase of Development Rights program averaged $1,100 per acre in 1980. (The cost has been lowered somewhat at this time.) The $1,100 per acre payment if amortized over twenty years at 10% interest would correspond to a payment of $129 per acre per year for twenty years.

With Pennsylvania's State revenue levels down and the pressures to keep the lid on most new spending proposals, it is doubtful if state funding for the purchase of development rights can be initiated for several years.

Therefore, it seems prudent to explore how far a country could go in funding a purchase of development rights effort.

Our goal in Lancaster County is to retain 278,000 acres in agricultural production. This would allow more than 100,000 acres now being farmed and most of which are located near major highways existing or planned water and sewer facilities, to be used for development.

If a united goal would be set to purchase development rights on one-fourth of this acre 70,000 acres, at $129 per year for twenty years, this would require an expenditure of over nine million dollars per year for twenty years from county tax revenue or approximately nine-tenths of the county's current tax revenue.

Even with a 40% county and 60% state arrangement as in Maryland, Lancaster County's annual cost of $3,612,000 would represent more than one-third of the county's current tax revenue.

Although, the citizens of Lancaster County in numerous polls have expressed great interest in and concern for the preservation of farmland, we are not at all sure the costs that have been outlined would be acceptable.

Therefore, we thought a more affordable program should be attempted. We call it an "Incentive Payment Program." The Lancaster County plan of incentive payments to landowners who dedicate their land to agriculture use for twenty-five years is a "take-off" of the Wisconsin plan where landowners with moderate incomes and whose property is located in a municipality with certain zoning restrictions become eligible for income and property tax credits. Wisconsin's plan, initiated in 1977, now has more than three million acres enrolled in their program.

Since Pennsylvania's constitution contains the equality of taxation provision, we cannot apply the provisions of the Wisconsin law in Pennsylvania. This is the reason we are using the incentive payment concept instead of the tax credit arrangement.

The Lancaster County Agricultural Preserve Board is recommending an incentive payment of $250 per acre to any property owner located in a preserve area. This would represent a county expenditure of $29.37 per acre if amortized over a twenty-year period of 10 percent interest. It would follow then, that by using the $250 incentive payment plan, the 70,000 acres could be retained in agriculture at a cost of $2,055,900 per year for twenty years and would represent a four mill tax increase at current assessment.

It has been said the best way to eat an elephant is one bite at a time! In line with that thinking, the following proposal is made.

PROPOSAL: Let's get 1,000 contiguous acres in three preserve areas offering $250 per acre at an annual cost of $88,095 per year for twenty years. Also take any donated deed restrictions and buy at public sale any properties that come up for sale in these preserve areas, where a change of use is anticipated.

This would then establish a track record for Lancaster County with nearly as much use restricted land as Suffolk County (3,193) at a cost in Suffolk of nearly $10 million as compared to Lancaster County $750,000.

Pennsylvania Council of Farm Organizations, Harrisburg

I made this presentation on January 21, 1980, to the Pennsylvania Council of Farm Organizations meeting held in the Penn Harris Motor Inn, Harrisburg. I tried to bring out the point that there is a lot of talk but not much action.

Most farmers want to preserve agricultural land. Most township supervisors, county commissioners, and state legislators say they want to preserve agricultural land. Penny Hallowell and Governor Thornburgh want to preserve agricultural land. Most citizens want to preserve agricultural land.

The question might well be asked, if everyone is in favor of preserving agricultural land, why then is not more happening?

I recently heard of a survey conducted by *Esquire* magazine. This survey was directed toward young males between the ages of eighteen and forty.

1. The first question in the survey was: What is the thing you desire most in life? What one thing would give you the greatest satisfaction?

    Answer. 90% responding replied: I would like to have a son . . . a son to bear my name.

2. The second question was: Do you plan to get married?

    Answer. 50% responded: No . . . I do not plan to marry.

3. The third question: Are you willing to assume the responsibility of a mortgage or other financial responsibility required in raising a family?

    Answer. To this question, only 45% were willing to make this commitment.

Nearly all these young men wanted a son, but most of them were not willing to assume the responsibility of marriage and carrying a mortgage to achieve their goal.

In our land use efforts, most of us want to preserve farmland, but few of us farmers and public officials alike are willing to make those difficult decisions, bear what seems to many to be unreasonable sacrifices needed to preserve on a long-time basis, this increasingly valuable resource . . . our productive agricultural land.

I am not saying we are doing nothing; I am saying we are not doing enough.

I realize there are agricultural districting bills in the House and in the Senate. I hope they will be passed early in this session. Except for former

Governor Shapp's veto, Pennsylvania would have an agricultural district act in place today.

I guess the thing that bothers me is, we are eight or ten years too late with the agricultural district legislation. Eight years ago, agricultural district legislation would have been useful in Lancaster County and much of southeastern Pennsylvania. Now, it is too late for us.

New York passed their agricultural district enabling legislation in 1971. Former Governor Sheafer's Committee for the Preservation of Pennsylvania's Agricultural Land recommended the use of agricultural districts to preserve farmland in 1969. California passed their agricultural district act in 1965.

Nearly all the provisions in the New York District Act, that protect farmers from increased tax assessments, sewer taxes, and some state regulations including condemnation proceedings, have now been enacted as separate pieces of legislation by the Pennsylvania Legislature.

The problem with Pennsylvania's land use efforts to date, as I see it, these benefits go to every one in the State.

No one can argue about the fairness of this approach. However, there is little incentive to make a long-term commitment to retain farmland in agricultural production. Obviously, a contract is signed under the provisions of Act 515, and 319; however, it is generally agreed these acts provide in most cases short-term benefits rather than long-term commitments.

It is generally agreed that of the forty-four states in the nation offering preferential taxation, only Michigan and Wisconsin require a significant commitment by farmers if they are to receive tax relief.

The tax credit or payment program in Wisconsin is tied directly to the level of land-use planning and zoning present in a certain county and the level of income of the property owner.

As of July 1, 1979, only nineteen months into the program, nearly 10,000 farm families owning over two million acres are participating in Wisconsin's program.

The numbers are impressive, but the significant thing about the Wisconsin experience is that the legislature in that state refused to grant preferential taxation to farm property owners without requiring a meaningful commitment from the landowner.

In a 1974 referendum, the voters of Wisconsin removed the uniformity of taxation clause from the state's constitution. In June 1977, the Wisconsin Farmland Preservation Act was passed and amended in May 1978.

The requirement of an exclusive agricultural zoning was a very controversial provision, and an unsuccessful attempt to block it was made by two influential senators. They claimed that the state has no right telling the counties to implement zoning. They pointed out local governments as well as farmers have a tremendous stake in this because it will affect their income, their taxes, and home rule.

Nevertheless, a determined state representative was successful in amending the bill to give a majority of the towns the power to veto an exclusive agricultural zoning ordinance adopted by the county.

Thus, towns can reject agricultural zoning, but such action would cancel local farmers' eligibility for an income tax credit.

Recently, I was discussing the possibility of getting House Bill 1983, a bill of great importance to many of us in Lancaster County, up for consideration in the House Agricultural Committee.

I was surprised and a little shocked when I was told, not by a legislator, but by several friends of mine, that a number of individuals who serve on the House Agriculture Committee do not want anything to do with land use legislation. It is too controversial.

I would raise the question, if not the House Agricultural Committee, then who? Who will provide the needed leadership to preserve Pennsylvania's prime agricultural land and guide growth toward less productive soils and encourage more concentrated development near sewer and water lines in our towns and our cities.

In Lancaster County, our Comprehensive Plan shows that within a five-mile radius of the center of the city, there are 33,000 acres of undeveloped land. This is enough land to provide for the projected population and industrial growth in Lancaster County for the next thirty years if the recommended housing densities in our Comprehensive Plan were followed.

To those who say a land use program for Pennsylvania is only acceptable if it is entirely voluntary, I would say very little of these 33,000 acres will be used for development in the near future with a voluntary approach, because it is cheaper and easier to buy a farm somewhere and develop there. This is true, notwithstanding the fact that most roads, sewer and water lines, and other utilities are in place in the 33,000-acre area within a five-mile radius of center square of the city.

I am certain the same situation prevails in many towns and cities in which most of you live.

If not the House Agricultural Committee, then who will provide the leadership to slow down the loss of Pennsylvania's farmland to nonagricultural uses?

According to a report issued by the ESCS, USDA in 1978, Pennsylvania ranked third highest in the nation in the percentage of land taken out of agricultural production during the years 1975-1979.

The loss of 700,000 acres of farmland in the four years between 1975-1979 should be troublesome to all Pennsylvanians.

Pennsylvania has to do much more to protect its farmland for the next twenty-five years and beyond. Pennsylvania has a lot at stake. According to the 1976 United States Census of Agriculture, Pennsylvania surpassed New York in gross farm income and now leads all twelve northeastern states in the realized gross income from farming. In fact, the gross income Pennsylvania farmers received in 1976 was greater than the combined gross income of all the farmers in the states of Delaware, Maryland, New Jersey, and West Virginia.

With Pennsylvania in this position of agricultural leadership, you can understand why I was surprised and a bit shocked when I was told some members of the House Agricultural Committee do not want to touch any land-use legislation because it is too controversial.

As I said early in my remarks, farmers are in favor of the preservation of agricultural land. However, there is little agreement as to how best to accomplish this.

It has been said of us farmers that we like to have our cake and eat it too. It has also been said, if you scratch a farmer deep enough, you will discover a land speculator. I suppose in many cases both statements are true.

Farmers do not like to be told what they can and cannot do. I am sure this applies to most individuals, but it is particularly true with farmers.

In spite of this, Pennsylvania did pass the Clean Streams Law. This law certainly spells out clearly what farmers cannot do. I distinctly remember how upset my friend Eddie Hopkins was at the prospect of someone telling him, as he put it, when to plow, how much, and in what direction to plow on his farm in Lackawana County.

However, with the appointment and impact of the Agricultural Advisory Committee to DER and the granting of some of the inspection function to county conservation districts, few of the anticipated problems were experienced.

Most farmers and farm organizations do not like zoning. Yet, in two Lancaster County townships, an Advisory Committee of farmers recommended strict agricultural use only zones be established in their townships. It was not that these farmers like zoning more than most farmers, they liked far less the alternative of checkerboard development near their farms and the problems such development can cause.

Eight townships in Lancaster County have adopted strict agricultural use only zones. Four more are working toward establishing similar zoning ordinances.

Farmers in Lancaster County and in other southeastern counties and possibly in other points of the state, are looking for solutions. They do not want the solution to destroy the equity they have in their land, their pension fund. They are concerned about their property rights. They want any proposal to be voluntary.

However, as I see it, overriding all these concerns is the concern for the wise use of our limited natural resource, prime agricultural land. One can be justly concerned when development, that could occur elsewhere, takes place on our best agricultural land just because it is cheaper and easier.

But, an even greater concern to me is the buckshot development, the sprawl-type development, that is taking place all over this state.

For example, according to our county comprehensive plan, Lancaster County's average population increase to the year 2000 is 4,000 people per year. If the recommended housing densities in the plan were followed, the housing and other needs of these 4,000 people could be provided on 1,000 acres per year, or four people per acre . . . not an unreasonable goal.

However, over the past five years, an average of 7,000 acres of farmland is lost annually to provide for these 4,000 new people. We are using seven times the farmland for development than what should be needed because we are allowing growth to take place in a buckshot pattern; we are not adequately guiding growth.

If we are able to guide growth in our county, the 100,000 acres set aside for development in the county could provide for all projected residential, commercial and residential growth for ninety years and still have 278,000 acres left for agricultural use.

If we continue as we have in the past few years, all of Lancaster County's 386,000 acres of farmland will be gone in fifty years.

Pennsylvania needs broad land use legislation that will fit the needs of those counties where urbanizing pressures are not great and at the same time, allow and encourage counties like Lancaster where urbanizing pressures are very great to guide growth and preserve our prime agricultural land. I am sure very little will happen unless we make it happen!

Table 7. Realized Gross Income from Farming, 1950-1976[1]

State	1950	1960	1970	1976
		——Millions of Dollars——		
Delaware	106.8	123.0	154.5	295.3
Maryland	266.3	325.6	447.5	773.3
New Jersey	324.4	332.0	276.2	379.4
New York	917.7	999.4	1,227.6	1,917.4
Pennsylvania	831.8	970.4	1,179.3	2,044.4
West Virginia	174.8	151.4	133.8	200.6
Regional Total	2,621.8	2,901.8	3,418.9	5,610.6
Percent of U.S.	8	8	6	5
U.S.	32,291.0	38,497.0	58,569.0	103,643.0

[1] Realized gross income includes cash receipts from farm marketing, government income, the value of farm products consumed directly by farm households, the values of housing provided by farm dwellings and farm income from machinery hire and custom work.

SOURCE: U.S. Department of Agriculture, *State Farm Income Statistics*.

Table 8. Number of Farms, 1945-1974.

	1945		1954		1964		1974	
State	No.	Pct.	No.	Pct.	No.	Pct.	No.	Pct.
Delaware	9,296	2	6,297	2	4,401	2	3,400	3
Maryland	41,275	8	32,500	9	20,760	10	15,163	4
New Jersey	26,226	5	22,686	6	10,641	4	7,409	5
New York	149,490	30	105,714	29	66,510	30	43,682	31
Pennsylvania	171,761	35	128,875	35	83,086	38	53,171	38
West Virginia	97,600	20	68,583	19	34,504	16	16,909	12
Reg. Total	495,648	100	364,656	100	219,902	100	139,734	100
Percent of U.S.		8		8		7		6

SOURCE: *U.S. Census of Agriculture*.

Spring Meeting of Pennsylvania Section of the American Society of Agricultural Engineers

On May 2, 1980, I made a presentation to the Pennsylvania Section of the American Society of Agricultural Engineers on land use planning. The meeting was held at the Penn Harris Motor Inn, Camp Hill. This was an elite group. I appreciated the invitation. My presentation follows:

As I was preparing my remarks for this occasion, I was quite aware that I am speaking to a very knowledgeable group. You folks know what is happening in the area of land use.

For example, Al Best who was kind enough to provide me with transportation to your meeting has sent me numerous papers on land use that have crossed his desk. One I particularly liked was the paper by Lester R. Brown on "The World Wide Loss of Cropland."

Those of you with an SCS background have seen the same papers I have seen. They come from Norm Berg and many other writers. I am sure others of you with a different background have read extensively on the problem of the loss of prime agricultural land.

I am sure most of you followed with a great deal of interest and with considerable hope the various methods used to slow down the loss of our nation's best farmland.

However, some disturbing things have happened recently.

In New York, over six million acres are enrolled in agricultural districts and are under contracts which carry with them numerous benefits to farmers including preferential taxation. However, the state court of New York has recently ruled that all land must be assessed at full market value. As a result, some farm taxes have more than doubled. Unless the New York legislature can give farmers some tax relief, it may be very difficult for some farmers in that state to survive.

The New Jersey pilot program in Burlington County testing the concept of purchasing of development rights was abandoned, not only because it was judged by many New Jersey legislators as being too costly, but also because of the possibility that the assessed value of land to farm would have increased from a present average of $230 per acre to somewhere between $900-$1,100 per acre. This would have caused a tax increase of sixteen million dollars in the first year for New Jersey farmers. Naturally, farmers opposed this!

In 1978, Connecticut enacted a two-year program to purchase development rights in that state. The rights to three farms have been purchased. The state paid $320,000 for the development rights to the first farm, a corn and dairy operation. The owner then sold the farm for $250,000, or a total of $570,000, and moved to West Virginia to take advantage of low property taxes. The new owner of the property is a farmer who wants to build a 400,000-bird poultry operation. The neighbors are demanding an environmental impact study. The state is saying a large poultry operation is not an agricultural use, but a commercial use. Now, the governor of Connecticut has stopped the development right purchasing program.

And, finally, it was reported in the April 2 issue of the *New York Times*, that the farmland preservation effort in Suffolk County, Long Island, has fallen on bad times.

John Kline is no longer the County Administrator. The new administrator does not share Mr. Kline's enthusiasm for the development rights purchase program.

The presiding officer of the county legislature is also critical of the program as being too costly and too rewarding to land speculators who own nearly 50% of Suffolk County's farmland.

So what am I saying? Can't we get there from here?

No, I do not take a negative view in regard to the preservation of Pennsylvania's farmland. However, I feel strongly that we will have to chart some new courses. We will have to strengthen things like zoning that have short time value and make them work better. This is what Wisconsin did with their farmland retention program and they have enrolled over two million acres in their program in less than nineteen months. The Wisconsin plan may be the best plan in place in this nation today.

I believe it is good because the Wisconsin legislature did several things. The legislature refused to provide preferential taxation for the landowner without rezoning a definite commitment from the landowner.

To initiate their program, the legislature had to amend the state's constitution removing the uniformity of taxation provision contained therein. Pennsylvania would have to do the same thing.

Landowners in Wisconsin can earn up to $4,200 annually in tax credits depending on the strength of zoning present in a county and the level of the combined farm and off farm income of the landowner. I believe Lancaster County's deed restriction program will work well in our county and quite likely other counties as well.

The deed restriction program builds on the County Comprehensive Plan passed by the county commissioners in 1975.

The goal is to preserve 278,000 acres of the best farmland in the county. This would allow more than 100,000 acres, now being farmed, near major highways, sewer and water lines, for development.

I would then raise the question, if it is possible to provide housing for the 4,000 additional individuals per year in our county through planned development and guided growth, why should we continue to take 7,000 acres or more each year out of agricultural production for whatever reason? We have to do better!

Of course, those of us interested in implementing the Deed Restriction Program are particularly interested in what happens to the 278,000 acres designated to remain permanently in agriculture. I am certain of one thing. Very few of those 278,000 acres will be retained in agricultural production unless the farmers living in the proposed preserve areas want them to be preserved. It is a safe bet at this point in time, that many of our farmers are not sure.

Most farmers want to preserve agricultural land. There is little agreement on how best to do it. Ten years ago, quite likely most farmers would have opposed having their farms included in a district zoned for agricultural use only by their township. Today, there are nine townships in the county with agricultural districts. We are making progress!

Some farmers accept the strict agricultural district concept, but are skeptical about being included in a proposed agricultural preserve area because, they point out, zoning can be changed and our proposal is permanent.

The permanent provision of our Deed Restriction Plan, while viewed as a weakness now, quite likely will be viewed as an outstanding strong point in years to come.

In the future, it will become increasingly important to have reasonably large, contiguous areas devoted permanently to agricultural production if farming is to survive in Lancaster County which has now become the second fastest developing county in the state and now also has become the fifth most important industrial county in the state. People and today's Lancaster County's animal and fowl agriculture just do not mix.

There is a lot of interest in having the "right to farm" provision included in any bill proposed or act that is passed. This provision is included in our bill.

However, these "right to farm" provisions may not prevent one or more urban residents from bringing a civil suit against a farmer. Even if the farmer wins, he may have legal costs to bear and considerable time would be lost in court. Again, I repeat, it is most important to separate people and Lancaster County's animal and fowl agriculture.

After the proposed legislation is passed, we hope to approach first those townships in which the farms are owned predominantly by Amish and the plainer Mennonite farmers.

However, we will discuss our proposal with any township officials who are interested.

It should be noted that no preserve areas will be officially designated within a township without a legally publicized hearing in that township at which time farmers and other citizens can testify. Following the hearing, the township officials will make the final decision whether or not they wish to participate in the program.

Our Deed Restriction Proposal is criticized by some as not being voluntary enough. We think it is as voluntary as it can be and still be effective. Remember, farmers and other individuals can let their feelings be known at a township hearing. I am sure the supervisors will listen.

The procedure is as follows: An approach would be made to supervisors and the Planning Commission of a township to determine their level of interest.

We would discuss the County Agricultural Preserve Map and the proposed preservation area in their township. Reasonable changes would be allowed. The preserve area could be expanded, contracted, or the shape could be changed in a reasonable manner.

The next step would be a public hearing which would meet all legal notification requirements. In addition, a certified letter will be sent to all property owners living within the proposed preserve area, notifying them of their inclusion in the area and of the meeting. At this point, any and all farmers or other landowners opposed to having their farms included in the preserve area could let their wishes be known. If there is sufficient objection, farmers can and should sign a petition in opposition and/or testify at the hearing.

The point has been made that since farmers make up only a small percentage of the total population of most townships, they cannot make their voices be heard.

The Barley Brothers' petition opposing the use of their farm for a landfill is an excellent example of what can be done. 10,000 signatures, most of them by urban residents, petitioned township officials to disallow the use of the Barley Farm for a landfill. With the support of their urban neighbors, the Barleys won their fight.

I will repeat a statement I made earlier, I think our proposal is as voluntary as it can be and yet be effective.

Any plan, and this includes most plans being used today, except Wisconsin's plan, that allow the voluntary withdrawal from an agricultural district and the sale of the withdrawn farmland for development and, consequently, results in a checkerboard of development and farming is not a very good plan. Again, let me repeat, people and today's fowl and animal agriculture do not mix very well.

This brings us to the other major criticism of our Deed Restriction Plan. We are told property values in the preserve area will be reduced if there is no opportunity to sell for development. This may or may not be true.

Since to our knowledge this plan, although used in France since 1964, has not been tried anywhere in this nation (we would like the legislature to allow us to try it in Lancaster County), we don't have any experience to draw from.

We do know that Amish and Mennonite farmers have outbid developers for land to farm in Lancaster County.

We also know there is an increasing concern by farmers to have the "right to farm." While "right to farm" laws and ordinances may help, they will not protect the farmers from civil suits.

In my opinion, relatively large (at least 1,000 acres) of contiguous farmland is the best assurance that farmers will have the right to farm. At the risk of becoming boring, let repeat once more, people and today's fowl and animal agriculture just do not mix. Few farmers can afford to own farmland in southeastern Pennsylvania without the additional income received from fowl and animal agriculture.

In the past, the highest and best use of land was considered by many to be the use for development. This point of view may be changing. Quite likely, the use of land to accommodate an industrial plant will still remain a very valuable use. However, I doubt if land for residential development in rural areas can long compete with farming, especially if the true costs of poorly or unplanned development is accurately appraised.

To get the job done, quite likely different approaches have to be used to preserve farmland in various parts of the county.

Wisconsin built on Michigan's land use plan and made innovative changes. They find the plan is working well in that state.

We believe our Deed Restriction Plan will work well in Lancaster County and possibly our other counties as well. We wish the legislature would give us a chance to try. The unusual thing is, we are not asking for any money from the state. We wouldn't turn it down, but we are ready to try our plan on our own, using county funds.

Special Meeting on Farmland Preservation
At the Penn Harris Motor Inn

I made this presentation on September 22, 1980, at the Penn Harris Motor Inn in Harrisburg. It was a rather negative presentation. Perhaps, I was a bit discouraged at the time.

At the most recent meeting of the Lancaster County Agricultural Preserve Board, our invited speaker, Marian Deppen, Cooperative Extension Director for the capitol region, stated that he may have held the first land use meeting in Pennsylvania while he was Assistant County Agent in nearby Montgomery County. He held that meeting in the fall of 1953. There were more than thirty farmers in attendance.

Aaron Stauffer, Vice-Chairman of our Agricultural Preservation Board, asked this question: "If you started that early in 1953, why has not more happened?" After reflecting a short time, Mr. Deppen replied, "I suppose it is because farmers value their independence of action, their freedom to do what they want with their land, far more than is their concern for the loss of farmland."

I am afraid this attitude hasn't changed a great deal up to this time.

To a large degree especially here in the east, farmers are loners. They want to make decisions independently and not be bound by the wishes of others.

Quite likely, this is one reason, with the exception of milk marketing cooperatives, there have been few successful marketing cooperatives in the east.

A number of years ago, Lancaster County farmers tried to develop and operate a tobacco marketing cooperative. Although some success was achieved, it finally had to be dissolved because of lack of member support. Too many exercised what, they conceived, their individual right to sell outside the co-op, rather than support their organization.

Service and commodity purchasing co-ops have fared much better in Lancaster County and in the east because farmers can compare prices and choose.

Another reason a farmer may be reluctant to relinquish the right to sell his or her land for development is that over the past thirty years, except for a brief period in 1973, farmers have not gotten an adequate price for their product.

Not adequate when one considers a fair return for their investment, reasonable allowance for the depreciation on their equipment and buildings, and at least a minimum wage for himself and his wife and any of his family who assist in the family farm operation.

To illustrate the point, when one looks at the total farm income between 1971 and 1977 in the United States, the total net farm income of all farmers in the nation ranged between $15 billion and $33 billion annually. The six-year total was $136 billion.

This represents the fruit of his back-breaking labor, his risk taking, and his management skills.

During the same six-year period from 1971 to 1977, with little or no effort on the farmers part, the value of his farmland rose over $223 billion . . . an amount 1.6 times greater than the net earnings from the family's labor, management and risk taking. It is little wonder that land is sometimes referred to as the farmers last cash crop . . . his pension fund.

A farmer readily responds to changing corn prices, selling when prices are high and withholding the crop from the market when prices are low. The level of product prices determines whether many farmers plant corn or soybeans or whether he keeps calves or slaughters them.

But when it comes to land, high prices have little impact on a farmer's land-use decisions. The decision to sell out and leave farming tends to be made because of retirement or death, not in response to fluctuating land prices.

On the other hand, the high stakes involved make farmers protective of their land asset, even when they have no intention of selling immediately. The price of a farmer's acreage is seen quite accurately as a function of supply and demand, and the free market forces (which often seem to buffet him unfairly when it comes to selling his crops) have done well by him in producing a high price for his land.

"In the farm product market," as one West Virginia poultryman put it, "the farmer has to take the other man's price." In the land market, by contrast, the farmer often finds eager buyers hammering at his door. It is a satisfying feeling.

Property tax relief programs or preferential taxation for landowners is offered to farmers in forty-two of the fifty states. Theoretically, this reduction induces the owner to keep the land in agricultural production. However, the capital gains which can be obtained from selling the land usually outweighs any tax benefit.

In a report from the U.S. Controller General to the U.S. Congress issued September 20, 1979, studies of the effects of preferential taxation in two states were reported in some detail.

Illinois, one of the states studied, has thirty-six million acres. As of 1976, 81% of the state's total land area was in farmland with 90% of the cropland classified as prime farmland. Illinois lost 1.6 million acres between 1960 and 1976. Much of this was converted to residential and industrial use (Pennsylvania has 8.2 million acres in farmland). Quoting from the report: "Illinois passed their preferential tax law for farm owners in 1972 with customary rollback penalty provisions.

"The law's primary purpose was to give bona-fide farmers near urban areas property tax relief to prevent the premature sale of farmland, and to control urban growth. On both aspects, the law has been less than successful.

"A Northwestern professor, who studied the effects of differential assessment in five Chicago area counties . . . Cook, DuPage, Kane, Lake, and Will, noted that in four counties where there was participation, about 32% of participating landlords were non-farmers. Non-farmer participation ranged 65% in Cook County to 25% in rural Kane County." He concluded, "Differential assessment did not seem to have retarded the loss of farmland.

"The SCS Illinois State Conservationist reported in 1977, there is nothing on the horizon to indicate that Illinois will not lose the equivalent of another five or six counties (of farmland) by the turn of the century."

California is an important agricultural state. California supplies 25% of all the table food and 40% of all fresh fruits and vegetables consumed in the United States.

California has forty-five million acres of privately owned non-urban land, about 12.6 million of these areas are prime land. As of October 1976, fifteen million acres were under the Williamson Act, passed in 1967 to prove, among other things, preferential taxation to farm property owners.

Of this fifteen million acres under the Williamson Act, 6% was prime farmland in rural/urban transitional zones, 24% was prime farmland in rural areas and 70% was forested, non-prime open-space land.

It can be concluded that the purpose of the Williamson Act, to preserve prime farmland near the urban fringe has not been achieved and most of the land under contract would not be developed whether the land is under contract or not.

Gov. Dick Thornburgh glances toward Millersville's Amos Funk, far right, after signing an important farm bill on Funk's farm. Seated next to Thornburgh are Rep. Joseph Pitts, left, and Sen. Richard A. Snyder. In the back row, from left, are Penrose Hallowell, State Secretary of Agriculture; Rep. Noah Wenger; and Rep. Gibson Armstrong.

The Farmland Preservation Bill That Became Law in Our Farm Market Greenhouse December 1980

From the beginning, getting legislation passed to promote farmland preservation has been very difficult. As seen on the photograph on the preceding page, my smile of satisfaction is a clear indication of the very substantial lift the signing of this bill gave me. It will be a very useful tool for many dedicated farm families in Lancaster County and elsewhere in the state.

I am deeply touched that in addition to Governor Thornburgh, the bill's chief sponsor, Representative Joseph Pitts, and co-sponsor, Representative Gibson Armstrong, were present. Also present were Senator Richard Snyder, Representative Noah Wenger, and Pennsylvania Agriculture Secretary Penrose Hallowell.

These important individuals traveled considerable distances to come to our farm market greenhouse to witness Governor Thornburgh's signing of the Farm Inheritance Tax Reduction Bill.

I feel highly honored and am most grateful.

GOVERNOR INKS FARM TAX BILL IN MILLERSVILLE

by Rick Sauder
Intelligencer Journal Farm Writer

In another effort to protect the family farm from development pressures, Gov. Dick Thornburgh signed a bill in Millersville Wednesday afternoon that gives farmers a break when paying inheritance taxes.

The signing ceremony took place at the Century Farm of Amos H. Funk, Millersville R1, who is chairman of the Lancaster County Agricultural Preserve Board and a long-time preservation advocate.

The new law will allow farms subject to inheritance tax to be assessed according to their value as agricultural land rather than as a development property on the open market.

To be eligible for the tax break, the inheriting farmer must maintain his land in agriculture.

Thornburgh said the bill will prevent farmers from being forced to sell prime agricultural land in order to pay the six percent inheritance tax based on the value the land might have if used for other purposes.

"It is a minor change in the law, but a major change in direction," said Thornburgh as a crowd of government, business and farm officials looked on.

"The pressures of urban sprawl, inflation and taxation have been pushing families off the farm," he said. "This law will help discourage the commercial or residential development of prime agricultural and forest reserve land."

Thornburgh went on to praise the farming community and its contribution to the state's economy. Farming is the second leading industry in the Commonwealth.

The law is one of a series of legislative efforts by the General Assembly to slow the loss of prime farmland in the state. Earlier this year, a bill was passed allowing the establishment of agricultural districts.

There was no clear picture Wednesday of what the inheritance tax amendment will mean to farmers in terms of dollars and cents.

The bill's prime sponsor, Rep. Joseph R. Pitts, Chester County, said his legislation contains no guidelines for determining either the "market value" or "use value" of land. Making that determination will be placed in the hands of each county's board of assessments, according to Pitts.

Rep. Gibson Armstrong, Refton, a co-sponsor of the bill, said Lancaster County is "on the edge" of areas surrounding Philadelphia where market value is significantly higher than agricultural value.

The 1978 Census of Agriculture placed the average value of farmland here at $3,375 per acre, but farms in prime locations have been sold at public auction for more than $8,000 per acre.

Those prices, however, reflect the effects of farmers bidding against developers for land desirable to both interests.

Millersville Lions Club

This is a presentation I made on January 13, 1981, to the Millersville Lions Club at Andy's Catering, Manor Street, Lancaster, Pennsylvania. My subject: Farmland Preservation.

When Bill Miller invited me to speak to you tonight, he was not too specific as to the subject. He indicated it would be all right if I spoke on conservation-preservation of farmland or any other subject I might choose. He certainly did not make it too difficult for me.

Perhaps, after the scary robbery that took place in our home on the night of December 14, I should discuss the importance of adequate security to prevent armed robbery. However, I want to assure you as soon as it is possible, I want to erase from memory the sight of those three young armed hoodlums advancing toward Esta and me with guns drawn after they had come in through our kitchen door. Perhaps I never will forget that terrible night.

Therefore, I will not speak to you about the robbery. The subject I have chosen is "How does farmland preservation in Lancaster County and elsewhere and the wise use of land affect members of the Millersville Lions Club?"

Quite likely, if we think about only the next ten to twenty years, we need not be too concerned. Doing nothing may not cause drastic consequences in the short term. Our concern for our children and our grandchildren is something else again. Here, the picture is not at all clear. However, this nation will not run out of food. It would be remembered that the United States exports the production of one out of every three acres of cropland in use today. All we would have to do is reduce exports.

However, there are many people who feel the volume of United States agricultural exports will have to grow and not be reduced in order to offset United States trade deficits incurred because of the high cost of importing oil.

In fiscal year 1978, for example, agricultural exports amounted to $27 billion, while oil imports cost the united States $42 billion. Without agriculture's offsetting influence, the overall United States trade deficit would have doubled.

United States farmers now export agricultural products from 100 million acres of cropland each year . . . twice the acreage dedicated to meet export demand a decade ago. In 1978, United States grain exports accounted for sixty-one percent of the world's grain trading. In 1980, agricultural exports were a record forty billion—the percentage would be still higher.

To meet this growing export demand, the land in crops increased from 333 million acres in 1969 to 376 million acres in 1977. These 376 million acres represent ninety-one percent of all the available cropland in the nation.

What a contrast to the 1950s and 1960s when the federal government paid farmers to idle between thirty-seven and sixty-five million acres each year.

Another problem regarding exports is the problem of how to feed the eighty percent additional people expected to be added to the world population in the next twenty-five years.

It is rather difficult to ignore this problem, especially in light of the fact that even with today's population level, fifteen percent of the world's population (between 400-600 million) human beings regularly go to bed hungry and are never far from starvation.

Added to this problem is the fact that, because of large population increases during the 1970s, these developing countries are losing ground in their own food production efforts. In fact, their per-capita food production in many countries is lower now than it was fifteen years ago. A shocking thought, to say the least!

It has been often said: "Why should we be concerned with the loss of farmland. There is so much of this nation's land not now producing crops that could be converted to cropland." All of us wonder about this as we fly over western United States.

Here again, there are problems. The National Land Use Study, now being conducted by eleven federal agencies at the direction of Congress, revealed that there is a continuing conversion of nearly one million acres of cropland to non-crop uses each year, as well as the loss of two million acres that produce agricultural products and in the future, could be used for cropland, but will never be available due to their conversion to non-agricultural use. This study reveals that the United States is losing at least three million acres of agricultural land each year to non-agricultural use.

Part of this lost agricultural land to other uses could be taken out of the 541 million acres of pasture and range land. This will quite likely happen; in fact, it is estimated that sixty million acres of pasture and rangeland will be converted to cropland in the next twenty years. Although this indeed will make more cropland available for the production of corn, wheat, soybeans, etc., it will reduce the availability of livestock as a result of reduced pastureland by 1.33 billion pounds per year. The result, undoubtedly, will be higher meat prices and this will affect nearly everyone in this room.

One might look at the 370 million acres of forest land in the nation. Incidentally, Pennsylvania has fifteen million acres in forest land. Some might say, "Why not convert some of this forest land to crop production?" This may happen. The problem with this approach: There is a need to have more, not less, producing forest land to meet our nation's lumber and pulp needs in the near future. Any reduction in the supply side can only have one result—higher lumber and pulp prices. Again, this will affect everyone in this room.

If something drastic and meaningful is not done to significantly reduce the conversion of agricultural land to non-agricultural uses, it is inevitable that the costs of producing agricultural products are going to rise drastically and the price of food will rise faster than the average rate of inflation, as a result of the loss of agricultural productivity.

The combination of land losses and increased demand for food products will mean that the land available for commercial agricultural production will be in full use within the next twenty years. The age of "surplus cropland" will be gone, perhaps forever. Again, this will affect everyone in this room in as few as five years, or possibly as early as 1983.

Well, what can be done about the problem? Obviously, we can do very little to prevent the unwise use of land in Illinois, Florida, or California. However, we can do something about it in the borough or city in which we live, or in our own township and in Lancaster County. What is more important, we not only can, we are doing something about this problem.

I would like to cite several examples. When the Millersville Planning Commission and the Borough Council approved the density levels set forth in Manny Murry's planned development across from our farm market, an important forward step was made. Sewer and water facilities are available on this tract, and more people will be housed on fewer acres. I am sure this was not an easy decision for many of the borough officials. This is not the way we have been accustomed to doing things in Lancaster County in the past.

We like single houses with a lawn around our home. Many of us do not want to live too close to our neighbors. In fact, I have a brother and a brother-in-law who each bought an additional lot next to his home. Although they may never admit it, their interest was to control who, if anyone, shall live immediately next to them. This is an attitude shared by many residents in our area and it must be changed if we are to use our land more wisely. Quite likely, it will not be easy!

Another example is Manor Township. After a considerable amount of committee input from farmers and others, Manor Township is nearly ready to declare a portion of the township an agricultural district.

By this action, Manor Township will stay, within this designated agricultural district, an area of approximately 9,000 acres; farming will be the predominate use. Any development in the agricultural district will be restricted to three percent of the land area of each farm. In addition, and very important, a minimum of 20,000 square foot lot size is permitted. This a bit less than one-half acre.

In some townships, the minimum lot size is three acres. This results in great waste of valuable farmland.

Obviously, a farmer in an agricultural district will be restricted in the number of acres that can be sold for development. Ten years ago, Manor Township farmers would never have accepted such an ordinance. Farmers do not like to be told what they can or cannot do with their land. However, today, farmers are even more interested in "the right to farm." Farmers are beginning to realize that in mixing people with animal and fowl, agriculture does not work! Frequently, urban people object to the manure and other smells and the noises that often are present in the day-to-day operation on many of our farms.

Increasingly, ordinances are being proposed that would severely limit the size and location of modern chicken houses, dairy barns, and hog houses. The adoption of such ordinances would make it difficult for many farmers to stay in business. Therefore, slowly but surely, attitudes in Lancaster County, at least, are changing. Farmers are willing to accept some restrictions on the use of their land in return for the farmers' "right to farm," provided recommended best management practices in manure handling and other farm operations are used.

Progress is being made at the county level, also. Early in April 1980, the Lancaster County Commissioners appointed a nine-member Agricultural Preserve Board. This is the first such board appointed in the state and perhaps in the nation.

The purpose of the Board is to assist in the implementation of the County Comprehensive Plan adopted by the county commissioners in 1975.

The long-term goal is to preserve 278,000 acres of our best agricultural land for agricultural use.

The plan would also provide for over 100,000 acres now being farmed to be available for residential and commercial uses. Much of this 100,000 acres is prime farmland—our most fertile soils. However, many of these soils are located along major highways and/or have sewer and water available. It just does not make much sense to attempt to save land so situated. It would be very difficult.

The thrust of the county plan is to preserve for farming reasonably large areas not under severe urbanizing pressures.

Under the Deed Restriction Plan we are proposing, farmers located in an agricultural district in a township will be offered an incentive of $250 per acre if they will voluntarily place a deed restriction on their farm, limiting its use to agricultural production only for at least twenty-five years. After twenty-five years, the property owner may ask for a review, at which time a request to terminate the agreement will be considered. The termination will not be automatic, but will be an option offered to the property owner.

At present population growth levels, our problem is not one of too much industry or too many people. Our problem is one of housing too few people on too many acres of land.

For example, Lancaster County's population growth to the year 2000 is projected at 4,000 new people per year. The County Comprehensive Plan recommends we should house these 4,000 new individuals on 1,000 acres per year, or four people per acre—not an unreasonable goal.

There have been periods in our recent past when Lancaster County lost 8,000 acres of agricultural land to non-agricultural use each year. This agricultural land loss has dropped to somewhere between 3,000 and 5,000 acres in 1979.

However, we can do better. Our goal should be to reduce this conversion to 1,000 acres. If we can do this, we would have enough land for 100 years for residential and commercial growth and still have 278,000 acres preserved for farming. This surely is a goal worth striving for!

You can be assured very little will happen unless we make it happen!

Adams County Extension Association

"Farmland Preservation, What It Will Mean To You," was presented to the Adams County Extension Association, January 22, 1981. The invitation for me to speak was made by my good friend, Adams County Agricultural Agent Tom Piper. My presentation follows:

I appreciate the opportunity to come to Adams County to share with you some of my concerns and my thoughts on this matter of farmland preservation—what it will mean to you.

I am not certain what the level of interest in farmland preservation is in Adams County. It should be high. You have a lot going for you in this county. Over the years you have developed an outstanding fruit-growing industry. The supporting agribusiness establishments are here. There are few anywhere in the state that are better.

You have the processing and marketing services here to move the fruit. You have the fruit lab at Arnesville. You also have so many outstanding farm families in Adams County. The individual I have known best and really appreciate is my long-time friend, Bob Lott. Bob, who has served his county, his state, and now as an NACD director, is making an important contribution at the national level. Then, too, there are Bill Lott, John Peters, John Pityer, their respective families, and, of course, many more. Nearly every year Adams County has a Master Farmer winner. Few counties can claim that honor.

I realize there are other things going on in Adams County beside fruit growing. You have dairying and other specialized agricultural efforts.

Over the past two years, I have gotten to know two members of another outstanding Adams County family, Horace and Dick Waybright. Last month I was able to visit their dairy and manure handling operation for the first time.

I was very impressed with the many innovations used in their methane production and related activities. I was even more impressed with the manner in which they refused to accept all advice and reports indicating the production of methane gas from cow manure cannot be achieved in a cost-effective manner; but, instead, these men looked for reasons why other attempts failed and proceeded to make needed procedural corrections.

Perhaps a lesson can be learned here and applied to efforts to develop a workable plan to preserve agricultural land.

Tom Piper sent me some information on Adams County. The fact that you are first in the state in apple and peach production was not surprising; nor was I surprised to learn that you are first in the value of fruits, nuts, and berries sold. However, I was not aware of the fact that you are first in the number of turkeys sold and third in the state in the number of broilers raised and in egg production.

The $70 million value of agricultural crops and products produced in Adams County is, in itself, an important contribution to the economic health of the county. It should be further pointed out that, if the same multiplier as was used by the Pennsylvania Department of Agriculture in Pennsylvania's RCA report is applied, the presence of agriculture in Adams County could contribute more than one-half billion dollars to the economy of the county each year.

I am not at all sure agriculture is given as much credit as it should have in many of our counties. A great deal of attention is paid to tourism in Adams and Lancaster Counties, and yet, in 1978, farmers spent more for their supplies and other production needs in Lancaster County than the total amount of money spent by tourists in that year.

I am not sure how the numbers would work out for Adams County. Quite likely, they would be similar.

I fear that too often agriculture is taken for granted. Farmers, the production from their farms, and the agribusiness establishments that serve them have been around for years; and the assumption is made they will always be there in the future.

In the southeastern counties of Bucks, Montgomery, and Chester, where the land area in farms has been severely reduced because of urbanizing pressures, some farmers have to drive 75 to 100 miles to get parts for their equipment and other supplies. Implement and feed dealers have moved out due to lack of sales volume.

I asked Tom Piper to send me a copy of your County Comprehensive Plan. I wanted to see what your planning commission projected as the role of agriculture in the future plans for Adams County. I assure you I was pleased with what I saw!

In the first of four major objectives stated in the plan, this statement of purpose was set forth. I will quote from the Plan: "To conserve and protect highly productive agricultural land. Agricultural activity, in addition to being the most appropriate use in many areas, has a direct influence upon other major activities."

In another part of the plan, it is also pointed out: "Local implementation policies will determine the success or failure of the plan."

Under Pennsylvania law in many instances, counties can prepare plans and recommend implementing procedures, but the townships are most often the real implementing bodies, particularly in many land use efforts.

Based on the most recent information I have available, Adams County still has 192,000 acres of land in farms and over 93,000 acres in cropland. This is approximately the same amount of cropland you had available in 1974; therefore, it would not seem you have an immediate problem.

However, there is a problem revealed by the most recent census. This census revealed that in the 1970s, Adams County was one of the ten fastest growing counties in the state, based on the rate of increase in growth.

According to the most recent census figures, with the exception of Bucks County, percentage wise, all ten fastest growing counties in the 1970s were non-metropolitan counties. Monroe, Pike, and Wayne led the list, with growth increases of 33%, 25%, and 21.7%. Wyoming, Perry, Bucks, Butler, Adams, and Indiana all led Lancaster County with 10.6% population increase.

These new settlement patterns could have a very disruptive effect on farmers living in a formerly predominantly agricultural area.

Does Adams County have a farmland preservation problem? I would suggest you may have one. I am not sure where it is, but it is somewhere in the county. Perhaps there are only several townships in which there is a need to guide growth away from the best farmland to other areas.

Perhaps one of the first goals that should be established is: How much farmland should be designated to remain in farming to the year 2000 or 2010? And, where should that land be located?

One of the things I failed to notice in your Comprehensive Plan were areas of agricultural land designated for agricultural use on the Future Land Use Map. I did see large holding areas designated. I have problems with the designation of "holding areas" or farmland-rural residential.

We have thirty-one townships in Lancaster County using the same farmland-rural residential designation in their zoning. I much prefer the procedure used in ten of our townships that have designated certain areas in the township as agricultural districts where agriculture is the predominate use and a farmer may sell, in most cases, a one-and-one-half-acre lot for each twenty-five acres of land in the farm. In return for this restricted use of his land, farmers are not hampered by restrictive ordinances increasingly common in some townships. A farmer's "right to farm" is definitely enhanced in these agricultural districts.

In our county, a farmer living in a farmland-rural residential zoned area could sell his entire farm for development, provided the designated minimum lot size is met. There could then be a situation where 100 homes could be built next to a 60,000-bird laying house and a modern dairy barn, and on the other side, a modern hog confinement barn.

In Lancaster County, with rather high concentrations of animal and fowl agriculture, the problem of mixing people and farming is becoming increasingly troublesome. I am not sure what your situation is here in Adams County. Quite likely, based on census information and your own population projections contained in your County Comprehensive Plan, if you do not have a problem mixing people with agricultural operations at present, you soon may have one.

If there is enough interest in farmland preservation in Adams County, you may want to follow the procedure we used in Lancaster County. We requested that the county commissioners appoint a farmland preservation task force to study the problem and come up with some recommendations. In our case, we had a fifteen-member task force consisting of three farmers, two women, a banker, a builder, and eight other interested individuals.

One of the recommendations you may want to consider is to revise the County Comprehensive Plan, or at least make a new map on future land use needs; and break out some of the county's orchard lands and other productive agricultural lands from the farmland-rural residential designation and designate these areas as areas to remain in agricultural production until 2000 or 2010.

In Lancaster County, we have designated 278,000 acres about sixty percent of the total county's land area to remain in agriculture to 2000, and also have designated 100,000 acres now being farmed to be used for development.

Even if no action is taken at the county level, Adams County farmers and others living in a township where productive farmland is under pressure for development could request their township supervisors to create an agricultural district. Certain legal procedures have to be followed, including township hearings, etc., but it can be done. This was done successfully in Millcreek Township in Lebanon County several years ago.

We hope to persuade one-half of our forty-one townships in Lancaster County to designate agricultural districts in the next five years. This is an important first step.

The nice thing about this approach is that it can be started at once. No new legislation is needed. In addition, it costs very little. The problem, as with all zoning efforts: It is politically vulnerable.

In 1967, Bob Lott and I were appointed to an eighteen-member committee and given the charge by then Governor Shafer to develop a plan to preserve Pennsylvania's agricultural land. In making his charge, he included the following remarks, and I quote: "In the past ten years, more than three million acres of Pennsylvania's farmlands have been converted to other purposes . . . continued loss of prime farmland in this manner will seriously affect our ability to provide food for future needs."

In 1978, eleven years later, then Governor Shapp said this: "In 1960, we had 12.3 million acres in farms. By 1975, Pennsylvania had only ten million acres in farmland, a loss of two million acres in fifteen years."

In 1980, we are told, if current land use trends continue in Pennsylvania, the National Land Use Study, currently being conducted by eleven federal agencies at the direction of Congress, projects that by the year 2000, Pennsylvania will lose an additional two million acres of farmland and have only six million acres of land left for agricultural production. This represents a loss of fifty percent of the State's 1960 farmland acreage in forty years.

With two former governors, the National Land Use Study, and others calling our attention to this very significant loss of farmland in the state, and the implied consequences, why is not more happening?

I believe Marion Deppen stated it well in an answer to a question raised during one of our Agricultural Preserve Board meetings. Marion, as you know, is cooperative extension director for the capitol region. Marion had just told the group that he may have held the first land use meeting in Pennsylvania while he was an assistant county agent in Montgomery County. He held the meeting in the fall of 1953 with more than thirty farmers in attendance.

Aaron Stauffer, vice-chairman of our Agricultural Preservation Board, asked this question: "If you started that early in 1953, why has not more happened?" After reflecting a short time, Mr. Deppen replied, "I suppose it is because farmers value their independence of action and their freedom to do what they want with their land far more than is their concern for the loss of farmland."

I am afraid this attitude hasn't changed a great deal up to this time. To a large degree, especially here in the east, farmers are loners. They want to make decisions independently and not be bound by the wishes of others.

I am not sure how helpful I have been. I have tried to share some of my concerns and my thoughts on this matter of farmland preservation: what it will mean to you.

I am certain very little will happen in Adams County unless the farmers want to preserve certain portions of the county's agricultural land and the supporting industry. The job would be a lot easier if farm prices were more favorable, and I believe they will be. I just hope our costs do not rise faster than our prices.

We plan to start our deed restriction program in one township in Lancaster County. You may wish to concentrate your preservation efforts in one or two townships and see what happens.

County commissioner support is vital. Township supervisor support is very important.

I will leave you with one parting thought. I am certain that if we do not do something to preserve and conserve our productive land resources in this nation, someone at the state or national level will do it for us and, quite likely, it will not be done as well as we could do it at the county or township level. By the year 2000, all surplus cropland will be in use. An annual three-million-acre conversion of cropland to non-crop uses will not be tolerated. It cannot be!!

National Association of Conservation District Directors' Annual Meeting San Francisco

I made the following presentation at the National Association of Conservation District Directors' Annual Meeting on February 2, 1981, held in San Francisco, California. The presentation was made to the Natural Resources and Development Committee.

My sister, Anna Mae Kritscher; her husband, Andrew; and their friend, Jack Pickett, former editor of the California Farmer *magazine, were kind enough to come and hear my remarks.*

Before I discuss Lancaster County's approach to preserving agricultural land, I would like to make it plain that I am aware that what we are proposing will not work everywhere in this nation. It may work in only a few places, or it may work in quite a number of places. However, I am certain it will work in Lancaster County.

I have read with a great deal of interest what has been tried and appears to be working quite well in other parts of the nation.

I am amazed at the apparent success of the large lot size approach: in San Luis Obispo, California, with a minimum lot size of 360 acres; in Weld County, Colorado, with two minimum lot sizes: 80 acres in irrigated areas and 160 acres in non-irrigated areas; in Kendal County, Illinois, in an agricultural area, a sixty-acre minimum lot size is required up from twenty acres in 1977. These lot sizes are as large or larger than many of our Lancaster County farms.

The quarter/quarter zoning in Minnesota is interesting. In this state, five counties and several townships have adopted this system of guiding growth by allowing one dwelling unit, usually less than two acres in size, for every forty acres (1/4 of one-quarter section) or possibly four two-acre lots on 160 acres.

Quite likely, the award for persistence has to go to Walworth County, Wisconsin. Under considerable development pressure from more than nine million people living in nearby Chicago and Milwaukee, Walworth County found it was losing far too much agricultural land to development. After seven years of effort, and more than 500 meetings, an ordinance was adopted that folks in Walworth County could live with.

I am also aware of the fact that in some parts of this nation, land use planning are "dirty words." Jim Bush, a NACD director, and a member of the NACD Outlook Committee, on which I serve, told me recently about a situation in a certain county in Idaho: The three commissioners were defeated for re-election, the Planning Commission was abolished, and the County Comprehensive Plan was torn up. Now, what caused all this furor? The county commissioners attempted to move ahead with a new land use proposal. Moving ahead means different things to different people.

Now, let me tell you about Lancaster County, Pennsylvania. The total land area in the county is 604,000 acres (943 square miles). As of 1980, we had 5,250 farms and just under 400,000 acres of farmland, averaging a bit under eighty acres per farm. The total value of agricultural crops and products produced in the county in 1979 was more than $557 million. Dividing the value of the agricultural production into the farmland acres (400,000) reveals that the average dollar-per-acre production exceeds $1,350.

Clearly, this kind of income is not generated from crop production alone. Although fifty-five percent of our soils are Class I and II soils, less than twenty percent of the value of our agricultural production is generated directly from crop production. The remaining eighty percent of the agricultural income is derived from animal and fowl production. This animal and fowl production totaled more than $460 million in 1979.

Lancaster County ranks first in agricultural production among the nation's non-irrigated counties (our average rainfall is 42 inches).

Our county is the second fastest growing county in the state. Our population now stands at 362,000, with a population growth rate in the 1970s of nearly eleven percent and most of that growth taking place in the rural agricultural townships of the county. Fifty percent of the farm families are of the plain sect—either Amish, Mennonite, or Brethren. They want to retain their farmland.

The 1977 production of the 560 industrial establishments in the county had a value of $3.1 billion.

Lancaster County, tenth in the nation in value of tourism, averages four million visitors per year. In 1978, tourists spent $233 1/3 million in Lancaster County.

Industrial and residential growth, plus the effect of tourism, has placed severe pressure on those 400,000 acres of agricultural land.

In 1975, the county commissioners adopted a County Comprehensive Plan, which designated 278,000 acres of land to be retained in agricultural use, and also designated more than 100,000 acres now being farmed;

but they are near major highways or near sewer and water lines for residential and commercial and industrial development. Now it is great to have a comprehensive plan; the trick is to get it implemented.

Working with the County Planning Commission, our county conservation district has been encouraging townships to create agricultural districts containing at least 1,000 contiguous acres in which farming is the predominant use. Development will be restricted to one one-half-acre lot per twenty-five acres, or about three one-half-acre lots per farm. While this will work for us, it has already proven unsatisfactory for some of the western states where farms are much larger. Nine out of forty-one townships in our county now have designated agricultural districts. Our goal is to have twenty-one townships with designated agricultural districts by 1985.

In April of 1980, the county commissioners appointed a nine-member Agricultural Preserve Board to build on the program established by the county and cooperating townships and our conservation district.

The original thrust of what we chose to call our "Deed Restriction Program" was as follows: The effort to secure covenants or deed restriction would be in three tiers. First, donated covenants would be sought. Where donations were not made over land thought to be significant in the district, the Agricultural Preserve Board would seek to purchase such covenants for a flat fee per acre. The price offered would be significantly less than the "development rights" and would restrict the use of the property to agricultural use only for twenty-five years. The price that will be offered is $250 per acre and can be raised in future years to compensate for increased land values if needed.

In November 1979, a bill generally conforming to this description was introduced in the Pennsylvania legislature. The bill, House Bill 1983, failed to be reported out of the Agriculture and Rural Affairs Committee.

Since we did not get what we wanted, rather than wait for several years, our Pennsylvania legislature does not move very fast on land use legislation; we are going with half a loaf. We are going forward with two of the three parts of our plan.

In a township-created agricultural district, we will offer the voluntary covenant on the land and we will provide the $250 per acre incentive to farmers who voluntarily place a deed restriction on their land, limiting its use to agricultural use only.

Compared to the $3,300 per acre PDR cost in Suffolk County, New York, the projected $2,100 per acre PDR cost in New Jersey, and the nearly $1,000 per acre offer for PDR in Maryland, the $250 incentive payment is not high. It is not high and for this reason, it is affordable.

Even at the $250 per acre, as an incentive, to retain in agricultural use the designated 278,000 acres of agricultural land in Lancaster County, the cost to our county government would be nearly $70 million.

Although there is a great deal of interest in preserving farmland in Lancaster County, I do not think it would be wise to use that $70-million "price tag" to develop additional support for farmland preservation in the county.

The resistance to increased taxes is present nearly everywhere in this nation. It has been said, "The best way to eat an elephant is one bite at a time." We hope to use this one-bite-at-a-time approach to sell our program.

Our goal is to preserve relatively large contiguous areas, 1,000 to 5,000 acres in size. By providing these large contiguous areas designated as preserves, our plan offers the only real assurance farmers have to provide for themselves "the right to farm."

The designation of these exclusive agricultural preserve areas by the county in cooperation with interested townships is, in my opinion, the reason House Bill 1983 failed to move in the Pennsylvania legislature.

I believe the expression, "Farmers like to have their cake and eat it too," applies here. Farmers want to have the "right to farm," but do not want to forego the sale of all, or part, of their farm for development. Many of them resist being included in the preserve area because they want to retain that right to sell for development. This is true, in spite of the fact that in 1978 and 1979, of all farm sales reported in the State of New Jersey, only one out of 100 were sold for development.

Because of the lack of development potential, property owners inside a proposed preserve area express concern that property values will be severely depressed. There is very little information on how property values are affected by the inclusion in a preserve area.

In the November-December issue of *Aglands Exchange*, Richard Benner discusses the Oregon experience. In 1973, the Oregon legislature passed Senate Bill 100, creating the Land Conservation and Development Commission to oversee a thorough zoning of all lands in the state—a type of state-imposed zoning law.

Although Oregon is the nation's eleventh fastest growing state, as the result of use of exclusive farm zoning areas, or agricultural districts consisting of Class I, II, III, and IV land, and the use of urban growth boundaries into which residential and other development is directed, since 1974 Oregon is one of the states with the lowest rate of converting agricultural land to non-farm uses.

In his summary statement, Mr. Benner makes these points: What makes Oregon's program successful is a combination of zoning, farm value assessment, and a growth strategy that puts lines on a map to separate land needed for development from farmland.

Mr. Benner also points out that farmland, in the exclusive farmland zones, have gone up in value, but only one-half the national rate. For anyone wishing to remain in farming, I am not sure that is all that bad. If you are a farmer-speculator, that is another thing again.

In our part of the country, it is expected by those who have considered it carefully, that farmland inside the preserve area will go up faster than surrounding land because farmers inside the agricultural preserve area will, indeed, "have the right to farm;" they will be removed from developing areas.

Again, in the November-December issue of *Aglands Exchange*, Mr. Edward Thompson, Jr., an attorney and director of National Association of Counties Agricultural Lands Project, took an interesting look at "right to farm" legislation. In one of his opening statements, Mr. Thompson says: "A close reading of these laws seems to indicate that they do not really offer much protection to farmers, and that amending them to provide real immunity from suit or nuisance liability would raise constitutional problems that could render the laws invalid."

Mr. Thompson examines closely the North Carolina "right to farm act" passed in 1979. Similar laws were passed by Delaware, Florida, Georgia, Mississippi, Tennessee, and Washington, and are now being considered by Kentucky and Virginia.

Charlie Boothby brought along copies of the most recent issue of *Aglands Exchange*. Any of you interested in right-to-farm legislation should read Ed Thompson's article. You may not agree with him, but he does raise some interesting points.

He concludes his article with this statement: "The most that can be said for the 'right to farm' laws, based on the North Carolina model, is that they offer just a bit more protection to the farmer than does the common law of nuisance. Whether this increment of protection makes a significant difference to the future security of agriculture remains to be seen. The worst that can be said about the 'right to farm' laws is that if, indeed, they are constitutional, they hold out for farmers a false promise of security that cannot be fulfilled. In this sense, they are a poor substitute for the one method of protecting agriculture from land-use conflicts that offers real hope for its future security and that is discouraging agricultural development in agricultural areas in the first place."

In summary, I would say there certainly are many ways to preserve farmland. What will work for us in Lancaster County may not work for you where you live. I have tried to go into some detail regarding the pre-emptive sale procedure as contained in House Bill 1983; I am certain it will work well in our county when enabling legislation is passed. I have several copies of the bill here if you would like to help yourself to a copy.

Since we cannot get the enabling legislation we want, we will take what we can get and move ahead to save as much of Lancaster County's farmland as we are able to preserve.

The Pennsylvania Young Farmers Association, Hershey, Pennsylvania

I made this presentation to the Pennsylvania Young Farmers Association on February 10, 1981. The meeting was held at the Hershey Motor Inn, Hershey, Pennsylvania.

I appreciate this opportunity to share some of my concerns and thoughts on the preservation of agricultural land with your Pennsylvania Young Farmers Association. No group has a greater stake in this matter than you—young farmers.

Let us take a look at what we have going for us. A recent Louisiana Extension Report reminds us that agriculture is the nation's biggest industry. Its assets total $920 billion, and are equal to nearly three-fourths of the capital assets of all manufacturing corporations in the United States.

Agriculture is also the nation's biggest employer. Between fourteen and seventeen million people work in some phase of agriculture, from growing food and fibre to selling it at the supermarket.

We live in northeastern United States where approximately seventy-five percent of the nation's population reside. The 159,000-plus farmers living in the northeast cannot begin to supply all the food and fibre needs of the more than 53 million people who live here. In the Northeast, we have twenty-five percent of the United States population, a bit over seven percent of the farms, and three percent of the actual farmland.

Our northeast farmers do produce most of the apples and eighty percent of the total dairy products consumed in the region. Eggs and broiler producers do almost as well; however, we fall off drastically in many other areas of agricultural production. As a result of such shortfalls in production, we import trainloads of lettuce from California; truckloads of elongated potatoes from Idaho; and truckloads of hogs, beef, and sheep from the midwest.

At current transportation rates, this is poor business. It costs nearly $3 per hundred to move potatoes from the great northwest to the wholesale docks in New York City. It costs $2.70 to move a hundred-weight of milk from Wisconsin to Baltimore.

Two years ago, it cost 46¢ to move a bushel of corn from Toledo, Ohio, to Lancaster, Pennsylvania, and this has certainly gone up.

Transportation costs have risen so rapidly that there are times when it costs more to transport a head of lettuce from California than the grower received for that lettuce in California.

Quite likely, if we concern ourselves only with the next ten to twenty years, we need not be too concerned. Doing nothing may not cause drastic consequences in the short term. Our concern for our children and our grandchildren is something else again. Here, the picture is not at all clear. However, this nation will not run out of food. It should be remembered that the United States exports the production of one out of every three acres of cropland in use today. All we would have to do is reduce exports.

However, there are many people who feel the volume of United States agricultural exports will have to grow and not be reduced in order to offset United States trade deficits incurred because of the high cost of importing oil.

Farmland Appreciation

The problem with land appreciation is that the increased value cannot be realized unless the farm is sold. A farmer has to sell out to collect.

At a meeting in Texas recently, I was discussing farmland preservation with a friend of mine from Elizabethtown, Kentucky, who owns 1,000 acres of land and rents 1,000 additional acres. He has two sons in college who want to return to the farm.

This friend of mine pointed out that for any farmer who wants to remain in farming, and particularly farmers who have sons coming back to the farm, farmland appreciation has a negative effect on the ability of a farmer to remain in farming, and especially if he wants to expand the farm operation. He went on to point out that the 1,000 acres he rents is costing him more each year because of land appreciation and, in most years, crop prices have not increased sufficiently to make up for this increased rental fee. In addition, when those two sons come back to the farm, quite likely he would like to buy additional acreage. It may be difficult, or impossible, to do this with escalating land prices.

Appreciated land values make it possible for farmers to borrow additional money. This can be viewed as "good news" or "bad news" for farmers. For the careful farm operator, needed new equipment can be purchased, or additional operating capital is made available to permit the farmer to be more effective in the farm operation. For this individual, appreciated land values may be "good news."

For the less efficient operator, purchases of many kinds might be made that are not operationally cost effective; and with increased interest rates, a severe cash flow problem may result and part or all of the farm will have to be sold, as is happening in a number of cases this year in our county. For these individuals, farmland appreciation could be viewed as "bad news."

Quite likely, because of the appreciation of land and other resources, farm debt in relation to net farm income will continue to increase. J. Bruce Bullock, manager of the Farm Credit Systems, Farmbank Research Information and Service, reports that the total farm debt during 1956-1958 was $1.70 for each dollar of net farm income. By 1975, that debt increased to $2.80 per dollar net farm income and now has reached $5.60 for each dollar net farm income. At the depth of the Great Depression in 1933, the ratio was $3.53 for each dollar of net farm income. The present debt load of all United States farmers is over $136 billion, more than two and one-half times as great as just ten years ago. No wonder some farmers are having cash flow problems. (Total United States farm assets: 671 billion.)

What is the solution to this matter of wise land use? Or, in a free competitive society, is there any solution? There are numerous plans and programs to restrict or stop the conversion of agricultural land to non-farm uses. Some of them seem to be working; others have failed.

But, the question still remains: Should a farmer be penalized by losing his options to sell or transfer the land into some other use? If farmland use and sales are to be restricted, why not restrict the use and sales of all lands?

These land-use issues are no more simple or palatable than are energy issues; but, one thing is certain—this country always operates from one crisis to another. When the land crisis fully develops, and we no longer produce more food than we need, the politicians will try to find instant solutions to a problem that cannot possibly be solved in a short time.

Garden Spot Young Farmers

Robert Anderson and Donald Robinson were advisors to young farmers of all ages. Each year they held a series of winter educational meetings for interested farmers. I was invited to speak to this group by Don and Bob on February 18, 1981. My presentation follows:

I appreciate the invitation extended to us by Bob Anderson, working with Don Robinson, and the Eastern Lancaster County School District, to participate in the Adult Farmer meeting to discuss farmland preservation.

First, I would like to commend farmers and other interested citizens living in Brecknock Township, the Brecknock Township Planning Commission, and the Brecknock Board of Township Supervisors on the progress you have made in your efforts to designate an area in the township as a district zoned for agriculture in Brecknock Township.

To those of you who live in other townships in the school district, I would like to suggest that you consider creating a district zoned for agriculture in the township in which you live. A district zoned for agriculture is an area where agriculture is the predominate use, and development in the agricultural district is limited by using the sliding scale approach as suggested in the Brecknock Ordinance; or one-half acre for each twenty-five acres in the farm as used in the farm as used in the East Donegal Township Ordinance; or one lot every twenty-five years, as proposed in the soon-to-be acted upon Ephrata Ordinance.

More and more Lancaster County farmers are beginning to support this agricultural district approach. Based on the two hearings I have attended in Manor Township in which I live, Manor Township will soon designate approximately 9,600 as a district zoned for agriculture, allowing a farmer to sell off three percent of his farmland acreage for development up to a total not to exceed 60,000 square feet, or about three lots per farm.

I am sure some of you, after reading about the Manor Township hearings in the newspapers, may have gotten the idea that Manor Township farmers are against the creation of a district zoned for agriculture. This is not true! Some very vocal individuals did speak out against the idea at the first hearing.

At the second hearing, most comments concerned reducing the proposed setback to 250 feet and other changes in the ordinance that would make it easier for farmers to farm in the district zoned for agriculture. The problem with agricultural districts is that they are relatively new. People do not know what to expect.

One of the very strong arguments for the creation of an agricultural district in a township is that the designation of these districts, and the reduction of the development potential in these districts, is the one sure way by which township officials, working with farmers and with the support of farmers, can assure all farmers living in a district zoned for agriculture the "right to farm." The "right to farm" is very high on the list of what farmers want and need.

I believe a "right to farm" bill will be passed by the Pennsylvania legislature. Townships like Brecknock, Ephrata, and Manor will remove from their ordinances language that would make it difficult for farmers to farm.

However, unless townships adopt a district zoned for agriculture ordinances that prevent the conflicts between farmers and non-farmers—conflicts over incompatible uses of land that arise when too many residential dwellings are mixed with working farms—farmers will be plagued by an increasing number of civil suits, suits brought directly by the non-farm residents against the farmer, civil suits that eventually may be won by the farmer, but at considerable cost to the farmer, not only in time lost in court, but in expensive legal fees as well.

One Lancaster County farmer spent $6,000 in legal fees during a number of zoning board hearings and other meetings, attempting to get a permit to build a 500-hog farrowing house. He won the case, but decided not to build the structure because of the possible continuing harassment by his non-farm neighbors. "You know we farmers are getting more neighbors and fewer friends."

Most townships in Eastern Lancaster County School District have the rural residential zoning classification for those areas in which much of the farmland is located.

In some of the townships this zoning is working fine, principally because farmers living in the townships refuse to sell their land for non-farm uses. However, most zoning ordinances will not prevent a farmer from selling to a developer. The developer could then build homes on the entire farm, provided the minimum lot zoning requirements is met. Thus, it is possible to build a considerable number of homes mixed in among working farms. The result is bound to be conflict and trouble sooner or later.

There are some townships in which some of the county's best farmland is located that require a minimum lot size of three acres for a house. Three acres for a home seems like a waste of good farmland. The one-half-acre lot size makes more sense to me. Does it really matter if the lot size is one-half acre or three acres? When one looks at a single transaction, the difference does not seem that great.

However, when you consider providing homes for the 4,000 new people expected to be added to the county's population each year to the year 2000, the differences are very great.

Today, the average persons per household has dropped to 2.8 per household. The 4,000 annual increase in the county population will require nearly 1,500 homes per year. If these new homes are placed on three-acre lots, nearly 4,500 acres would be required annually. However, if a bit over one-half acre per house is used, less than 1,000 acres would be needed.

Projecting the use of these lot sizes forward, the larger lot sizes would use up all of the 368,000 acres now being farmed in eighty-one years. Whereas, the smaller lot size would provide for all the needed growth for 100 years and still have 278,000 acres left in agricultural production. With these choices before you, there should be little doubt that we should make an all-out effort to guide growth in Lancaster County.

Some of you may say, "Many of these new people will not come out and build on our farmland. They will choose to live in the city, boroughs, or towns." There was a time when this was true; however, today, many cities are losing population. According to the most recent census figures in Lancaster County, in the four suburban townships near the city of Lancaster, the average rate of population growth decreased from twenty-five percent in the 1960s to twelve percent in the 1970s.

In seven of the very rural townships in our county, the average growth rate increased from fifteen percent in the 1960s to forty-one percent in the 1970s.

These new settlement patterns could have a very disruptive effect on farmers living in a formerly predominant agricultural area. This is the reason we are urging the adoption of agriculturally zoned districts in Lancaster County.

Pennsylvania State Association of Township Supervisors, Pittsburgh, Pennsylvania

Gilbert L. Longwell, Jr., special projects director for the Pennsylvania State Association of Township Supervisors, invited me to speak at their annual meeting held at the Pittsburgh Hilton on April 15, 1981. My assigned subject was "Farmland Preservation." Under Pennsylvania law, this group of individuals is very powerful, especially in the area of farmland preservation.

Naturally, I was delighted to speak to them. My presentation follows:

First, I would like to assure you I appreciate this invitation to participate in your state convention. I consider it a privilege and an opportunity. It is a privilege because I consider your organization one of the most important organizations in the state. It is an opportunity because I **now** believe you, the township supervisors, are the only group who can do something meaningful about the conversion of so much of our productive farmland to non-agricultural uses.

Back in 1967, I was appointed to an eighteen-member committee and we were given the charge by then Governor Shafer to develop a plan to preserve Pennsylvania's agricultural land. In making his charge to the committee, he included the following remarks: "In the past ten years, more than three million acres of Pennsylvania farmland have been converted to other purposes. Continued loss of prime farmland in this manner will seriously affect our ability to provide food for future needs."

I assure you, serving on that committee was a learning experience for me. Although we did produce a good-looking report, I do not think our efforts resulted in the preservation of much farmland.

As I look back, I believe much more would have been accomplished if then Governor Shafer would have made his appeal for help to the township supervisors of Pennsylvania at their state convention.

I say this because in 1978, eleven years later, at a land use conference held at the Penn Harris Motor Inn, then Governor Shapp made this statement: "In 1960, we has 12.3 million acres in farms. By 1975, Pennsylvania had only ten million acres in farmland, a loss of over two million acres in fifteen years."

In my opinion, Governor Shapp was also talking to the wrong people; or, putting it differently, he did not make his appeal to the one group in our state who can really turn things around in our farmland preservation efforts. Governor Shapp, also, should have requested help from Pennsylvania's township supervisors.

Now in 1980, twelve years after the Governor Shapp statement, the National Agricultural Land Study, conducted by eleven federal agencies at the direction of Congress, made the following projection—not a prediction; there is a difference. "If the trends existing in Pennsylvania through the years 1967-1977 continue, by the year 2000, Pennsylvania will lose one-half of the agricultural acreage that was available for farming in 1960." Putting it differently, the 12.3 million acres in agricultural production in 1960 will be reduced to six million acres by the year 2000—a fifty percent loss in forty years.

I know you township supervisors can do something to stop this trend, if you will. You can do things in your townships that were not being done during that period, 1967 to 1977. There are a number of things you can do to guide growth away from our best farmland. However, I would like you to consider one method that I feel could be quite helpful, and that is the delineation of zoned agricultural districts in your township. In these zoned agricultural districts, agriculture would be the predominate use. Other uses would be restricted, just as other uses are restricted in those areas zoned for industrial development and commercial uses.

There are numerous examples of this zoned agricultural district concept now in use in Pennsylvania. There are nine zoned agricultural districts in Lancaster County; eleven in York County; at least two in Berks County and Millcreek Township in Lebanon County.

Although the language is different in many of these township ordinances, the one prevailing thread running through all of them is the restriction of development in that part of the township where soils are productive, where development pressures are not yet too great, and, most important of all, where farmers indicated a desire to use the land for farming rather than speculation.

I would quickly point out that it has been said, "If you scratch a farmer deep enough, you will find a land speculator." I believe for many farmers, this may be true.

However, increasingly more and more farmers are willing to give up that speculative value of their farmland that might accrue to them some day for the right to farm today. The right to farm may be fully afforded by an ordinance passed by a municipal or other governmental body, but the right to farm assured by having reasonably large contiguous areas designated for the agricultural use and in which development is restricted offers much more protection for the farmer.

Quite likely, the reason this zoned agricultural district concept has not been used more extensively is, first, there are some who think preserving agricultural land in Pennsylvania, or particularly in your township, is not all that important. Food and fibre can be grown elsewhere. However, all over this nation, development is taking place in every state and most often, on the most productive agricultural land. I can expand on that during the question period if you like.

The second and most important reason the zoned agricultural district approach has not been used is because it is not easy to implement.

In the past, farmers have opposed this concept, referring to it as a taking without just compensation. You recall I said earlier: If you scratch a farmer deep enough, you may find a land speculator. However, as more and more urban people move out into our rural areas, quite likely more and more civil suits will be brought against the farmer, protecting against the smells, noises, and other perceived nuisances objectionable to them—suits the farmer may win because of existing right-to-farm ordinances. However, the farmer will have to pay his attorney and he will surely spend some time in court when he would much prefer to be in the field. Then, too, there is the matter of harassment—snowmobiles, motor bikes, bottles, and cans.

I would now like to suggest a number of things you township supervisors might consider at your next meeting. No new legislation is needed. First, consider the National Agricultural Land Study Projection in Pennsylvania is projected to lose another two million acres of agricultural land by the year 2000 if something is not done to alter the trend during 1967 to 1977. Again, let me repeat that you supervisors can make a difference if you decide to help.

Why not test the waters in your own township. Why not do what the supervisors in Manor Township and Warwick Township in Lancaster County did. In these townships, a special committee of farmers was appointed as advisors to the township planning commission to see if there is interest in preserving farmland in the township; and if so, let them propose a plan to do so. In most townships, very little can be done without the support of farmers.

The following story, written by John Risser, appeared in the June 1980 issue of The Susquehanna *magazine, published by the* Susquehanna Times and Magazine. *It is used with their permission.*

Why Amos Funk Has Worked Hard to Preserve Farmland

by John Risser

Before Amos Funk became deeply concerned about farms being sold for residential development, he was very active in the soil conservation movement. In fact, he was one of the pioneers in soil conservation in Lancaster County in the 1930s. He talked his father, also named Amos, into terracing their family farm and planting rows along contours to keep the soil from washing away.

Slowly, over the years, Amos has succeeded in building up the topsoil on his farm, and has used his own farm as a model to teach other farmers the value of soil conservation. From the 1930s through the 1950s, Amos Funk became known far and wide as a soil conservationist and was appointed by the U.S. Secretary of Agriculture to soil conservation commissions.

Meanwhile, Lancaster County was growing industrially and, as a result, increasing in population. More and more farmland was being sold for suburban development. The loss of farmland from 1954 to 1964 was only about 3,000 acres per year, but from 1964 to 1969 the loss approached 8,000 acres per year.

Amos Funk, the soil conservationist, became aware that the most serious threat to the soil of Lancaster County was not erosion but the conversion of farms into residential developments.

What was most disturbing about this change in land use was that the very best soils for agriculture were the ones being sold for development. The richness of Lancaster County soil has been recognized for centuries; Lancaster County, even with severe losses from its best farm acreage over the last twenty years, still leads the non-irrigated counties of the nation in the dollar value of its agricultural production.

Amos asks, "Can the U.S. economy afford a loss in agricultural productivity? This year, the U.S. is exporting 33 billion in agricultural products, enough to make up half the cost of the country's oil imports. Last year the United States' grain exports accounted for 61 percent of the world's grain trading.

"How about our moral obligation to all countries, including the developing countries that depend on us for food.... Every time we lose a couple million acres of cropland, there are a million people who aren't going to be fed."

Most people literally don't know where their food comes from. Amos Funk, of course, has always known. When he took over his family's farm outside of Millersville, he devoted it to production of fruits and vegetables. Getting up often at four a.m., he and his wife, Esta, used to "stand" in as many as thirteen different farmers' markets in the area. In 1963 he opened his own market on his farm, which is now operated by his son Fred. Over the years, he has derived great satisfaction from hearing his customers tell him how much they liked his celery, asparagus, strawberries, etc.

He keeps in close touch with agricultural experiment stations, and every year tries out newly-developed hybrid fruits and vegetables. Always, he is thinking of his customers, of what they will like to eat. For Amos Funk, farming is a way to serve people.

Amos's liking for people must have a lot to do with his untiring work to save farmland. His friend since boyhood, Nelson Wallick, calls Amos a "philanthropist."

Aaron Stauffer, supervisor of Ephrata Township and vice-chairman of the Agricultural Preserve Board (of which Amos is chairman), says Amos is a "unique fellow." Aaron says that Amos once told him, "If I can be instrumental in preserving this prime agricultural farmland, I will be ready to die and feel I have made my contribution to mankind."

Nelson Wallick sees Amos's work to preserve our farmland as growing out of a sense of "heritage." Amos lives on the same farm that his father, also Amos H. Funk, and his grandfather, Amos G. Funk, farmed before him. Amos's ancestors have lived in Lancaster County since 1711. Nelson says, "Amos doesn't want to see our heritage lost. He wants to preserve the heritage handed down to us. He wants to keep on handing it down and, if possible, to hand it down in a better condition than we received it."

Amos's grandfather, as well as his father, exerted a strong influence on his life. His grandfather, more than his father, shared Amos's joy in raising fruits and vegetables. Amos's sister, Grace (Mrs. H. H. Kauffman), says that her grandfather planted trees not for his own pleasure, but for other people's pleasure, including the people still to be born.

At a meeting in Ephrata Township, where Amos presented the plans of the Agricultural Preserve Board to farmers, architect Charles Conrad, also a member of the board, talked about "stewardship" of "God-given" land. It is possible that Amos's motivation in preserving farmland may be partly religious, too. At least, he is a very active churchman, being president of the board of trustees of Grace United Methodist Church in Millersville; but Amos does not wear his religion on his sleeve, and does not mention God in his many talks on saving land.

In addition to appreciating the economic and social value of land,

and possessing a very deep sense of the heritage of Lancaster County, Amos Funk has at least one other characteristic necessary for his unceasing effort to save our farmland—courage. Fortunately, it is becoming more fashionable to speak up for saving the farmland of Lancaster County, but when Amos Funk first spoke up, his was a lone voice, aggravating to some powerful economic interests.

There is an underlying toughness in this gentle and humane man who speaks in a calm and reasoned voice, and relies more on logic than emotion in his crusade to save farmland.

This same toughness was evident in an earlier part of Amos's career, which most people today have never heard of. At the old Manor Township High School, Amos Funk was once known as a star athlete. He played basketball with Nelson Wallick and Sherman Hill (the former state legislator from Millersville) on the team which won the county and district championships in 1929. Amos had developed a shot which was written about in the Philadelphia papers. Starting with his back turned to the basket, he would leap, turn in the air, and get it off with both hands. He was captain of the freshman basketball team at Penn State, where he studied economics. He was also state champion in pole vaulting, establishing a record that stood for many years.

What most impressed his coaches and fellow athletes was the amount of effort Amos put into practicing. He was never content with his present level of performance, and was always trying to better it. Sherman Hill remembers that Amos ran the several miles from his farm to the school every day to improve his condition.

Amos says, "I have always liked a challenge." Taking on the impersonal, seemingly irresistible economic forces that were transforming his native county from the "garden spot" it used to be called, into an endless suburbia, was certainly a challenge. Amos has shown the same pluck in battling rampant development that he used to show in athletics.

Amos's persistence seems to be succeeding in farm preservation, just as it used to succeed in sports. At the recent meeting of the planning commission of Ephrata Township, the commissioners and the farmers attending responded favorably to his presentation of the plans of the Agricultural Preserve Board to create agricultural preserves by means of deed restrictions limiting land use to agriculture.

An elderly farmer with snow-white hair and sunburned skin was asked by Township Supervisor Aaron Stauffer, "Would you sell your land to a developer?"

"No," said the elderly farmer, with some disgust in his voice.

"Why not?" asked Stauffer.

"Because it goes against the grain," said the elderly farmer.

Amos Funk, listening, grinned broadly.

Farmer Attitudes and Their Effect on Putting Together a Deed Restriction Program in Lancaster County

I made this presentation to the Lancaster League of Women Voters on September 15, 1981. My presentation follows:

During the past fifteen years, I have read about, talked to many people about, and attended many meetings to learn about ways to preserve Lancaster County's farmland and the important agricultural industry it supports.

The question might be asked, "Why is Amos Funk so interested?" I suppose I am so interested in what happens to Lancaster County's farmland because our land and our people are so special.

Lancaster County's farmland is twice as fertile as the average of all the rest of Pennsylvania's farmland. Fifty percent of the agricultural production in the county is produced on farms operated by Mennonite, Amish, or Brethren farmers. Most of them want to retain their land in agricultural use.

As many of you know, Lancaster County is the leading non-irrigated county in the nation. The value of the county's agricultural production now has jumped to nearly two-third of a billion dollars in 1980.

Several weeks ago, our Lancaster County Conservation District hosted 250 Louisiana bankers and conservation farmers. We arranged a brief tour of the county and visited five Amish farms.

Most Louisiana farmers on the tour had farms ranging in size from 400 acres to more than 4,000 acres. The question asked most frequently by the folks from Louisiana was "How can these farm families make a living on sixty to eighty acres?" Of course, the answer is, they use their land intensively and carefully.

The average per-acre gross return on our 5,200 Lancaster County farms is more than $1,500 per acre. Although eighty percent of this income is derived from animal and fowl production, adequate land is needed to support our dairy, livestock, and poultry industry. Gross income from cotton production in Louisiana is between $500 to $750 per acre.

In addition to the above comparison, you may find the following comparisons interesting:

In 1978:
- The value of Lancaster County's hog production ($18.1 million) was greater than the total value of the entire state of New York ($17.4 million) and greater than the value of the combined hog production of the entire states of Delaware and New Jersey ($17 million).
- The value of layers and eggs produced in Lancaster County ($43.9 million) was greater than the value of the combined production of the entire states of Delaware, New Jersey, and West Virginia ($38.4 million).
- The value of Lancaster County's dairy products ($113.5 million) is greater than the value of the combined dairy production of the states of Delaware, New Jersey, and West Virginia ($108.9 million).

Yes, I repeat, our land and our people are indeed special.

I would point out we get this agricultural production with very little use of irrigation. In contrast, eighty-five percent of all the water used in California is used for irrigation. In Lancaster County, less than two percent of the water used is used for irrigation.

Irrigation requires energy, a lot of energy. In fact, more than five times as much energy is required to irrigate a crop of corn in Nebraska than is required to plant, care for, and harvest that corn. If and when energy costs increase, undoubtedly irrigation costs again will increase dramatically.

Transportation costs, an insignificant cost consideration in the past, is becoming increasingly important to those of us who live in the east. In fact, there are times when it costs more to transport a case of lettuce to the east coast than the California grower received for the lettuce at harvest time.

The question might be asked: If Lancaster County farmers have all these things going for them, why is it a problem to preserve farmland? There are a number of reasons, and I will attempt to speak to some of them.

The first problem that surfaces when one talks to a farmer about preserving farmland is low prices for farm products of all kinds. While most folks are paying more for many food items at the supermarket, farmers are getting very little of that increase. If you work for the county or in most establishments in the County, quite likely you received salary or wage increases of at least seven percent to eight percent in 1980. The average United States farmer took a decrease of twenty percent to twenty-five percent in the net income received, as compared to 1979. Unfortunately, 1981 will not be much better as things look now.

United States Secretary of Agriculture John Block stated in the August 17 issue of *U.S. News and World Report* that he lost money on hogs on his farm in Illinois during the past two years. He also pointed out cattlemen faired even worse.

Some poultrymen in Lancaster County with 60,000 laying hens lost $1.50 per bird in 1980. Few, if any, of us can withstand a $90,000 annual loss for more than one year.

This ability and willingness by farmers to produce abundantly, even at times to their own disadvantage, is a contribution to low cost food made by our farmers in behalf of our urban neighbors which, in many instances, is not fully understood and not adequately appreciated.

If the question is asked, "Why do farmers continue to produce so abundantly?" the answer is simply that a farmer is an eternal optimist. We are sure next year will be better. As an example, Aaron Stauffer continues to tell his son, Clark, that prices and farm profitability will get better soon, and Clark continues to ask the question, "When?"

Another problem we have when we are trying to persuade a farmer to keep his or her land in agriculture for an extended period of time is the problem of the property's potential value when sold for development, as compared to the possible reduction of the rate of appreciation when a farm is located in an agricultural preserve area where development is restricted or excluded.

At least some of you have heard the expression: "This is a good farm; it has a lot of road frontage;" or, "the price of the farm is not too high because it has a lot of road frontage." These are expressions I have heard since childhood. So have most young and older people living in most rural communities.

Now, when one hears a thing often enough, one starts to believe it and, in this instance, it becomes part of one's attitude regarding land and land values.

The ability to sell part of a property for development quite easily could influence one's decision to buy a property and, thus, it becomes one of your rights as an owner. The right to sell for development is a right many farmers do not wish to give up. It seems to me, very little has been done to date to change this attitude of farmers; however, we are making a start.

Using some farm sales' records of transactions that are not father to son or daughter, properties over ten acres in size that are used for farming, and from which the value of the buildings were excluded, it was found that averaging these sales, farmland increased in value from $861 per acre in 1967 to $3,199 per acre in 1979. If the values are rounded off to $900 per acre in 1967 and $3,200 per acre in 1979, based on the 1967 land value of $900 per acre in Lancaster County, farmland sold for farming and not for development has more than tripled in value in twelve years.

Putting it differently and, again, based on the 1967 value of $900 per acre, farmland in the county has appreciated more than twenty percent per year in the past twelve years.

As for the opportunity to sell for development, in New Jersey in 1977 and 1978, and in Lancaster County in 1979, less than one farm in 100 was sold for development. Putting it differently, a farmer's chances to sell for development are one in 100. In most cases, there is no assurance when that big price will be offered by a developer.

However, by joining other farmers in a preserve area in which development is restricted, and in which farming is the predominant land use, farmers who want to farm very likely will gain more than they lose by being so located.

These are some of the things we are pointing out to our Lancaster County farmers. It is important to convince farmers that preserving their farmland will benefit them, their children, and grandchildren. It is not easy, but we will keep trying.

I wish to thank the League of Women Voters for holding this meeting. I especially want to thank Christine Brubaker and her committee for their contribution. We need a great amount of help if we are to be successful in putting together a deed restriction program in Lancaster County. We hope the League will continue to help in this effort.

I would like to conclude my remarks with a written statement by Bob Colver in the *North Carolina Charlotte News*. Mr. Colver writes: "We have in this county a resource of land and water greater than any other nation on earth. And we have had the genius to develop it. The question now is, "Do we have the wisdom to keep it?"

"We are a young country compared to India or China. Our agricultural system developed when land was plentiful and labor scarce," reminded Poehlman.

"What would be our land and population situation when we are as old as India or China? Or just fifty years from now? Individually, we can't have much influence on increasing food production in India, Bolivia, or Mali, but we can have some influence on maintaining a productive agriculture at home."

Speech to the National Farm City Council

At a regional seminar of the National Farm City Council, held at the Marriott Inn, Harrisburg, Pennsylvania, on May 29, 1981, I made the following presentation:

Following dinner last night, we heard Robert Rodale share with us his concern for the future of agriculture in Pennsylvania.

He is concerned about the rapid conversion of farmland to other uses in this state, and the alarming loss of the productive capacity of the land as the result of severe erosion.

There are those who may dispute the findings of the study conducted by Mr. Rodale's organization. However, the recently completed National Agricultural Lands Study conducted by eleven federal agencies at the direction of Congress, arrived at similar conclusions. Both studies were based on the same premise.

The Rodale Study concluded: "If the amount of land being farmed continues to decline as it has since 1950, Pennsylvania will have no farms by the year 2030."

The National Agricultural Land Study concluded: "If the trends existing between 1967-1977 continue, Pennsylvania will lose fifty percent of the acreage in farms in 1960 by the year 2000. The 12.3 million acres in farms in 1960 will be reduced to six million acres in the year 2000—a fifty percent loss of farmland in forty years. Quite likely, the remaining six million acres will be gone by the year 2030."

The key words here are: If present trends continue, certain things will happen. However, a few new things are already happening. House Bill 143 is making good progress in the Pennsylvania legislature. This is good! This is important because it will be one of the first major pieces of land-use legislation ever enacted when it becomes the law of the Commonwealth.

The language in Section II of the bill is especially significant: "It is the declared policy of the Commonwealth to conserve and protect and to encourage the development and improvement of its agricultural land for the production of food and other agricultural products."

I wish the bill were a bit stronger. I wish the bill would require a greater degree of contiguousness in the agricultural area. I worry about the ease with which a farmer may sell his property in the preserve area for development.

However, this is what most farmers are telling their farm organizations and their legislators. We farmers want to preserve farmland, but don't interfere with our right to sell for development, if the opportunity presents itself.

I do not think farmers can have it both ways. Farmers cannot have their cake and eat it too.

Looking at the situation from the farmer's point of view, it is not easy for a farmer to make a commitment to keep his or her land in agricultural use when it is so difficult to make a profit these days in any farming enterprise. Prices are so low in comparison to production costs.

In the March 1981 issue of the *Agricultural Report* from the Federal Reserve Bank in Chicago, it was pointed out that hogs were marketed at a loss in fifteen out of the past twenty months.

Steer feeders faired even worse, experiencing losses in eighteen of the past twenty months, averaging a loss of nearly $80 a head in January and February of 1981.

Recent action in Washington regarding dairy support prices will surely have an impact on dairy farmers.

The appreciation of farmland at twice the rate of inflation also adds to the problem of farmland preservation. Why should a farmer dedicate his or her land to remain in agriculture for a certain number of years when, according to one study, the appreciation of farmland over a five-year period averaged 1.6 times greater than the net income derived from farming the land—net income that was realized as a result of the farmers back-breaking labor, his management skills, and his risk taking.

I suppose the reason we farmers keep going is because we are eternal optimists. We are sure things will get better, and I believe things will get better and soon.

In this period of low prices and high land appreciation rates, how do we develop interest in preserving farmland? First, it must be realized that not all the land in Pennsylvania will be needed for development for a long time to come. Naturally, it will be used up much more quickly if leap-frog development continues.

In Lancaster County, if we could guide growth and use land more wisely and follow the guidelines set forth in our County Comprehensive Plan, increasing the average housing density of four people per acre—not an unreasonable goal—we could provide for the projected annual population growth of 4,000 people in the county and for the land needed for commercial and industrial growth for the next 100 years and still have 278,000 acres of our best farmland left for farming.

In the past, we have not done very well. According to United States Census figures, during 1969 to 1974, Lancaster County lost 7,000 acres each year to development of all lands. This translates not to four people per acre, but to 1.75 acres per person. What a waste of our land resource!

Happily, we are doing better now; we are losing 4,000 and 5,000 acres per year, still too much, but better.

In 1967, when I first started thinking about farmland preservation, as a member of Governor Shafer's Committee on the Preservation of Pennsylvania's Agricultural Land, I thought agricultural districts were the way to go. I so testified at a number of hearings held in Pennsylvania. The legislature felt Act 319—the Clean and Green Bill—would best meet the State's needs at that time. I supported that effort!

I later supported the concept of the purchase of development rights. Although this idea received considerable verbal support, it has not been too successful. This is true largely because of the perceived high cost of this program.

Some Maryland farmers have been willing to accept development-right values as low as $1,000 per acre. Perhaps at this level the purchase of develop easements program can move forward in Maryland.

Still, a great deal of public money will be required to purchase large viable areas of farmland. At the $1,000 per acre rate, more than $270 million would be needed to preserve the area designated to remain in agriculture in Lancaster County. This is more than five times the $50 million bond issue recently proposed and then withdrawn in New Jersey. The funds were to be used for the retention of agriculture in New Jersey and was slated to be put on the November ballot.

Royd Smith, a Frederick County, Maryland, leader, speaking in this room on January 29 at the Agricultural Leadership Conference, pointed out that, in his opinion, there is too much worry and apprehension about adequate funding for the Maryland program.

In Frederick County, Maryland, they plan to control development and guide growth by county zoning, and only use the purchase of the development rights for special cases.

This is about where I come down at this time. We have to use the tool of zoning at this time because it is about the only affordable tool we have. I did not think this way as late as November 1979. I thought zoning was a taking without just compensation and, I suppose, I now say zoning is taking without adequate compensation. Many farmers put it much more strongly.

Granted, zoning is a temporary solution, and it is politically very vulnerable. However, like it or not, in most places where it has been tried, it has worked. It is a start, hopefully, toward something better.

The State of Oregon's imposed zoning law has been in effect since 1974, and has worked rather well. Although Oregon is the eleventh fastest growing state in the nation, as a result of the use of "Exclusive Farm Zoning" areas and the use of urban growth boundaries into which residential and other development is directed, since 1974, Oregon is one of the states with the lowest rate of farmland conversion to other uses in the nation.

It has been suggested that what makes the Oregon program successful is a combination of zoning, farm value assessment, and a growth strategy that puts lines on a map to separate land needed for development from farmland.

There are a number of successful zoning efforts working well in Pennsylvania, a few of them since 1974—Millcreek Township in Lebanon County; Heidelberg and Middle Heidelberg Townships in Berks County; and a number of townships in York County.

In Lancaster County, twenty of our forty-one townships now have designated agricultural districts where farming is the predominate use and residential development is restricted—as residential development is restricted in industrial or commercially zoned areas. If these townships, zoned agricultural districts, are 1,000 or more acres in size, and if residential development is restricted as it is in East Donegal Township in Lancaster County (to one one-half-acre lot to each twenty-five acres in the farm), this restricted residential growth in a designated agricultural district will indeed provide the farmer with the right to farm, since the number of non-farm residents will be very limited.

The problem with the right-to-farm ordinances, as important as they are to assist the farmer in his efforts to remain in business, I am not aware of any ordinance or any law that will protect the farmer from civil suit brought by a small group of unhappy urban neighbors where there has been an attempt to mix farmers and urban dwellers.

We are doing our best to persuade the remaining twenty-one townships in Lancaster County to designate agricultural districts where there is farmer interest. If there is little or no farmer interest, quite likely no township-zoned agricultural district will be created by the municipal officials.

After needed state-enabling legislation is passed, Lancaster County, through its newly appointed Agricultural Preserve Board, will encourage interested farmers living in an agricultural zoned district, to place voluntary deed restrictions on their land dedicating it to farming for twenty-five years.

This will add a greater degree of permanence to the zoning effort and will help to retain a viable agriculture in the county. Hopefully, there can be maintained the desirable mix of agriculture, industry, and people living together, and yet, with needed separation. It is a worthwhile goal; I trust we can reach it!

Open Market Committee of the Federal Reserve Bank

The Open Market Committee of the Federal Reserve Bank held a round-table meeting at the Lancaster Country Club on November 10, 1981. The subject to be discussed was the farm crisis of 1980-1981. Input from individuals living in Lancaster County was sought. My remarks, presented to the group, were as follows:

The farm sector of the United States economy is in a crisis, a crisis unlike any we have seen for decades—some say since the Depression era.

The situation has been brought on by a drop in United States net farm income from over thirty-two billion in 1979 to less than twenty billion in 1980. 1981 is expected to be only slightly better.

The problem has been made still more difficult by very high interest rates and sharply increased costs of farm production expenses.

Unlike the automobile industry, this situation was not brought about by a lack of productivity. Quite likely, farmers lead all other Americans in their increase in productivity. According to a recent USDA calculation, a market basket of food which takes fifty-three minutes of labor to buy today, took a consumer one and one-half hours of labor to buy in 1950.

Nor is the problem caused by excessively high labor costs. On most family farms in the nation, labor income and net farm income are one and the same. Contrary to the accepted practice in most small and intermediate-sized businesses, relatively few farmers take out a specified weekly or monthly salary from the farm income. Monies for family living are taken from the milk check, from the egg check, or some other like income. In most cases, if the farm income is down, less money will be used for living expenses. During the past two years, many farm families have done with much less of everything.

A Nebraska farmer put it this way: "The more we raise, the less we get." It is different to shut down the assembly line in most farm operations.

Since January 1, 1981, wheat prices are down 58¢ a bushel; corn is down 67¢ a bushel; grain sorghum, by $1.40 a bushel; soybeans $1.51 a bushel; and cotton is down 14¢ a pound.

At a national meeting I attended in Memphis, a friend of mine, who serves on a bank board in Louisiana, told me that unless there is a good cotton crop in his state and the crop can be sold at a good price, fourteen farmers whom the bank has been carrying for more than a year will face foreclosure. I asked him what the bank will do with the farms. He said that quite likely the bank will hold them until an interested buyer is found; and, unless the economy turns abruptly more favorable for agriculture, it is doubtful if many of those farms will be sold to operating farm owners.

From what I can learn, this happening could be repeated in a great many areas of our nation, including Lancaster County. This, then, will add to a problem that concerns me very much—the decline in the number of owner-operator family farms. The United States General Accounting Office, in a report issued recently, pointed out that less than one-half of the United States farmland is owned by the people who farm the land. A 1980 study by a Sioux City, Iowa, Roman Catholic group, dedicated to preserving the family farms, found that in some of Iowa's richest farming counties, as much as seventy-seven percent of the farmland is rented.

The president of the Lancaster County Farmer's Association rents one-half of the land he farms. Another Lancaster County farmer friend of mine rents two-thirds of the acreage he farms.

While it is true that a healthy agriculture should have a mixture of farm-owned and rented land, I am concerned about the increasing amount of rented land and by the fact that land will be less carefully stewarded if it is held by a non-operator owner.

The recent announcement by USDA that food prices might be expected to increase in price up to nine percent in 1982, with little or no increase to farmers, leads me to state that, if this projection turns out to be true, there is great need to do something quickly to improve the economic position of the nation's farmers.

One action that could be very helpful is the lowering of interest rates from three percent to four percent. I appreciate the concern for the effect such action might have on inflation. I believe most farmers would favor limiting the amount of new money made available, if that is possible, and reducing the interest payment on their present debt load.

Interest outlay by United States farmers exceeded $16.5 billion in 1980, a thirty-eight percent since 1979. Net farm income in 1980 was $19.9 billion.

Many Lancaster County dairy farmers are now carrying a debt load of $3,000 to $5,000 per cow. Although I am certain this per-cow indebtedness does not apply to all of the 94,000 cows in the county, it would be interesting to know what the total Lancaster County dairy indebtedness would be.

There is no question that high interest rates and reduced milk prices are causing an increasingly severe problem for many dairymen.

Rapid expansion in the poultry and hog industry in the past three years has required very substantial capital outlays in Lancaster County. Quite likely, most of this expansion is made possible through some form of financing subject to prevailing high interest rates.

Three million laying hens, an eighty-eight percent increase in laying hen numbers since January 1978, now brings the number of laying hens in the county to over seven and one-half million birds. At $9.00 per bird for housing and equipment costs, it is readily apparent that Lancaster County poultrymen have a sizable investment in their poultry industry. At least $27 million have been invested in buildings and equipment in the past three years.

It is also quite likely most of this expansion was made possible through banks or other financing subject to current interest rates.

As of September 1, 1981, the above and other investments in buildings and equipment, plus the relatively high price of Lancaster County's farmland, account for the following levels of indebtedness to major lenders in the county.

These numbers were supplied to me by Mr. Paul Whipple, Customer Finance Manager for Pennfield Corporation.

	Mortgages	All Other Loans
Banks	66.4 million	99.9 million
FHA Farm Credit Assoc.	145.2 million	70.6 million
Equitable Life		
	(55%) 211.6 million	170.5 million (45%)

TOTAL: 382.1 million

It is my opinion, and the opinion of a number of people with whom I have discussed the matter, that for Lancaster County's agricultural industry, and quite likely for agriculture in most parts of the nation, a reduction in interest rates of three percent to four percent would reduce our cost of production and enable most farmers to survive during this very difficult period of low prices for most agricultural products for a period of two, and possibly three, years.

Farmers are so deeply in debt that most farmers would apply any interest savings to the reduction in current loans, which in many cases, is not now possible. Few farmers would borrow money for new capital expansion until prices improve substantially. Most farmers have learned their lesson! At least, I hope they have.

Effect of the New Federalism and Reduced Spending on the Capitol Region

On March 17, 1982, Penn State's Capitol Campus at Middletown, Pennsylvania, held a meeting on The Concerns of the Capitol Region, as related to the "New Federalism" as announced by the federal government. The greatest impact, or problem: How would reduced federal spending affect the capitol region?

My remarks on this subject follow:

The New Federalism quite likely will have a negative effect on one area of concern that I have, and a positive effect on another. I am certain the New Federalism will impair the ability of conservation districts in Pennsylvania to reduce the rate of soil erosion that is taking place in our state. In Lancaster County in 1981, we lost ten tons per acre from our cropland, up from three tons per acre in 1952; but that's another story. There is a proposal in OMB that would reduce the level of funding for ACP, federal cost sharing for pollution abatement associated with agricultural related activities in the United States from 160 million in 1981 to fifty million in 1984—a 300 percent reduction.

In addition, any cost-share proposal, whether it be 75 to 25 or 50 to 50 federal-state, to be used to fund all or part of SCS operational budget in Pennsylvania, will be of little value to us because at least, in the view of Penny Hallowell (and he ought to know), there are not now, and quite likely will not be in the near future, any state funds available for federal cost sharing for this purpose. Therefore, Pennsylvania's conservation program is bound to suffer.

However, in the area of farmland preservation, I think the New Federalism will help. It will help because many federal agencies and the programs they administer have contributed directly to urban sprawl and the loss of farmland.

According to the Compact Allies Report issued in 1981, there is twenty-two to twenty-five percent of the privately owned land vacant in the central cities of this nation. I know Harrisburg has a lot of vacant land and Lancaster has some undeveloped land.

In the decade of the 1970s, the City of Lancaster had a population loss of over five percent. In three townships nearest to Lancaster, the average population growth of thirty-five percent in the 1960s dropped to sixteen percent in the 1970s. However, in seven rural townships, in which farming is the predominate land use, the average population grew from sixteen percent in the 1960s to forty-eight percent in the 1970s. To me, the scary thing is that this is happening all over this nation. In the 100 most important agricultural counties in the nation, population increased at two times the rate that occurred in the less important agricultural counties.

How does this relate to the New Federalism? Quite likely, lower levels of funding will reduce the number of new highways that will be built, many times through the best farmland in an area. In addition, it would appear that we, in this nation, have built more federally funded highways and bridges than we can maintain, or at least more than we have had the wisdom to provide funding for proper maintenance.

Highways are one of the federally subsidized large-scale investments that contribute mightily to urban sprawl and the loss of good farmland. Fine highways make it so easy to travel great distances to get to work. This makes it possible to live in the country and work almost anywhere. Shopping is made easy by the fact that new convenient shopping centers are often built adjacent to these new highways. The problem these new shopping centers cause for downtown merchants is well known.

Another area of concern is federally subsidized housing. No problem with the concept, just the thrust and direction. Hopefully, the New Federalism will change the direction of those federal or federal-local subsidies to encourage housing—a very important segment of our economy and a vital contributor to our economic health.

In the past, most subsidized interest rates and lower down payments were only available to those who built single-family detached houses, many times on large lots. Subsidy payments usually are not available to build apartments, or dense compact settlements. In other words, our housing finance subsidies promoted a demand for space.

In addition, I have a great deal of confidence in our local officials, two of whom are serving on this panel with me. Many proposals under the New Federalism concept are grants to, or cost-share with, state and local officials. If these officials are not expected to do too much with too few dollars received, these local officials may just get more out of those dollars than has been the case in the past. In addition, the programs chosen might better fit local needs than those programs mandated by Washington.

I would now like to share with you some thoughts on the quality of life we have here in the capitol region. Will our region be a more or less desirable place in which to live by the year 2010? As I view it, to a large degree, what happens is up to those of us who live in the region.

The perception of a great many people that the quality of the environment is better and, therefore, more desirable in some other location is interesting, to say the least. The problem associated with this type of thinking is quite clearly illustrated by a recent survey of California attitudes, which indicated that twenty-nine percent of those surveyed said they wished to leave California and of this group, more wished to go to Oregon than to any other place. To put this in perspective, it is helpful to know that twenty-nine percent of California's population is double the present population of Oregon.

People are attracted to Oregon because of the state's special laws for environmental protection. One has to wonder what would happen to the quality of Oregon's environment with a 300 percent population increase.

The capitol region of Pennsylvania is generally referred to as a nice place to work and live. We have a nice mix of people, industry, and agriculture. In fact, the region contains more than one million acres of prime farmland.

Many, if not all, of the eight counties are experiencing considerable pressures on their farmland. We are told that many industries pass up locating in other counties, less important agricultural counties, and locate in the capitol region because it is a nice place for their executives to work and live.

I am not aware of the population growth in the other seven counties in the region. However, I know the projected and actual population growth in Lancaster County is 4,000 persons per year. I hope it remains at this level. Within certain bounds the population increase is not as important as the number of acres of agricultural land needed to provide shelter for these new persons. Our County Comprehensive Plan has set as a goal the use of 1,000 acres per year to provide adequate shelter for the 4,000 increase in population. That works out to four people per acre—not an unrealistic goal.

However, in the past we have not met this goal. The Lancaster County Planning Commission's Annual Report shows a steady increase in subdivision and land development activity from 1,513 acres in 1971 to 5,114 acres in 1978. The present level is under 3,000 acres due to lack of building activity.

I am concerned about what happens in Lancaster County and partially what happens to Lancaster County's farmland. Our son, Fred, who bought the home farm in 1976, is now the fourth-generation full-time farmer to have owned our family farm in Millersville.

As some of you know, Lancaster County ranks first in agricultural production among the nation's non-irrigated counties. The value of agricultural products produced in 1981 was $664 million.

Our county is the third fastest growing county in the state. Our population now stands at 365,500 with a population growth rate in the 1970s of nearly eleven percent and most of that growth taking place in the rural agricultural townships in the county.

Fifty percent of the farm families are the plain sect, of either the Amish, Mennonite, or Brethren. They want to retain their farmland.

The 1977 production of the 560 industrial establishments in the county had a value of $3.1 billion.

Industrial and residential growth, plus the effect of tourism, has placed severe pressure on those nearly 400,000 acres of agricultural land.

You recall, I mentioned the value of agricultural products produced in Lancaster County in 1981 was more than $664 million. Eighty percent of this income was derived from animal and fowl production. We have a great concentration of animals and fowl in the county. These animals and fowl produce a great deal of manure. In fact, according to a soon-to-be-published study conducted in the county, in 1979 there were five million tons of manure produced in the county. How much is five million tons?—enough to apply sixteen tons per acre to every acre of cropland in the county.

Now manure is great for crop production. It's great for strawberries, raspberries, and celery, but I never liked the smell of the stuff. Neither do most non-farmers who move out into the country to enjoy what they perceive to be a better environment. This is the reason we in Lancaster County make so strong an effort to separate farmers and non-farmers through the use of agriculturally-zoned districts. We do not think farmers and non-farmers can live together without conflict. The level of conflict depends on the individuals involved.

To strengthen our zoning effort, the recently appointed Lancaster County Agricultural Preserve Board is developing a program patterned after the Wisconsin plan where farmers will be offered an incentive payment to keep their land in agricultural production for twenty-five years.

This matter of resource conservation has been challenging, frustrating, and yet rewarding. I am glad to have been involved during these past thirty years.

I wish to thank Irving Hand and the committee for inviting me to share some of my thoughts with you during this Conference.

How Modern Man Has Created His Own Farming Problems

The Chesapeake Marketing Association, on December 9, 1982, held a meeting at the Penn Harris Lodge Conference Center in Camp Hill, Pennsylvania. I was asked to speak on the subject, "How Modern Man Has Created His Own Farming Problems." My remarks follow:

Ever since the North American Continent was inhabited by European settlers, the notion of a limit on land supplies has been unthinkable. The fact that the best soils were plowed out first as settlers spread across the nation was of little consequence: There were other lands where only slightly more investment was needed.

Thomas Jefferson thought it foolish to fertilize on his Virginia plantation because he could buy an acre of new land cheaper than he could manure an old acre.

Then came the great movement west—the establishment of land grant colleges and the use of water to make the deserts bloom. There were always other lands to move to.

There is still plenty of desert land that would respond to water, but now water is either in short supply, or is too expensive to use for many crops at prevailing energy costs.

In 1980, when I was last in San Diego County, California, a vegetable grower friend of mine was paying $110 an acre-foot for water to irrigate his strawberry, tomato, and other crops. This compares to $20 an acre-foot in the early 1970s. No wonder growers are switching to drip irrigation where far less water is used.

World War II brought another revolution to American agriculture. Urged on by labor shortages, high prices, and the need for food to rebuild much of the world, farmers greatly accelerated the mechanization of their farms and added new techniques that would intensify the use of each acre.

In addition to newer and more powerful tractors that would cover more acres, farmers shifted to methods of gaining a higher yield from each acre. These methods included commercial fertilizers and pesticides, improved seed and livestock, and the expanded use of irrigation water.

As a result, United States cropland production in 1970 was forty-eight percent higher than it had been in 1950. American agriculture was cited as living proof that the free enterprise system really worked.

Then, as now, the "farm problem" facing national policy makers was not one of too little production, but one of too much production, agricultural surpluses, and low farm prices. In fact, American public opinion and policy spent the entire half century from 1920 to 1970 (with the exception of the war years) trying to reduce crop surpluses and cropland acreage.

Then came the Arab oil embargo. Oil prices went from $2 a barrel to $30 to $40 a barrel.

Next came the Russian grain purchase—twenty-eight million tons—eighteen million from the United States. By 1975, the farm surpluses were virtually wiped out.

The value of agricultural products exported increased from $7 billion in 1970 to $40 billion in 1980—nearly a 600 percent increase in ten years. Americans sold forty percent of their grain abroad.

United States Secretary of Agriculture Earl Butz encouraged farmers to plant from fence row to fence row.

Many fields with a high wind and rain erosion hazard were plowed. Most of these fields should have stayed in prairie grass, or whatever was their native grass, and should not have been plowed. Many of these acres are among those acres that make up the thirty-two percent of the nation's cropland with very high erosion problems.

Having known former Secretary Earl Butz, and having served with him on a national committee, I am sure he acted in good faith when he urged farmers to plow fence row to fence row.

Over fifty million acres of cropland (two times the present cropland acreage in twelve northeastern states) were added back into intensive cropping from set-aside between 1967 and 1977. Most of it was added between 1973 and 1975 during this plow "fence row to fence row" era. Many of these fifty million acres were erodable acres—erodable from excessive winds or rainfall. Now we are paying the price!

As I mentioned before, thirty-two percent of this nation's cropland is losing ten tons of topsoil per acre per year. This translates to an inch of topsoil lost every fifteen to twenty years. This loss is more troublesome when it is pointed out that at least 100 years are required to create an inch of topsoil through natural processes.

Whether or not this is a serious problem depends on how far we look ahead. For the farmer producing crops on six inches of topsoil, research shows corn yields will be reduced about three bushels per acre per year, with the loss of one inch of topsoil. A yield reduction from 100 bushels to ninety-seven bushels. Few farmers will get upset by this kind of yield reduction.

However, eighty years from now, with an inch of topsoil lost every twenty years, that original six-inch layer of topsoil will be reduced to two inches. The productive capacity of such soils may be so low they may have to be returned back to pasture.

Few people are willing to look eighty years ahead, and herein lies the problem. Unless we look twenty-five to fifty years ahead, there is no problem as far as the quantity or quality of the nation's productive farmland is concerned.

Don Paarlberg, former chief of USDA AES, speaking at the Pennsylvania Farmer's Association Annual Meeting in November 1982, took issue with the position that we are running out of farmland; water is becoming scarce; and erosion is a serious problem. He went on to say that we are losing less than one-fifth of one percent of our farmland each year, and erosion is serious on only twenty-five percent of our cropland; and there is ample water.

Now, Dr. Don Paarlberg is a distinguished economist. However, with so many of them disagreeing with each other regarding the same subject, sometimes one has to wonder about them. I first started getting suspicious of economists in 1950 when our local vocational-agriculture teacher went to the Agricultural Economic Research people in Washington to get some information on a certain subject and he was asked the question: Do you want favorable or unfavorable information? Most of us are aware that there can, indeed, be effective arguments made on both sides of a position taken.

I also lose a little confidence in economists when I reflect on how poorly most of them have done in predicting when the current recession will end.

I get particularly upset by economists like William Fischel of Dartmouth, and Jullian Simon of the University of Illinois. They not only use old data to refute the findings of NALS; they also take the position: Don't worry about the amount of farmland we are losing or how much erosion is taking place on our cropland. They point out that as soon as good agricultural land becomes scarce enough, commodity prices will rise to the point where the market needs will be met and everybody will benefit.

Higher commodity prices are badly needed and will be welcomed by our farmers who, for too long, have received too little compensation for his or her labor, capital investment, and management skills.

But, how high can food prices rise before consumers rebel? Remember the beef boycott? Consumers have become accustomed to spending only seventeen percent of their disposable income for food purchases. How much higher can that percentage rise before consumers may be pitted against farmers in a battle that will make reasonable discussion about long-term farm and food policies virtually impossible.

American agriculture is one of the few industries that out-produces foreign competition. A productive soil factory can compete. Poor or depleted soils may not be able to compete.

Since the most recent census revealed that population in the nation's 100 leading agricultural counties grew at two times the rate of growth of the remaining counties, it would appear that the nation's best agricultural land is being converted to non-agricultural use much more rapidly than the less productive land.

Therefore, it can safely be assumed that each year the productive capacity of our nation's soils is being reduced not only by the conversion of some of our best land to non-agricultural use, but also from serious erosion problems.

Going back to Don Paarlberg's statement about the two-tenths of one percent farmland conversion number, this amount seems small until one multiplies it by the nation's 413 million acres of cropland and finds the resulting number to be nearly one million acres converted each year. Over a four-year period, four million acres would be lost. If that land were moderately productive, that land would produce the same amount of grain that is committed to foreign food assistance programs by all donor nations in the world. From the viewpoint of the world's needy people setting aside four million acres in Iowa for use later in the century would indeed be viewed as significant.

How about Don Paarlberg's statement that erosion is only serious on twenty-five percent of the United States cropland? Actually, the accepted number is thirty-two percent. Here again, the number becomes significant only when thirty-two percent is multiplied by the nation's 413 million acres of cropland. By so doing, we find there are over 130 million acres of the nation's cropland eroding at the rate of ten tons or more per acre per year.

How much is 130 million acres? It is an area more than four times greater than all the cropland in the twelve northeastern states. That is a lot of land.

Here in Lancaster County, when I was first appointed as a member of the County Conservation District Board in 1951, our cropland was eroding at the rate of three tons per acre per year.

Today, that rate has increased to ten tons per acre per year. A conservation district is supposed to develop programs and motivate farmers to prevent soil erosion, not increase it.

So, where did we go wrong? Simply stated, our farmers caused problems faster than we could find solutions. Many of our farmers discontinued their contour strips and rotations gave way to continuous corn. On too many farms, we have entire fields planted entirely to corn with slopes up to ten percent, and that spells trouble. Some farmers even removed terraces for which they received government cost-share payments.

What is the reason for the change to these erosion promoting practices? New and larger machines make farming uneven strips and point rows difficult to manage. When the choice was between the larger machines and the contour strops and terraces, the conservation measures had to go. This has caused our problem. It seems to me that here is a case where bigger is not better—at least not better when we look twenty-five to fifty years down the road and consider the long-term productivity of the land.

Conservation tillage may be the way to get back on tract. We certainly are going to give it our best effort through promotion and education.

Here in Lancaster County we are also developing a program to reduce the rate of farmland conversion taking place by guiding growth and by encouraging more dense development where there is water and sewer available.

Lancaster County has the dubious distinction of being the third fastest growing county, the fifth most important industrial county in the State, and is tenth in the nation in the value of tourism.

Lancaster County is also first in the nation in the value of its agricultural production among non-irrigated counties.

The value of agricultural crops and products in the county in 1981 exceeded $664 million from 326,000 acres. It is obvious we have serious competition for the use of the land.

However, we have a County Comprehensive Plan that designates 100,000 acres of land now being farmed for development of all kinds, and also designates 278,000 acres to remain in agricultural production.

The Lancaster County Commissioners have appointed and strongly support a nine-member Agricultural Preservation Board on which I serve as Chairman. Working closely with the County Planning Commission and other groups, we are doing our best to implement the County Comprehensive Plan, and guide growth in the county.

We hope to retain those 278,000 acres of prime farmland in the county through the use of township agricultural-zoned districts reinforced by a voluntary deed restriction program that offers four choices to landowners to retain their land in agriculture for twenty-five years or, in some cases, in perpetuity.

I have attempted to develop the idea that modern man has indeed created many of the problems we face today. Undoubtedly, it will take considerable time to turn things around. Without a doubt, a lot of attitudes will have to be changed, and this will not be easy. My hope is that we can do it before it is too late!

Can Lancaster County's Small Farms and Farm Families Survive?

A very positive **yes** by each of three respected, widely traveled observers with extensive natural resource experiences was given to that question.

These men are not "lightweights." The first individual is Norman A. Berg, former Chief of United States Soil Conservation Service. The second individual is Neil Samdson, former Executive Director of the National Association of Conservation District Directors and later Executive Director of the American Forestry Association. The third individual is Robert Grey, attorney for the American Farmland Trust, headquartered in Washington, D.C. These men visited the county in 1986.

Following their speaking engagements at three special meetings held in Lancaster County on farmland preservation, I asked each one of them to block out at least six hours for me to guide them on a tour in Lancaster County. We visited farms and farm families on three separate occasions—a number of Amish and Mennonite farms.

We visited in the kitchen; we went into the barns and stables; and we talked to the wives and children. Most of them told us that one of their goals, although increasingly more difficult to achieve, is to have a farm for each of their children. It is part of their religious heritage.

We were told by these farm families that they believe their children should be taught the value of work, to save, to be frugal, and to be honest in all their dealings. These values can be taught anywhere; however, they believe it is much easier to teach them on the farm.

Each of these very knowledgeable individuals, after visiting a number of Amish and Mennonite farms and farm families on separate occasions, came to the same conclusion: Lancaster County's plain sect, and other farmers, can survive in the future if the already favorable agricultural climate that now exists in Lancaster County continues at the present level.

In addition, Norman Berg pointed out that, in his opinion, still further improvement in the "favorable agricultural climate" may have to be initiated by state, county, and township governments to provide added assurance that Lancaster County's small farms will survive in the future.

The question might be asked: Is it worth it? Norman Berg answered with a resounding, "Yes!" In fact, he went so far as to say, "Amos, you have something very special here. Your Lancaster County's agricultural industry is a 'national treasure' similar to the Yellowstone National Park." He added, "Amos, work hard with others to preserve it!"

As of today, May 23, 1986, Lancaster County has approximately 5,000 farms, averaging eighty-six acres. We have been told these farm families can survive if certain new initiatives are taken. I agree; however, there are hopeful individuals who are losing that hope. They observe the too rapid loss of our farmland to development.

However, they are not aware of the new and helpful things that are being done as of May 23, 1986.

On May 21, Alan Musselman and I were discussing this matter with an individual living in Manor Township, in which our home farm is located and where we are working to develop farmer interest in order that the township supervisors can successfully designate an area as an effective agricultural zoned district of about 10,000 acres within the township. The individual to whom we were talking, together with members of his family, own ten farms comprising a total area of 1,000 acres.

Although this individual was interested in farmland preservation, he was sure that eventually most of Lancaster County's 368,000 acres will be developed. However, at the time he made that statement, he was unaware of the tools we now have to get the preservation job done. He was not aware of the federal income and capital gains provisions that exist and have now been clarified by the new regulations in the tax code.

He was not aware of the important boost Sam Morris's House Bill 806 will give to our preservation efforts. We can offer a much more attractive incentive to an individual who wishes to place a deed restriction, as we prefer to call it in Lancaster County, or to sell the development rights, as the procedure is generally referred to, instead of the present $250 per acre incentive payment we can offer, based on appraisal value we have encountered with our deed restriction efforts—an average of $1,000 per acre and, in several instances, $3,000 per acre to interested individuals.

It is obvious Sam Morris's House Bill 806 will help a great deal. We support the bill enthusiastically. Sam has worked hard to get House Bill 806 where it is today. We are indebted to him for his efforts. Our own representatives have also been most helpful.

If we are to reach our preservation goal, we will have to continue to have the strong support of our county government. We have had excellent support in the past.

The creation of the Farmland Preservation Board, the level of staffing, and our $350,000 budget for incentive payments is ample evidence of Lancaster County government's strong support. We trust it will continue.

In Pennsylvania, with our strong township form of government, we need continued support of townships. This is especially true in the area of the approval or denial of a request for rezoning in the agricultural zoned districts.

We will have to prove to farmers who want to continue to farm that the benefits of being in our agricultural zoned district outweigh the costs. This is our challenge. We must tell our story well.

My Meeting With the West Donegal Township Officials

At a meeting held by the township in the West Donegal municipal building on November 20, 1986, I found myself in a difficult position, caused by an action of the Lancaster County Planning Commission. The Lancaster County Planning Commission agreed to rezone part of Robert Kauffman's farm to residential. Although I had promised the Kauffmans I would not attend the township hearing meeting, I had to break my promise.

The remarks I made at the hearing follow:

The first thing I would like to do is to apologize to Bob and Miriam Kauffman for not keeping a promise I made to them. At their request, I made a promise not to appear at this hearing. In addition, I promised I would not ask Alan Musselman to appear. I broke both promises. Again, I apologize.

I know now I made a mistake in making those promises. What changed my mind? One of the reasons was the recent action by Lancaster County Planning Commission. By a six to two vote, they supported Bob Kauffman's request to rezone a major part of his farm from inclusion in the agricultural district zoning area to R-2.

Now, one county advisory group, the Lancaster County Planning Commission, has opposed the position of another county advisory group, the County Agricultural Preserve Board. This is the first time this has ever happened.

Obviously, the planning commission has the right to vote their convictions. However, it is counter-productive for two county-appointed groups to pull in different directions. Apparently Bob and his attorney made a strong case for their rezoning position.

If the supervisors of West Donegal Township would grant the request for rezoning, which they alone can do, it would seriously damage our preservation program. For this reason, we are here tonight to present reasons why this request for rezoning should not be granted.

Another reason I am here is because I was requested to be here by a long-time friend and a landowner in your agricultural district, who lives relatively near the Kauffman property. Since Alan Musselman and I are outsiders and might be considered intruders, I asked the permission of supervisors Barry Garman and Jack Lawson to attend and participate in this hearing. Permission was granted.

On September 17, at Bob Kauffman's invitation, I visited with him and Miriam at their home for nearly an hour. I took along a map outlining the provisions of Lancaster County's Comprehensive Land Use and Transportation Plan and pointed out that the Bob Kauffman farm in West Donegal Township is included in that area of the county, designated to remain in agricultural production.

The land zoned agricultural and included in the townships zoned agricultural district in 1979 by the township supervisors of West Donegal Township contains excellent soils. Eighty-one percent of the soil is Class I and II. This soil is level and will not erode easily. Only fifty-two percent of the agricultural land in Lancaster County is Class I and II soil. It is evident your township supervisors did a good job in 1979.

Bob Kauffman did not show much interest in, or enthusiasm for, the County Comprehensive Plan. I am not sure he approves of zoning as a tool to guide growth. I doubt it. He told me and the Lancaster County Planning Commission that he is in favor of agricultural preservation. Apparently he wants other farmers to do the preserving, not him.

Bob feels strongly about the rights of an individual landowner to make his or her own decisions. An individual's rights are very important, but so is the public good important.

If nearly 500 homes are built on the seventy-eight-acre tract on the Kauffman property, Bob's individual desire and right to do so will be granted. But what about the rights of the neighboring farmers? How will the residents living in those 500 homes react to the manure smells; the increased number of flies, whether real or perceived; the noise; and other related activities that are associated with farming? If they react as most urban dwellers react, farming practices will have to be drastically changed to satisfy the complaints, and even lawsuits, brought by the new residents. It is certain the rights of the remaining farm families will be infringed upon. Then there is the matter of increased traffic and the problem for farmers to move their large equipment on Bossler Road and other connecting roads.

Regarding the right to use land in the manner a landowner wants, I would like to cite two Manor Township examples where this right was denied. The first example is the Achey brothers' 110-acre farm with public sewer and water available. The Acheys wanted to increase the permitted zoning density to allow for a more dense development of their farm. Neighbors strongly opposed this request, and the township supervisors decided it was not in the public interest to rezone the property for this dense development. This action drastically reduced the value of the property for development.

The other example is Chet Haverstick, who owns a property on the corner of Stone Mill Road and Route 741. He has had a standing offer from a fast food establishment to buy his corner home at a very high price if the necessary zoning can be obtained. To date, the supervisors have ruled it is not in the public interest to grant this request. His request has been denied. There are many other examples that could be given if time permitted.

The point is often made, many times by developers, that being included in a township-zoned agricultural district makes it impossible for a farmer to sell five or ten lots to a developer to satisfy a debt that cannot be met by normal cash flow, either because of former high interest rates or because of today's very low farm prices on most farm commodities.

For example, a $50,000 debt could easily be satisfied by selling five one-acre lots at $10,000 each to a developer. Would it not be far better, especially from a long-range viewpoint, if a farmer with a $50,000 debt problem offers to a neighboring farmer ten acres at $5,000 per acre, or even fifteen acres at $3,300 per acre, in order that the land remain in agricultural production and thus avoid the urban-farmer conflict.

This would enable the farmer to keep the farm and concentrate a bit more on his or her livestock or poultry production. After all, isn't this where most of our net income is generated here in Lancaster County?

I would like to take issue with Bob Kauffman regarding his opinion expressed to me in his home, and again at the County Planning Commission hearing, that the future of agriculture is in large corporate farms and not in traditional family farms which comprise the core of Lancaster County agriculture.

I would agree that the trend toward fewer and larger farms will continue in Lancaster County and elsewhere. However, I think the vast majority of our Lancaster County farms will continue to be family farms somewhat larger, but still family farms.

The recent sale of an eighty-acre farm west of Lititz is a case in point. This farm was purchased by an Amish farmer for $5,537 per acre. He plans to farm it.

In March 1985, a Manor Township farm was purchased at a cost of over $5,200 per acre. A developer was next to the last bidder. This farm family, the purchaser, did not want a development next to their home dairy farm. This farm will continue to be farmed.

Whether I am right about the future of Lancaster County's agriculture or Bob Kauffman is right, only time will tell.

I trust we will do what we can to preserve our prime farmland for our children and our grandchildren. I would hope and pray we do not make all the land-use decisions for them. Let us give them a chance to make some decisions for themselves.

Bob Kauffman and others say each farmer should be responsible for preserving our farmland, and that zoning interferes with a farmer's decision making and is unfair.

There is little evidence to prove this theory is right. There is a great deal of evidence to prove zoning is an important tool to guide growth.

I do not have the most recent information; however, during one recent twenty-five-year period, the three nearby counties—Bucks, Delaware, and Montgomery—lost fifty percent of their agricultural cropland in twenty-five years. During the same period, Chester and Dauphin Counties lost nearly thirty percent of their cropland, and Lancaster County lost eleven percent. As you know, Lancaster County has twenty-five townships with effective agricultural districts.

The last point that is often made, and was made by Bob during my visit to his home, was: Why should we preserve farmland when we have too much of nearly all agricultural products, resulting in low prices and severe financial hardship for many of our farm families?

This is easily the most difficult question to speak to. However, let me try. Yes, United States farmers are greatly overproducing. We have huge surpluses stored in government storehouses somewhere. We are told there is enough dried milk in United States storage to meet domestic demand for sixteen months. There is enough wheat in United States storage—over 450 million bushels—to bake nearly seven sixteen-ounce loaves of bread for every man, woman, and child in the world.

However, we all know too few of those who are hungry or starving will get their share. In fact, too many will get none. There are a number of reasons for this. When consideration is given to future population projections, especially in developing countries, the challenge to feed the needy will become greater, not less. Today, global population is growing by more than 200,000 a day.

It is obvious to me this need to feed the hungry in the world can be best met if production costs can be kept as low as possible. Crops can be produced far more cheaply on prime farmland than on land that is less than prime. I think each of the more than 3,000 counties in this nation should do their best to preserve their best farmland. Many of them will not do this. I trust Lancaster County not only will continue to be the leading non-irrigated agricultural county in the nation; but also, I hope we will do the best job of preserving our prime farmland.

Testimony on
House Bill 442 and Senate Bill 156

On May 29, 1987, I attended a hearing held by the Pennsylvania House Agricultural Committee on House Bill 442 and Senate Bill 156. I testified in favor of both bills.

My testimony follows:

Ladies and gentlemen, my name is Amos Funk. I'm a vegetable farmer from Millersville, Lancaster County. For the past thirty years, I have been working to conserve and protect the soil and water resources of the Commonwealth.

More than twenty years ago, I realized that the conversion of farms to built-up sprawl and ill-placed suburbia was to become the serious perennial problem it is today, with permanent implications. I served as a member of Governor Scranton's Committee on Agriculture and Governor Shafer's Committee on the Preservation of Agricultural Land. During the Thornburgh years, we have initiated a farmland preservation program in Lancaster County based upon sketchy enabling legislation and local fiscal limitations which hamper our best efforts. Over these many years there has been agreement among us that agriculture is economically very important to the Commonwealth and that saving our best agricultural land resources for future generations makes sense.

Patience, however, is not one of Amos Funk's renowned virtues. We have talked and talked—for more than twenty years we have talked about farmland preservation in Pennsylvania. It is time to **do** something! That something is before you today with unanimous endorsement from the Senate. The House and Senate versions of the farmland preservation bill differ only in the extent of fiscal commitment.

Send on the more affordable of the two to the floor of the house; submit it to the democratic process of a floor vote. Opinion polls have shown that more than seventy percent of Pennsylvanians (farm and non-farm; Democrats and Republicans) support the expenditure of funds to preserve and protect our most important farmlands.

Voluntary agricultural areas have been established in every area of the State in accordance with the intents of Act 43. The commitment and the structure are in place at the grass roots. The commitment and structure on the part of the Commonwealth await your approval.

These bills represent to me your opportunity to make a natural resource commitment; an economic development commitment; a family farming commitment; and a commitment to the fresh food production—scenic, and environmental qualities our most productive countryside offers, with a single affirmative vote.

In the interests of the land which has provided us so abundantly, and the citizens of this generation and future generations of Pennsylvanians, ladies and gentlemen, it is time for you to act with foresight and leadership.

My Meeting With Elizabethtown Young Farmers

At a meeting held by the Elizabethtown Young Farmers on February 16, 1988, I made a presentation to those individuals present.
My remarks follow:

Tonight I would like to try to answer a number of questions often put to me. Some of you may have similar questions. Perhaps we can supply some answers.

Why preserve farmland in Lancaster County when there is too much of nearly all farm products to fill market demand, not only in the United States, but in most of the world?

These world surpluses are present today because of the lack of our ability to distribute the food and the lack of buying power by the world poor. United Nations Food and Agriculture Organization estimates that worldwide there are one-half billion people—more than one in ten humans—who suffer from chronic malnutrition.

The United States has provided by far the most food aid. Other developed nations have been even more generous according to their means. Sweden's per capita expenditure for food aid is $95 per capita. The annual United States Food aid contribution is $22 per capita.

Some members of Congress and others point out that we have a major hunger problem in United States also. This is difficult to understand in light of the fact we are told there is enough dried milk in United States storage to meet domestic demand for sixteen months. There is enough wheat in United States storage, over 450 million bushels, to bake nearly seven sixteen-ounce loaves of bread for every man, woman, and child in the world.

However, we all know too few of those who are hungry or starving will get their share. In fact, too many get none. When consideration is given to future population projections, especially in developing countries, the challenge to feed the needy will become greater, not less. Today, global population is growing by more than 200,000 a day.

It is obvious to me this need to feed the hungry in the world can be best met if production costs can be kept as low as possible. Crops can be produced far more cheaply on prime farmland than on land that is less than prime. I think each of the 3,000 counties in this nation should do their best to preserve their best farmland. So should each township. Many municipalities will not do this. I hope Lancaster County not only will continue to be the leading non-irrigated agricultural county in the nation; but, also, I hope we will do the best job of preserving our prime farmland.

I have been asked on many occasions, "Why are you so concerned about saving Lancaster County's farmland? Food and fiber can be grown elsewhere." James Michener, in his book *Centennial*, refers to Lancaster County as one of the three most fertile areas in the world.

Norman Berg, former administrator of the United States Soil Conservation Service, who traveled all over the world, made this observation after two days of traveling with me and visiting in Lancaster County with Amish, Mennonite, and other families: "Amos, what you have here is a national treasure similar to Yellowstone National Park." He urged me to work with others to save as much of it as possible.

We have the soil. We have adequate rainfall in most years. Several years ago I was serving as a member of the NACD outlook committee. We met in Nashville, Tennessee, that year. I asked several of the members about their annual rainfall. One member from Burlington, Colorado (east central Colorado), said, "twelve inches;" another from Hays, Kansas (north central Kansas), said, "fourteen inches;" yet another from Magnum, Oklahoma (southwest Oklahoma), said, "twenty inches." Lancaster County gets about forty-two inches of annual rainfall. We get nearly as much rainfall in one year as the combined average rainfall in Colorado, Kansas, and Oklahoma.

We have a very special people here in Lancaster County, including those of you in this room. We are hardworking and frugal. Over the years we have earned for this county the reputation: the Garden Spot of America.

Why should we save farmland when it is so difficult to make a net profit these days? Milk prices are down $.50 per hundredweight and many other prices lower than they should be.

> In 1970, value of agricultural exports $ 7 billion
> In 1980, value of agricultural exports $40 billion
> In 1987, value of agricultural exports _____

In 1972 the American farmers were paid to idle cropland. Two years later, due to corn blight and worldwide drought, the surplus had all but disappeared. Now we are back to surpluses.

Although weather and other factors play a part, I am convinced a lot of the problem can be attributed to what was depicted in a recent "Nova" program on public television entitled "The Politics of Food." Among other things, the film showed large combines in Brazil, harvesting soybeans in very large fields on corporate-type farms. Large fields of sugar cane were being harvested with as much mechanized equipment as possible. Then followed a series of shots of the displaced Brazilian small farmers and their families living in shacks that were clutstered together in rows. These families had very little income because of the lack of jobs.

This decision to replace people and small farms with corporate-type agriculture in order to finance foreign debt obligations may serve a short-time need. However, the long-time effect on ninety percent of the people living in Brazil is yet to be determined.

Possibly, the most important contribution to the agricultural surpluses in the United States is the sharp reduction in United States agricultural exports. An important reason for this reduction of our agricultural exports are high subsidies. European economic community countries, including Italy, plus Saudi Arabia, Japan, etc., place high internal subsidies on agricultural products grown in these countries. At one time European economic community countries were supporting wheat prices at twice the world market price. Some support prices of wheat were as high as $70 per ton, making it possible to offer European economic community wheat to importing countries at $35 to $45 per ton below United States prices for similar wheat.

The Italian government subsidized tomato producers at a per ton price equal to the price United States canners offered their growers in the United States. It is difficult for United States processors to resist accepting the lower priced Italian tomato pulp.

According to a February 5, 1988, *Farmshine* magazine article, Ralph Hofstead, president of Land of Lakes, insists that the American dairy farmers can compete in the world market if the playing field is even. It is not even now. United States supports milk at $10.60 per hundredweight, compared to $15.56 in Canada, and $15.75 in European economic community countries. In the article, Carol Brookings of World Prospectives, Washington, D.C., pointed out that if these inequalities of support could be phased out gradually, world market prices would rise and world trade would increase.

The bottom line is: There is growing evidence that if the playing field is even, United States farmers can compete and farm profitability will rise.

Why should we save farmland in Lancaster County when there is a major effort to take cropland out of production all over this nation? Much of the land now being taken out of production should never have been taken out of grass and other cover.

Thousands of acres were purchased by non-farmer investors for a quick profit. Prairie land was plowed to meet certain standards. Then it was sold as cropland at substantial profits. The investor would watch the soil blow and wash away. This is the reason for the sod buster bill.

Not all of this nation's 430 million acres of cropland are the same. I mentioned earlier about the differences in rainfall. Approximately ten percent of United States cropland is irrigated. However, from this ten percent of irrigated acres, twenty-five percent of this nation's food and fiber supply is produced.

Will there be enough water to irrigate the approximately forty-five million acres of cropland in the future? Let's take a look.

Ogallala Aquifer—a large underground lake spreading from north Texas through parts of Oklahoma, New Mexico, Kansas, Colorado, Nebraska, Wyoming, and South Dakota—supplies 170,000 irrigation wells for 14.3 million acres that produce fifteen percent of the value of wheat, corn, sorghum, and cotton, plus thirty-eight percent of the livestock in this nation.

Twenty-four million acre feet of water is drawn out of these wells each year.

Three million acre feet of water is replaced by nature each year.

Twenty-one million acre feet annual shortfall.

An acre foot of water is 328,811 gallons. In the middle 1960s, farmers in Arizona were paying $8 an acre foot. That amounts to less than three cents per 1,000 gallons.

There are those who complain about government subsidies to preserve farmland. We Pennsylvanians are pikers compared to those western farmers.

Arizonans pump out of the ground two times as much water as nature restores each year. Under a plan enacted in 1980, these farmers are required to pay sharply higher prices for water to irrigate their crops. The goal is to force them to sell their land for other uses by 2006. If not enough farmers sell out, the state will begin to buy up farmland and put the land to other uses. Officials feel hi-tech industry will replace the $2 billion per year income from agriculture.

Another water conflict is forcing major changes in California's San Joaquin Valley and it could eventually affect 148,000 farmers in seventeen western states who now receive cheap water from federal projects.

In order to resolve the conflict concerning strict enforcement of the 1902 Reclamation Act, a compromise was arrived at which will result in major changes in water costs, water use, conservation, and agriculture.

John Harris, who owns a large farm in the San Joaquin Valley, estimates the change in the 1902 Reclamation Act will double his water bill to $1.6 million a year without assurance of better yields or prices.

Since the early 1900s, population in the United States has increased 200 percent. Water use during the same period increased 500 to 800 percent. By 1980, the average use for all purposes, including household use, reached 2,000 gallons per day for each man, woman, and child in the United States, an increase of twenty-two percent in ten years.

I will repeat what I have said many times before. Who can be sure about the supply of our resources in the future? It behooves all of us to use these resources wisely, whether they be used for agriculture, home building, or any other use. We need to do our best. We need to look twenty-five to fifty years down the road if we are to avoid future problems.

The State's Role and History in Creating the Pennsylvania Conservation Easement Program

This statement was made November 15, 1990, to some state legislators in the House and Senate. Also present were quite a number of state and local political leaders. My statement to those assembled follows:

As most of you know, agriculture is, and has been for some time, Pennsylvania's leading industry. Pennsylvania also leads all twelve northeast states in the value of its agricultural production.

It was quite fitting, therefore, that on November 3, 1987, Pennsylvania voters approved by a nearly two to one margin the $100 million statewide bond issue for the purchase of conservation easements, a very positive procedure to preserve prime farmland.

In December 1988, Act 149, sponsored by Senator Noah Wenger, Lancaster County, and Representative Sam Morris, Chester County, and many others, was signed into law.

To my knowledge this $100 million bond issue is the greatest amount of money ever approved by any state to preserve farmland through the purchase of conservation easements.

There are many good reasons the above action took place. These may be referred to positive steps toward farmland preservation in Pennsylvania which led to the passage of Act 149.

The first major effort to preserve farmland in these United States started in 1965 with California's passage of the Williamson Act, an act to create agricultural districts and offer preferential taxation to participating landowners.

Pennsylvania was not far behind:
- In 1966 - Act 515 was passed with similar purposes.
- In 1968 - Act 442 was passed to strengthen several areas of the earlier act. Incidentally, Act 442 was used to authorize and guide the activities of the Lancaster County Agricultural Preserve Board at its creation in 1980.

    New York passed similar legislation in 1971: Virginia and Maryland in 1977; Illinois in 1979; and Minnesota in 1980.
- In 1968 - Pennsylvania Act 284 amended the municipal planning code to authorize municipalities to establish zoning ordinances for the protection and preservation of natural resources and agricultural land and activities.

- In 1973 - Pennsylvania passed a constitutional amendment permitting preferential assessment of farmland and forest land.
- In 1974 - Act 319, Clean and Green Act, was passed to allow farmland and forest land to be taxed according to use rather than market value.
- In 1976 - Act 71 exempts farmers from payment of assessments for municipal improvements, such as the installation of sewer and water lines fronting or crossing their land if the farmer does not make use of the facilities.
- In 1976 - Act 279 exempts family farmers from prosecution from the Environmental Quality Board when pursuing normal farming operations, such as spreading lime and from the creation of dust resulting from disking dry soil.
- In 1979 - Act 100 created the Agricultural Lands Condemnation Approval Board and set up guidelines regarding the condemnation of agricultural lands.
- In 1980 - Act 207 provides that farmland must be valued at its use value for inheritance tax purposes.

During all these twenty-two years from 1966 to 1988, Pennsylvania's legislature has been trying to create a climate in Pennsylvania that is favorable to farmers, and in which farmers can survive and stay in business and get a reasonable return for their labor.

As of 1980, forty-eight states have laws which, in some way or another, seek to reduce the burden of real property taxes on farmers.

Twenty-eight states, including Pennsylvania, have preferential current use assessment, with a seven-year roll back if the property use is changed from agricultural to other uses.

Lancaster County has only minor participation in the Clean and Green Act, due to the present low assessments and the high quality of our soil. Quite likely this will change if reassessment occurs in the county.

It is thought by many that differential assessment is an inefficient way to soften the income squeeze that may lead some owners to sell to a developer. It benefits all eligible landowners, whether they be rich or poor, private citizens or corporations, farmers, or speculators, in return for a supply response at the margin by a small number of prospective sellers who decide to postpone sales.

While the above is true, it is the best tool we have in Pennsylvania to protect farmers from overburdening annual taxes, including school taxes.

Do I sell my conservation easement? Possibly the most likely answer is: yes, if I can see a profitable future in farming not only for me, but for the individual who may wish to take over the farm in the future, whether it be son, daughter, or just a future buyer.

As we look to 1991 and beyond, there are a number of things on the horizon that make the climate less favorable for farmers, especially young farmers, to take over the family farm.

Concern #1) Taxes. One of the greatest concerns of farmers to whom I have spoken in Lancaster County is the problem of rising taxes. Not too many years ago a prominent farmer in Manor Township who owned several farms was the second highest taxpayer in Manor Township with Armstrong World Industries the highest taxpayer in the township.

Most farmers are willing to pay their fair share of taxes, including school taxes. However, even here in Lancaster County where property assessments are relatively low, many farmers think their taxes are disproportionately high when the taxes levied are compared to the services required or requested by farmers.

It is important in Lancaster County, and elsewhere, to create an agricultural climate as favorable as possible for farmers and farming. This is especially true if we hope to increase the participation of interested landowners in conservation easement sales.

For this reason, I plan to recommend to the Lancaster County Agricultural Preserve Board that we request the county commissioners to support a study of the present tax system as it relates to farm families and their ability to remain in farming, now and in the future here in Lancaster County, the second fastest developing county in the state.

Although the study would need the strong support of the county commissioners, I would hope the major cost of the study would be paid for by agribusinesses in the county. I think this is quite possible, because it is in the interest of agribusiness to have agriculture remain strong in Lancaster County.

Concern #2) Meeting environmental standards. Adhering to new and sometimes unrealistic environmental standards and goals will definitely affect in a negative manner the favorable agricultural climate needed to encourage farmers to participate in our conservation easement acquisition program.

In my opinion the original language in the Wetlands Protection Act is an example of an unrealistic environmental regulation for farmers. The revision of the language by the United States Corp of Engineers makes implementation less controversial and is fairer to the farmer. Wetlands need to be protected, but in a fair and reasonable manner.

Much safer use of pesticides and fertilizers, not the elimination of these agricultural tools, should be our environmental goal if agriculture is to survive in any community. It should be remembered, it took a considerable amount of time to create the present problems. It will take a reasonable amount of time to correct these problems we have created. Too often some regulators show less patience than they should.

The improvement of water quality should be the goal of all of us. However, this effort will take time and cost taxpayers, including farmers, a considerable amount of dollars. Farmers should not be expected to assume the entire cost of this effort that will benefit all our people.

The rate of soil erosion, a definite contribution to the pollution of surface water, has increased from three tons per acre in 1950 to nine tons per acre in 1989. This increase has not been due to the lack of activity by the Lancaster County Conservation District on which I serve; but instead, it is due to the change in farming practices in the past forty years. In 1950 when the conservation district was created by the county commissioners, sixty-six percent of the county's cropland was planted to close-growing, less erosive crops such as wheat, oats, and hay. Only thirty-three percent of the land was planted to corn. Today the planting pattern is reversed to sixty-six percent of our cropland planted to corn, a very erodible crop, and only thirty-three percent of our land is planted to close-growing crops that reduce soil erosion.

Many farmers use no rotation—the farm is planted entirely to corn. The County Conservation District, working with United States Soil Conservation Service, Penn State Extension Service, and other cooperating agencies, is addressing these problems by urging the use of conservation tillage, slit till farming, and the expanded use of terraces and diversions and, where appropriate, contour strip cropping to reduce soil loss. Are we reducing the size of the problem? Yes, we are. In 1989, as a result of erosion reduction activities, 143,000 tons of soil were retained in our fields and kept out of our streams.

Since 1985, USDA-EPA and the Pennsylvania legislature has made available to Lancaster County farmers more than $2 million in cost share funds to reduce soil erosion and improve safe manure storage and application. In addition, the district has hired a full-time nutrient management specialist to work with our farmers.

Any attempt to move too quickly to solve a problem that has developed over many years will result in having a negative effect on a favorable agricultural climate for agriculture to survive in Lancaster County.

Finally, there is the cost of land in Lancaster County. With land for farming bringing up to $10,000 an acre, when does this land become too expensive to farm? Who is wise enough to know for sure?

Perhaps the only way the $10,000-per-acre cost can be justified is that the repayment schedule needs to be spread out over a much longer period of time, maybe as much as two or more generations, and the expected return on capital needs to be quite low.

For many of our Lancaster County farm families, farming is a way of life, not a business with fixed capital return requirements.

In addition, the ownership of one, two, or three additional farms, purchased over the years at a much lower cost per acre, makes it possible to reduce the total cost per acre on the combined holdings, increases the efficiency of the machinery now being held and, if the management level is high enough, can reduce the per-unit cost of production on the combined holdings.

Some years ago, Fred Hughs, a very good farm management specialist from Penn State, suggested that Lancaster County farmers should not pay over $800 an acre for farmland.

In 1944, a friend of mine now living in Manor Township, moved from his father's farm in Leacock Township to a farm he purchased in Manor Township. He was twenty-six years old at the time. Remember, the year was 1944. He paid $167 per acre with crops in the fields. Although he thought he made a good buy, the farm, costing approximately one-third the cost of farmland in his home township, a number of older established farmers insisted he paid too much. They were certain he would go broke in two years and then be happy to go back home and join his father.

He did not go broke and today he and his family own four Manor Township farms. After each farm purchase he was told by older, more experienced farmers that he paid entirely too much for each farm. The fourth farm, at nearly $5,000 per acre is proving to be the most difficult farm to pay off. It would seem interest and other expenses have risen at a faster rate than prices received for the farm products produced on the farm.

Putting it differently, it is harder to pay off a farm purchased at $5,000 an acre today than it was to pay off a farm at $167 per acre in 1944, or $500 per acre in 1953. It should be remembered that the management level on the four farms has remained at a high level.

This would lead me to conclude that if we hope to preserve 225,000 acres (my personal goal) of desirably located prime farmland in Lancaster County, we need to make an all-out effort to create as desirable an agricultural climate as possible here in Lancaster County in order that farmers who want to farm can continue to do so and get a reasonable return for their invested capital and labor. The offer to purchase their conservation easement, a very important farmland preservation tool, however, by itself is not enough. We must do more.

It should be pointed out, as most farmers in the audience already know, farmers do not get, nor do they expect, as high a return on invested capital as is expected in most other business enterprises. In addition, the farmer and his or her family income is much lower per hour than experienced in most other businesses or professions. Farmers attempt to make up for the low labor income per hour by working a lot of hours, especially during peak period, and by being available for work seven days a week in many cases.

For the past twenty-two years, government in Pennsylvania has tried to create a favorable agricultural climate in the State.

The ten Acts mentioned are ample proof of that effort. Of course, the passage of Act 149 in December 1988 was the most important of all acts that were passed.

I have tried to outline some concerns that will undoubtedly affect the long-term acceptance and effectiveness of the conservation easement program. I feel strongly we have to maintain and even improve the favorable agricultural climate here in Lancaster County and in other counties in the state.

Over the years Lancaster County Commissioners have been very supportive of the county's agricultural industry. I am certain we will get their support in the future.

My purpose in outlining these concerns in this paper is to bring to the attention of anyone who will listen—there are some problems to be addressed. Many of them affect the future of agriculture in Lancaster County. As usual, I am optimistic. I feel the right decisions will be made and we will be able to keep Lancaster County Number One in non-irrigated agricultural production.

Congressman Walker's Hearing on the Environment at F & M College

My congressman, Robert S. Walker, asked me to participate in a hearing before the United States House Subcommittee on Natural Resources, Agricultural Research, and Environment. The meeting was held March 2, 1990, at Hensel Hall of Franklin and Marshall College in Lancaster, Pennsylvania.

My testimony at the hearing on H. R. 2456 follows:

My name is Amos Funk. I am an almost-retired farmer. I am Chairman of Lancaster County's Agricultural Preserve Board, member of the Board of Trustees of the Lancaster Farmland Trust, and for the past thirty-six years I have been a director of the Lancaster County Conservation District.

I favor the provisions contained in H.R. 2457 because there is very little information available to state and local authorities in planning and managing suburban and rural growth while preserving environmental quality.

There is some information available on the financial impact of growth, including sprawl type of growth, on a community. In many cases the above studies lack credibility because of the perceived bias of those who initiated the study. Information gathered from the procedure outlined in H.R. 2457 would have sufficient credibility to be considered seriously.

In Lancaster County and elsewhere, too many decisions are made to meet short-term goals or needs. In my opinion, far more of our decisions should be made with long-term—twenty-five to thirty years—objectives in mind. It is also my view that those communities that make decisions to meet long-term environmental and financial goals will be the communities that will be referred to in the future as desirable places to work and live.

It is obvious that unless adequate information is available, proper decisions cannot be made. There is an urgent need in our decision-making process to weigh costs versus benefits. This comparison cannot be done fairly without adequate information. Again the need for H.R. 2457.

The recent story contained in the February 14, 1990, edition of the *Intelligencer Journal* called attention to the ten million pounds of toxic chemicals discharged in 1987 into Lancaster County's environment. This story prompts the questions: How much can these discharges be reduced? What are the cost benefits involved? How much would further reduction of the stated emissions cost, and how would such costs affect the world-wide competitiveness of the industries involved? Jobs are important to the economy of Lancaster County and so is the environmental quality.

Lawrence Jensen, assistant administrator of EPA, in a speech delivered at the National Association of Conservation District's Annual Meeting in Reno, Nevada, in 1987, made a number of interest points. Speaking of ground water pollution, he said: "I believe that the emphasis on ground water protection should be on the prevention of contamination rather than cleanup."

An example of an effort to reduce air pollution through prevention would be the first of a three-tier anti-pollution plan to be implemented by the Los Angeles Air Quality Authority, where in that area after 1993, the area would outlaw new drive-through facilities at fast food and other outlets to avoid the serious emission problem caused by long lines of idling cars waiting to be served. This represents a simple and very doable effort.

EPA's Dr. Jensen also pointed out that although there is a great deal of interest, and deservedly so, in ground water quality (25% of EPA budget is devoted to ground water protection), he also stated, "There is a good deal of evidence which would suggest that, in terms of threats to public health, the risks are far greater from the air we breath in our homes than from some of the types of contamination we find in our ground water. I think before we risk judgment on how much protection of ground water is needed and how much can we afford, we need to take a moment to look broadly at the whole range of environmental problems we're facing and make our decisions from that perspective."

Although this statement by Dr. Jensen, assistant administrator of EPA, was made more than a year before Congressman Walker introduced H.R. 2457, it certainly can be considered a strong endorsement of the provisions of this bill.

Many, if not most, of Lancaster County's environmental problems are people-created problems. According to United Census Census data, from 1960 to 1984, Lancaster County's population increased by more than 100,000 people, a thirty-seven percent increase, making the county one of the top growth areas in the Northeast.

As of 1984, Lancaster County was the fastest growing metropolitan area in Pennsylvania. When the new census data is collected, quite likely Lancaster County will have earned the dubious distinction of being the fastest growing county in Pennsylvania.

While this growth puts tremendous pressure on Lancaster County's prime farmland, the effect on Lancaster County's environment is even more devastating. As one example, although the county's population increased thirty-seven percent between 1960 and 1984, the number of vehicles on the road increased nearly 100 percent. As further verification of these numbers, according to the Pennsylvania Bureau of Motor Vehicles figures, in 1984 Lancastrians paid for 276,000 motor registrations, nearly twice the number of vehicles registered twenty years earlier.

In addition to the traffic problems these vehicles create, there is the not-yet-assessed problem of the auto emissions on the environment in an area like Lancaster County.

Approximately fifty percent of the county's water needs are supplied by ground water sources. Although the adequate supply of ground water may not be considered an environmental concern, the quality of life is greatly enhanced by an adequate supply of ground water.

As an increasing amount of our farmland and some of our wooded land is covered with concrete and macadam to meet the increased population needs, the area left for ground water recharge is drastically reduced. According to a recent USGS study, one acre of open land is needed to recharge the ground water supply to meet the needs of every 3.5 people living in the area.

As an almost-retired farmer, I am aware that farmers are accused of polluting our ground water as a result of over application of manure, fertilizer, and other farm chemicals. While many farmers would have to plead guilty, we know we have done much better in 1989 than in 1987. We are getting the message. We will continue to do better.

However, we farmers believe that many malfunctioning septic systems, some old and some not so old, also contribute greatly to the ground water problem. We are concerned that urban overuse of fertilizer and pesticides for the lawn and garden also contribute to ground water contamination.

The technical people to whom I have spoken are certain that most assessments of the amount of pesticides and other farm chemicals used by farmers are based on assumption, not facts. These assumptions are arrived at by computing the number of acres of a crop planted, times the highest recommended application rate, times the greatest suggested number of times applied. The facts are: Most farmers use the least amount needed (because of cost), only apply when needed, based on weather and disease or insect infestation (again to reduce costs). Perhaps one of the greatest needs today is for farmers to supply accurate information to regulators and other decisions makers on the actual amount of farm chemicals used per crop and per acre in an average year.

Only California has provided EPA and others with this information. If this information is made available, the effect on the environment of pesticides and other farm chemicals could be made based on facts, not assumptions. I trust H.R. 2457 could assist in this information-gathering process.

I have long felt that having a strong viable agricultural industry in Lancaster County is important for many financial and aesthetic reasons. However, one often overlooked the contribution agriculture makes is the environmentally important carbon dioxide to oxygen exchange performed by our crops and trees. This, and the many other contributions that agriculture makes, far outweighs any negative effects of the reasonable application of manure and other farm chemicals, the application of which I am certain will be drastically reduced in the next five years.

Only with adequate information, such as will be provided by the provisions of H.R. 2457, can correct decisions be made in rapidly developing counties like Lancaster, that will enable such counties to maintain the needed balance between agriculture, industry, and people.

The following story by Lou Ann Good appeared in the February 22, 1992, issue of the Lancaster Farming *newspaper and is used with the permission of the* Lancaster Farming.

Funk Dedicates Lifetime To Conservation, Preservation, Ag Promotion

LOU ANN GOOD
LANCASTER FARMING STAFF

MILLERSVILLE (Lancaster Co.) — Most 80-year-olds retire from everyday labor. But Amos Funk and his wife, Esta, are not the average 80-year-olds.

"Why, I work all the time," Esta exclaimed. Dubbed the "Midnight Manager" by her son, Esta tallies up the day's receipts from Funk's Farm Market and takes care of late business at the store.

Her husband Amos is well-known for his conservation and preservation efforts for which he has received 35 awards nationally, locally, and regionally.

The Funks live in their century-old farmhouse, which has been in the family since 1848. It borders the rambling Funk's Farm Market and its 22 greenhouses, located at South Duke Street, Millersville.

In 1975, Amos turned the market over to his son, Fred. Although the

From left to right: Amos Funk; his sister, Gracie Kauffman; his son, Fred Funk; his wife, Esta Funk; and his sister, Anna Mae Kritscher.

responsibility no longer belongs to Amos, he still plays an active role in the management and keeps detailed records of planting through harvesting cost.

Fred said, "It's hard to replace Dad with all his knowledge. He's a hard worker and it's difficult to get someone else to fill his place."

When one considers that the Funks adapted a small chicken house into a roadside stand in 1963, which has expanded to include three farms, 22 greenhouses, a store with more than $2 million in sales last year, and with 150 employees during its peak season, it looks like success has come easy to Funk.

But Amos gives a more realistic evaluation of the business expansion: "It's been an uphill climb the whole way."

Over the years, the Funks have suffered big crop failures from hail and drought.

But in typical dry humor, Funk said, "After you live a certain amount of time, you get used to rolling with the punches."

The produce business, he said, especially in Lancaster County, is extremely competitive. Despite the challenges, it is still possible to be successful, according to Amos.

"You should start out small," he said. "You'll go broke if you start out too big and with new equipment. In this business, you can start with ten acres."

Even if you have the land and equipment, Amos cautioned, "don't try the produce business unless you love vegetable growing because it's a lot of work.

"Today the challenges are greater in produce marketing. The costs are higher, but you can make it," Funk said. "I wouldn't go back to the good old days even with all the problems we face."

And while many lament the tough economical times of today, Amos said, "People don't know what a Depression is. There is nothing like it now."

He views the future with optimism by saying, "I don't think things (economy) will ever get that bad (as the Depression)."

Although Funk's father was a dairy farmer and had a milk route with a horse and wagon, Funk preferred working with poultry and vegetables. His first crop was asparagus and he planted raspberries, which he sold at an "itty bitty" Central Market stand managed by his mother who sold chickens, eggs, and a few vegetables.

Funk's leadership skills surfaced early. While a junior in high school, he was elected as captain of the basketball team and when he went to Penn State, he was elected captain of the basketball team, although he was only a freshman.

Funk only attended one year of college because at that time there were no student loans or scholarships available.

In 1936, he married Esta. Even before they married, Esta got a glimpse of what life would be like as a farm wife when Amos was one hour late for their first date because he wanted to pick all the beans before a predicted frost.

"She's a very tolerant person and that's the reason we get along so well; otherwise I couldn't do as many things as I do," Funk said. After their marriage, Esta tended chickens, butchered and dressed them for marketing. As early as 1938, Amos experimented with farm terraces and contour strips. Only a few other farms did so at that time.

Amos, who took the biblical admonition seriously to be a good steward of the land, became an ardent supporter of conservation, although it took a while for neighboring farmers to become convinced of contour farming practices.

The couple purchased the family farm in 1950. Because Amos loved to watch things grow, he got rid of all but one cow and gradually planted more and more vegetables and fruit. At first, Funks sold their produce at farmers' markets. At one time, They went to 13 different markets. After the roadside stand became successful, they gradually eliminated farmers' markets except for Root's Country Market, Manheim, and Central Market, Lancaster.

In 1951, Funk became part of the Conservation District Board. In 1959, Funks purchased a Marticville farm, and in 1969 he purchased a Pequea Township farm, which he had previously rented. Although the farms are not neighboring, one is two and one-half miles and the other eight miles from the main farm, Funk said that it is more important to him that all three farms have access to a creek, which is important for irrigation. They use a traveler irrigation system, which they believe is the least labor intensive. They have three miles of underground irrigation pipe.

On the 240 acres, crops are rotated. The 125 acres are farmed with sustainable agricultural practice. Amos said that they had a 50 percent increase in the sweet corn yield after the field had been planted with rye grass for two years.

"We couldn't afford to grow things we do now without the use of herbicides, but we can use less per acre. We try to find a balance between no fertilizer and too much of it," he said. "We find when we rotate corn, we don't have as many problems with root worm and other corn funguses."

Currently, Funks plant twenty acres of peaches and nectarines, seven acres of red and black raspberries, five acres of strawberries, and one to ten acres of corn with twelve plantings.

Labor is very intensive. Amos likes to keep detailed records of costs, labor, and income. Sometimes figures show that certain crops are not profitable to raise, but that does not mean that the crop will be dropped from the program.

Amos said, "We had six crops that were not profitable. We changed our planting and managing practices and two of those are now our most profitable crops."

One of the crops to which adjustments were made is sugar peas. For 130 bushels per acre yield of sugar peas, figures showed that it took 550 labor hours to plant, grow, and harvest. That was too labor intensive for the prices charged. Funks can purchase sugar peas from neighboring farms at lower prices than it costs to raise them. Now Funks raise only 1/4 acre of sugar peas, which they plant early under plastic in order to get premium prices for the early crop.

When Funk first started farming, he hired high school youngsters to help in the fields, but today students are too busy with other things, Funk said. For the past 17 years, the market provides airline tickets for Puerto Rican laborers who come from March through October and are housed on the farm. The government has recognized Funks for their superior labor conditions.

During the Funk's years in business, they have noticed a difference in consumers.

"Customer loyalty is not as strong as it used to be. You must work week by week to get customers to return. You must give people a good product that is a bit different than supermarkets," Amos said.

Some of the different products that the Funks have offered to customers are cherry pudding with milk, stuffed sweet peppers, spiced bell peppers, watermelon rind, corn relish, chow chow, and home-baked items.

Funks are always on the lookout for innovative marketing ideas. They advertise corn roasts, craft fairs, pumpkinland, open houses, mushroom week, plant auctions, and spring garden weekends. Some of these promotions are not cost effective and others are extremely profitable. For example, Funks sell approximately 100 pounds of fresh mushrooms weekly, but during their mushroom promotion, they sold 1,000 pounds. Pumpkinland increased pumpkin sales 61 percent in one year.

Homemade soups and fresh fruit salads have proven to be popular. Funks make 16 varieties of soup.

Attractive displays are a prime requirement for the food area that has 8,000 square feet and for the 12,000 square feet of garden items.

"Spring bedding sales are unbelievable," Funk said.

The greenhouse employees are planting now for spring sales. Funks sell 80 to 90 percent of the plants retail. During the holidays, they sold 20,000 poinsettias.

One of the most surprising things he learned in merchandising is that people object when the prices of food rise, but not to the rising prices on ornamental plants and flowers.

Every March 20, the Funks plant ten acres of sweet corn under plastic so that it is available by June 17.

"This past year the average price of sweet corn was $4 in the state, but we can't get that around here," Funk said. "Too many other growers make tough competition."

To stay on the cutting edge, the Funks find that it is necessary to constantly change their program to meet the competition. They found they could make more money raising broccoli than tobacco. They grow asparagus, lima beans, brussel sprouts, cantaloupes, celery, sweet corn, gourds, pumpkins, peaches, and nectarines. For 20 years they had black raspberries, rhubarb, strawberries, sugar peas, tomatoes, and watermelon.

Amos said that he became aware in the 1960s that farmland was being lost to development. In 1978, he went to the county commissioners and requested that they do something about loss of farmland.

He said that the Conestoga Valley Association was formed when a former teacher remarked that he wished we could involve urban people in conservation.

Although Funk is highly praised for his conservation and preservation efforts, not everyone has been grateful for Funk's efforts to preserve farmland.

He said, "I've spent heated sessions in the courthouse. Some do not want ag preservation. It takes careful, slow, aggressive pursuit of disseminating knowledge to help people understand."

Amos is a charter member of the Lancaster County Conservancy and member of the Lancaster County Preservation Board.

Amos had opportunity to be on the National Board of Vegetable Growers and the National Board of Conservation, but did not do it because it required too much time away from home.

Of the 35 awards Amos received, he is most pleased with the Teddy Roosevelt Award given by President Bush in 1990. Other cherished awards include the 1984 National Association of Conservation Districts Special Service Award for his more than 30 years of conservation efforts at the local, state, and national level. In addition, he was awarded the 1985 Pennsylvania Farmer's Award for outstanding achievement and in 1966, the Pennsylvania Master Farmer Award.

Recently, Amos received the George Delp Award for being the most influential in promoting agribusiness within the county.

Although never a member of the Rotary Club or other service club,

Amos was honored by the Rotary with a Harris Fellow Award in appreciation of tangible and significant assistance given for furtherance of better understanding and friendly relationships between people of the world.

He is active in church work. Although he is no longer able to play all the sports he formerly did, he remains an avid Nittany Lions fan and has season tickets for the Philadelphia Eagles. The Funks have six children and eleven grandchildren.

Amos continues to set goals. He would like to get more farmland preserved and to get a handle on nutrient management without polluting underground water that would allow farmers to make money.

"Of course," Amos added, "I never get over trying to grow better watermelon and cantaloupe."